THE
BLOODY
ROAD TO
PANMUNJOM

THE BLOODY ROAD TO PANMUNJOM

EDWIN P. HOYT

MILITARY HERITAGE PRESS
New York

The photographs in this book are reproduced
courtesy of the United States Army Signal Corps
and the United States Marine Corps.
The map of the Korean theater on page 10
is from *The Encyclopedia of Modern War*
by Roger Parkinson, courtesy of Stein
and Day/*Publishers*. All other maps are
from U.S. government publications.

This edition published by Military Heritage Press,
a division of Marboro Books Corporation,
by arrangement with
Stein & Day/Publishers.
1988 Dorset Press

ISBN 0-88029-223-7
(formerly ISBN 0-8128-2999-9)

Printed in the United States of America
M 9 8 7 6 5 4 3 2 1

CONTENTS

Illustrations

Maps

THE
BLOODY
ROAD TO
PANMUNJOM

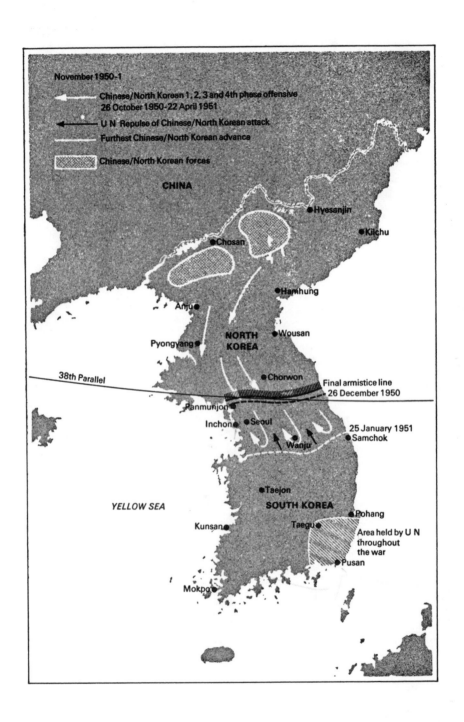

November 1950–1

← Chinese/North Korean 1, 2, 3 and 4th phase offensive
26 October 1950–22 April 1951

← U N Repulse of Chinese/North Korean attack

— Furthest Chinese/North Korean advance

▨ Chinese/North Korean forces

CHINA

●Hyesanjin

●Kilchu

●Chosan

●Hamhung

Anju●

●Wousan

Pyongyang●

NORTH KOREA

●Chorwon

38th Parallel

Final armistice line
26 December 1950

Panmunjon●

Inchon● ●Seoul

25 January 1951
●Samchok

●Wanju

●Taejon

SOUTH KOREA

YELLOW SEA

●Pohang

Kunsan●

Taegu●

Area held by U N throughout the war

●Pusan

Mokpo●

1

The Chinese
Change the War

The Korean War is notable in American and world history as the first confrontation of the "big powers" in the atomic age. It foreshadowed later and present conflicts. In Korea the USSR discovered the technique it has used successfully for more than thirty years to keep the United States off balance: the direct involvement of one of its satellites in a military situation, while the Soviets remain only indirectly involved, with all the freedom of action that implies. The USSR, until its Afghanistan adventure, did not have to commit its military forces beyond its own bloc; it achieved the same ends by committing those of other nations. Thus, the Korean War and its outcome represented something new; the most powerful nation in the world was musclebound, shackled by its own strength. The United States was capable of winning victory in a general war through the use of conventional and atomic weapons but was constrained by a national abhorrence of general war as well as by widespread public sentiment against the atomic weapons the nation had invented.

Had the eventual course of the Korean War been known at the beginning, an entirely different U.S. war policy would have ensued, and nearly three years of tragic and bloody struggle, costing fifty-one thousand American dead and over a hundred thousand American wounded, might well have been avoided.

In the summer of 1950 the Americans were ill-prepared to respond to the North Korean invasion. As late as January, the Truman administration had indicated that it had no stake in the defense of the South Korean republic. Secretary of State Dean Acheson had made a public statement to that effect to a group of journalists at the National Press Club in Washington.

When the North Korean army invaded on June 25, 1950, its forces cut through the meager South Korean defenses like a knife through cheese. In less than three days they took Seoul, the capital. In a week they had pushed the South Koreans halfway to Pusan, the southernmost port. Belatedly, President Truman reversed U.S. policy and announced that South Korea would be defended. He was lucky enough that the Soviet representative to the United Nations Security Council was off in an official sulk that week, and thus the open aggression of the North Koreans could be condemned by the council without a Soviet veto. That is what happened, and the administration was pleased that the American military response would carry the respectability of a UN "police action." The Americans sent in troops, but they were raw and green—no match for the highly disciplined and well-armed North Koreans, who possessed the second best army in Asia. (The first was that of the Soviets.)

The shock to Americans was enormous. Imagine—the troops of the most powerful nation in the world being pushed around by a bunch of "gooks." But there it was: the American army in Japan was soft, weak, badly commanded on the regiment and division levels, underarmed, and undertrained. When the men in power in Washington decided that South Korea would be defended, they soon discovered that the previous four years of demilitarization had stripped America of its defenses and that it would be weeks before any significant force could be sent from the U.S. mainland to Korea.

So, during the summer of 1950 Lieutenant General Walton Walker, commander of the Eighth Army, fought with inadequate and outdated weapons against a determined North Korean enemy. He only barely managed, through a sort of sleight of hand, to maintain a defensive line at the banks of the Naktong and Nam rivers, around the Pusan Perimeter.

In this, as in so much else that was unfortunate in postwar history, President Harry Truman found himself the victim of actions and decisions made by his predecessor, Franklin Roosevelt. In turn, Mr. Roosevelt was the victim of a Western reading of history and of an insufficient understanding of the Soviets and the Chinese Communists. As far as the Soviet Union was concerned, the end of the war against Germany and Japan did not mean peace. Soviet leaders perceived the world as composed of Communist bloc nations and enemies. The end of the European war, in particular, was seen from Moscow as no more than a point of departure, a breathing space in which Soviet Russia could regain strength, while surrounding herself with satellites and preparing for the continuation of the battle against the capitalist world. The fact that out of World War II emerged a world that was less capitalist, more social democratic in its leaning made no difference to them; only Communist states are acceptable to the Soviet Union, and, even then, they must be subservient to Moscow. The Soviet reaction to the breakaway of Yugoslavia in the summer of 1947 indicated the Kremlin outlook, as later did the schism that developed between the USSR and China. Actually, the latter was not really a schism, which presupposes earlier solid common ground, but a recognition by China of the reality: the USSR holds and covets millions of square miles of territory claimed by the Chinese.

By this fundamental error the U.S. foreign policy, which emerged in 1946 and continued at least until 1972, tended to push Marxist governments into the Soviet orbit. That is what happened in Korea and what has happened in Cuba, Nicaragua, and what will happen again until American politicians learn the difference between national communism and Soviet imperialism.

The result, in the Korean War, was that the U.S. government in October 1950 found itself faced with a major policy decision; yet the decision-makers did not recognize the nature of the problem. With the capture of Seoul in late September, and the easy drive north, the way seemed clear to achieve the ambition General MacArthur had announced in July: to destroy the North Korean People's Republic. That plan, attractive to the American government and its allies, was tempting enough to make them forget the announced UN purpose of the Korean "police action." Originally, the intent had been to force the North Koreans back into their own territory. But over the months, and particularly after the easy victory at Inchon and the capture of Seoul, the aim of the Americans changed, and they were supported initially by the British and other Commonwealth governments. The idea of stopping at the 38th parallel now seemed to be precluded by events as well as to be unattractive, because Republic of Korea forces had forged ahead even as Seoul was being liberated; on September 30 they had crossed the parallel. Ten days later the ROK troops were in Wonsan, the east coast port deep inside North Korean territory.

What was at stake went far beyond the perceived "police action" of the first three months, an action supported by most of the world. Few back on the Potomac seemed to recognize that the issue was whether or not the United States was willing to commit itself to an extended war across the sea from which it had little, if anything, to gain.

All this while, from September 25 on, the debate continued in the capital, but it was apparent that the "hawks" had the upper hand. The warnings of those who suspected the future were heard but not heeded.

The Chinese added other warnings; early in October Foreign Minister Chou En-lai announced that if the South Koreans crossed the 38th parallel, it would be acceptable to China. But if the foreign troops—the Americans, Australians, and British—crossed over and entered North Korean territory, then China would enter the war on the side of North Korea. In Tokyo this flat warning was regarded as a bluff and in Washington as probably a bluff. The Truman administration did not truly assess the possibility that the war might be expanded. Instead, General MacArthur was allowed to move on northward, to capture Pyongyang, the North Korean capital.

After Pyongyang, MacArthur vowed to drive to the Yalu River, the border between Chinese Manchuria and North Korea, and to destroy the North Korean army and government.

The difficulties posed by this war and the changed international situation and balance of power by 1950 were not foreseen by the Americans or even understood as they developed. Thus, in November 1950, when vital decisions about the conduct of the war had to be made, America's leaders set off from a totally false premise. They believed that the Soviet Union and China would allow the North Korean government to fall and be replaced on their borders by the fanatically anti-Communist government of South Korea's President Syngman Rhee. Why they believed this is still unclear, an indication of the peculiarly ethnocentric American world outlook. A glance at the interdependence of the Chinese and North Korean economies, particularly in the matter of hydroelectric development, should have given the American leaders second thoughts. Unfortunately, there were few among President Truman's advisors with enough knowledge of modern Korean and Chinese history to realize that the two countries were reaping what the Japanese had sowed in the establishment of their own empire; first they had taken Korea and then Manchuria, and then they combined the resources of those imperial provinces to the advantage of the homeland. Had a postwar South Korea been allowed a moderate government, had the United States not been going through paroxysms of all-embracing anti-Communism, had America's political leaders recognized the natural tension between China and Russia, it is conceivable that the Chinese might have sat by and allowed the conquest of North Korea by South Korea. Instead, American Pacific policy, which included the deadly embrace of Chiang Kai-shek's Nationalist government on Taiwan, which was still vowing that it would reconquer the mainland, threw the Chinese into the arms of the Soviets. That Chinese reaction is perfectly understandable; the United States was the professed enemy of the Chinese Communist government. It was not in 1949 the other way around. Nor did the American administration understand the nervousness of Mao Tse-tung's government; less than a year in power, its hold on continental China was far from complete, with guerillas still fighting in the south and southwest.

Add to that the presence of the U.S. Sixth Fleet in Chinese waters, which the Peking government found almost intolerable, one can begin to get a feeling for the Chinese position in the summer of 1950 when the North Koreans marched into the south. The Chinese would have been pleased to see the Rhee government eliminated and one potential threat to the security of Manchuria wiped out.

But China was not eager to pick a fight. As General MacArthur said later when rationalizing his mistaken belief that the Chinese would not enter the war, the logical time for the Chinese to enter, if they wished, would have been when the Americans were struggling at the Pusan Perimeter. Even a hundred thousand men sent to help North Korea at that point would have tipped the scale.

China did not enter the war that summer. Only after the capture of Seoul did the Chinese truly become upset. That is when the Chinese warnings about the 38th parallel began. They were ignored in the American euphoria over victory, a euphoria that had proved so catching at the UN that even powers not usually receptive to American advances saw a logic in using this occasion to restore a historic unity to Korea through elections under UN auspices. Why anyone believed that China, which smarted at being deprived of the UN seat it considered its own, would be sympathetic to any UN action is another unresolved question.

The UN drive north continued unabated in October. All the Chinese warnings were ignored. The North Korean capital at Pyongyang fell. The Eighth Army moved north, urged by General MacArthur to hasten to the Yalu River border with China. The ROK forces actually did reach the Yalu on October 25—the day that the Chinese finally took a hand. The ROK II Corps was driving north on the west side of the peninsula when it encountered strong Chinese forces. The UN commanders had no suspicion of their real strength: two Chinese armies, sixty thousand men, were involved. The Chinese had been entering North Korea quietly since mid-October, when Peking was issuing its warnings. In the following battle, the ROK II Corps was virtually destroyed. Elsewhere, in the center and on the right, UN forces encountered other Chinese units.

At that moment, there was still time to maneuver a settlement. The Chinese had brought several armies into Korea, but they were still largely concealed in the mountains of north central Korea awaiting events.

General MacArthur had first been shocked when the North Korean People's Army marched south across the 38th parallel and swiftly overran most of South Korea. With Washington's authorization, he had rushed in troops from his Japanese occupation force and with the utmost difficulty had managed to stem the tide at the Pusan Perimeter, a defense line drawn along two rivers north of that South Korean port city. During the summer the Americans and South Koreans had gained strength and on September 15 they were able to launch the counterinvasion by an amphibious landing at Inchon, the port for Seoul. Two weeks later the war had been turned around, Seoul was liberated and the drive begun toward Pyongyang, the capital of North Korea. So, bearing in mind MacArthur's enormous ego, it is understandable that the general believed the war was over. This, in spite of the several Peking warnings that if the Allies continued to advance, the Chinese would enter the conflict. The warnings were ignored and the Americans captured Pyongyang. Then Americans and South Koreans began the drive north to the Onjong area where the ROK II Corps was mauled.

But the major battle that proved the Chinese intentions was yet to be fought, and, because the first attacks had been made against ROK forces, the Americans tended to disbelieve the reports that the Chinese had entered Korea in force. They were soon to be enlightened at a little Korean town called Unsan.

The action began on the cold morning of October 25. The ROK 1st Division, the best fighting unit in the South Korean army, was moving on Unsan, led by American tanks. For nearly a month opposition had been slight, but on this morning the tanks were stopped at a bridge by mortar fire, and the advance of the ROK 15th Regiment was halted. Chinese captives were taken here as the battle developed. American troops of the 1st Cavalry Division came up to join the fighting, but the Chinese would not be budged. A major action was developing on the western side of the Korean peninsula, where the U.S. Eighth Army operated.

Meanwhile, on the other side of the peninsula, Major General Edward M. Almond's X Corps was moving up toward the Changjin Reservoir. The ROK I Corps attacked north from Hamhung (see map 1), but as they approached the hydroelectric plants of the Changjin Reservoir the Chinese attacked, and the drive was stopped.

At Eighth Army headquarters in Pyongyang, at General Almond's head-

ADVANCE TO THE NORTH (20—24 OCT 1950)

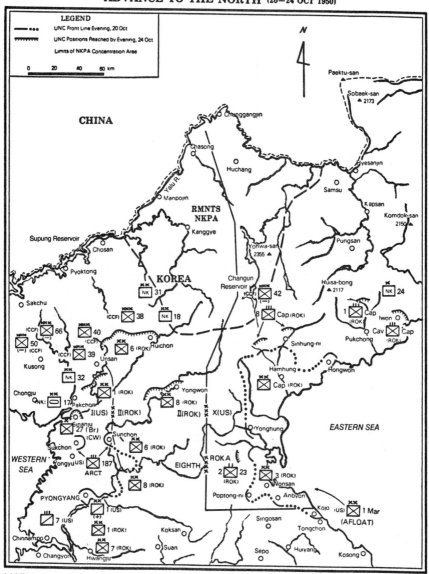

MAP 1

quarters in Wonsan, and at General MacArthur's headquarters in Tokyo the intelligence officers struggled with the questions: how many Chinese were there in North Korea, and what were their intentions? For a week they labored and got all the wrong answers. They spoke in terms of Chinese divisions; they should have been speaking of armies. They decided the Chinese were making a token effort to stop the UN forces. They were wrong. The Chinese had something quite different on their minds.

As October ended, great smoke clouds appeared in the mountains in the Unsan and Onjong areas. They were caused by forest fires. The first to notice them were the observation pilots. Soon artillery spotters moving up found they could not see anything through the smoke. The forest fires were a crude, but effective, Chinese method of masking their troop movements.

In spite of the smoke screen, the Americans in the field began to have uneasy feelings about the movements of the enemy. A Korean civilian working in a paddy nine miles southwest of Unsan saw a long column of troops moving eastward, toward the road below the town. He reported what he had seen to a South Korean military unit. Other Koreans reported seeing thousands of troops moving about the Unsan area. At noon on November 1 American artillery spotters saw a column of men, horse cavalry, and horse-drawn wagons on the road eight miles southeast of Unsan. The artillery opened fire, and then American fighter bombers attacked the column. Men and horses fell, but the survivors continued to march along.

Artillery spotters in the liaison planes in the air reported the same phenomenon; American artillery shells landed squarely in the middle of columns, and yet the Chinese did not stop or even hesitate. The dead and wounded fell by the wayside, and the rest marched on. Those who saw that had the feeling that a juggernaut was moving down on them.

By midafternoon on November 1, General Gay was becoming uneasy about reports of columns advancing around the 1st Division on all sides. He took action to tighten his ranks; he asked I Corps to send the 7th Cavalry up to join his headquarters at Yongsan-dong and to let him withdraw the 8th Cavalry back a few miles from Unsan.

Unfortunately, I Corps headquarters was skeptical about reports of heavy Chinese involvement, and General Gay's requests were denied. It had not been so many hours earlier that General Gay's own staff had ridiculed Colonel Percy Thomas, the intelligence officer of I Corps, who had warned of the Chinese threat. Now, with the Chinese approaching rapidly, the 1st Cavalry were becoming convinced, but the I Corps staff and commander were still not. This was true even though on October 27 Brigadier General Paik Sun Yup, commander of the ROK 1st Division, had warned General

Milburn personally that he was facing at least a division of Chinese soldiers, not a mixture of Chinese and North Koreans as Milburn believed.

I Corps was in for some shocks. The first came early on the afternoon of November 1, when General Walker telephoned General Milburn, the I Corps commander, to tell him that the ROK II Corps had been all but destroyed and that Milburn's right flank was virtually open. Milburn scurried into action, ordering engineer troops and anyone else he could corral up to positions around Kunu-ri. (See Map 2.) Their mission was to protect the right flank and particularly the bridges across the Chongchon River.

General Milburn went up front to Kuni-ri to see what was happening. The ROK II Corps was supposed to be operating from there, but Milburn found Major General Yu Jae Hung, commander of the II Corps, preparing to retreat to Sunchon. Yu said his corps was totally disorganized and that only three battalions of the ROK 7th Division troops in the Kunu-ri area were capable of fighting. General Milburn told General Yu that he had to fight to protect the American flank and that an American force would come up to support him.

Meanwhile, events were moving rapidly. A combat patrol from the 1st Battalion of the 5th Cavalry moved north from Yongsan-dong but found its way blocked six miles below the position of the 8th Cavalry. The Chinese had moved in and held a strong position on a ridge that extended across the road

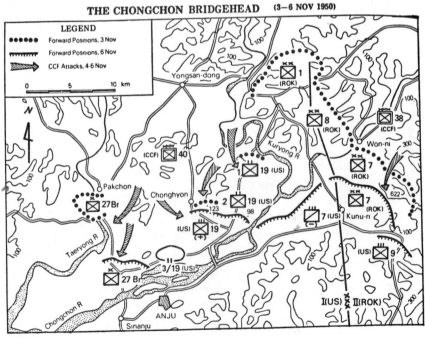

THE CHONGCHON BRIDGEHEAD   (3—6 NOV 1950)

MAP 2

south of the Turtle Head Bend of the Kuryong River. (See Map 2.) That afternoon they attacked the 1st Battalion of the 5th Cavalry and drove them back with the loss of several heavy mortars and some machine guns. They were now on three sides of the 8th Cavalry, north, west, and south. On the east, the flank was protected by the ROK 15th Regiment.

All day long on November 1 the Chinese had been attacking the ROK 15th Regiment. Something new was added to the Korean War that day—the Katushka rocket launcher. This weapon had been developed by the Russians during World War II and was used effectively against the Germans. It consisted of four multiple tubes, mounted on a truck for mobility, which fired 82mm rockets in clusters. The rockets did considerable damage; one barrage struck an ammunition truck at the command post of the 8th Cavalry's 1st Battalion and blew it skyhigh. The rocket launchers were located north of the Samtan River and were hit by U.S. artillery and forced to move out.

The Chinese kept up the pressure. By dark they had infiltrated between the ROK 15th Regiment and the 8th Cavalry. Later that night they overran most of the positions of the ROK 15th, and by midnight that regiment had fallen apart. Their right flank in jeopardy, the Americans prepared for a fight.

The Chinese attacked all along the line of Major Millikin's 1st Battalion. The Americans held. But the Chinese then found the gap in the ridge line between the 1st and 2nd battalions and moved through. Just before midnight tanks holding the bridge across the Samtan River reported a large body of troops moving down on them. General Milburn sent an aide to see what was happening, and the aide found that the ROK 15th Regiment had disappeared, and the Chinese were on the American flank, preparing to move down on the east and surround Milburn's force. So Milburn moved his supply trains and noncombat forces south through Unsan toward Ipsok, on the south side of the Kuryong River.

If the Americans had not previously known they were fighting the Chinese, they now did. The Katushka rockets were one sign. Another was the fearful racket made by the Chinese bugles, which sounded like no other bugles in the world. The Chinese method of attack was also something new. They came in droves, apparently unmindful of the automatic fire that cut the front down. Shortly before midnight they encircled the 2nd Battalion and drove back the 1st Battalion from its ridge position. Both battalions were now desperately short of ammunition.

While this fierce hand-to-hand battle was raging north of Unsan, General Milburn was holding a command conference with the leaders of the U.S. 24th Division and 1st Cavalry and the ROK 1st Division. He ordered all units to go on the defensive and to withdraw south of Unsan. The ROK 15th Regiment was to fight the rearguard action. When the meeting ended, the commanders returned to their posts, only to learn that the Chinese had destroyed the ROK 15th Regiment and were working on the 8th Cavalry.

When the orders were received, the 1st and 2nd battalions were heavily engaged. Major Millikin said his 1st Battalion would try to hold Unsan while the 2nd Battalion came through, and then the 3rd Battalion, not yet engaged, would hold while the 1st Battalion escaped south.

But by this hour Colonel Walton had lost all communication with the 2nd Battalion, except for Company H. That company had to inform the other rifle companies. The troops then began withdrawing eastward.

At Major Millikin's area north of Unsan, Company A had been forced from its left flank position, and the Chinese were infiltrating along the ridge line into Unsan. On the right the Chinese were pressing Company B and the tanks along the river that guarded the right flank. Soon the tanks were forced back to the road junction at the northeast edge of the town. Shortly afterward the Chinese took Unsan. When the men of A and B companies arrived at the road fork, they were fired on by Chinese troops in the town, and some men went down. Major Millikin ordered his troops to march south of the town and wait for him at another junction. He and his staff remained on the northeast edge of the town, directing other units as they retreated through. Four tanks fought their way through Unsan to the south edge and established a position at the junction. Two tanks were sent on with the wounded and the mortar vehicles, but the column ran into a burning truck, which stopped them. One tank tried to get around it and slid into a shell crater where it stuck. The Chinese overwhelmed the tank, killing the commander, and blew off the treads of the second tank. Most of the crews of both tanks were killed or wounded, only three men escaped. None of the mortar carriers or the wounded escaped.

Major Millikin was still holding the road junction northeast of Unsan. Little groups of stragglers appeared, some from Company C and some soldiers from the ROK 15th Regiment. He sent them south, and, as the Chinese closed in, he and his men moved west, circled Unsan, and came south themselves, trying to reach the roadblock south of the town.

The roadblock, a mile and a half south of Unsan, was commanded by Colonel Edson, the regimental executive officer. The regimental trains passed through safely. So did many soldiers of the 1st and 2nd battalions. Four tanks arrived shortly after midnight, and two more came along later. Edson sent four of the tanks south to hold the ford over the Kuryong River.

At about two o'clock in the morning of November 2, artillery units came up to the road junction, bound eastward. The headquarters and service batteries of the 99th Field Artillery came first. Then came B Battery and, finally, C Battery. Captain Jack Bolt, commander of C Battery, was riding in a jeep, leading twenty vehicles with six towed 105 mm howitzers.

The road ran east from the fork for about a mile along an embankment above rice paddies. Then it turned southeast to ford the Kuryong River, and then it ran to Ipsok, their destination, which was four miles south of the river. North of the road were more rice paddies, which extended to the Samtan River, to a point where it turned east in a bend and flowed into the Kuryong. On the south the paddy fields rose to a hill line, which included Hill 165 and Hill 119, which stood close above the south side of the road nearly all the way along. It was a nice place for an ambush, but no one was much worried because the enemy had not been seen in this area.

Captain Bolt turned his column east on the road and went on. When he was about two hundred yards down the road, he looked back and saw that he was alone. The second vehicle was a 2½-ton truck, hauling a 105 mm howitzer. The driver had missed the turn and had to back up, not an easy task with the heavy howitzer behind him. This move had jammed up the column of vehicles. Bolt told his driver to stop. As the jeep stopped, Bolt looked across the paddy in the bright moonlight and saw a group of men approaching the road. He thought they were retreating Americans until they reached a point about fifty yards from the road and opened fire. Bolt shouted to his driver to get out of there, and they sped down the road. They went around a curve, and Bolt saw about twenty soldiers in the middle of the road. They opened fire on the jeep. Bolt returned the fire with his submachine gun, and the soldiers scattered and jumped into the ditches on the roadside. Bolt's jeep rushed on through several small groups of soldiers; he fired as they went. In a few minutes they caught up with the end of the regimental column that included the four tanks of that first tank platoon. Bolt asked one of the tanks to go up and clear the road, but the tank commander said he was out of ammunition. So there was no help for Bolt's column.

Meanwhile, the Chinese soldiers had taken possession of the roadside. As the 2½-ton truck came up, leading the column, they opened fire. The driver lost control of the truck, and it slipped over the bank into the ditch by the paddy field, and the howitzer slewed across the road, blocking it. One of the two tanks at the roadblock came up to try to help, but it came under fire at the point where the howitzer sat. A Chinese satchel charge broke one of the treads. The tank crew disabled the tank and then climbed out and escaped. For all practical purposes the road to Ipsok was now closed. The howitzer and damaged tank became the Chinese roadblock.

At the junction Colonel Edson tried to rally his troops, but they were a mixture of men from many units, and they did not respond. In small groups they left the roadblock and escaped in various directions. The enemy began to close in on the junction. At about this time Colonel Walton and the men of the 2nd Battalion arrived from Unsan. He led the men south across the hills.

Major Millikin was still up north, but he met elements of Company H and put his wounded in their vehicles and came down to the road junction. By the time he got there it was empty, except for a mass of shattered vehicles and equipment.

Behind Millikin was chaos. The rest of the 2nd Battalion never reached the road junction southeast of Unsan because the Chinese cut the road just outside the town. When Millikin reached the junction, he found Major Robert Ormond there with part of Ormond's 3rd Battalion. Ormond told Millikin that he had been ordered to put a platoon at the junction until the other battalions came through and that Millikin must represent the last of them. So Ormond went south with his men to join up with his battalion and retreat to Ipsok.

Millikin collected all the men he found around the area. They discovered one operable tank and traveled with it, until enemy fire caused them to scatter into small groups and infiltrate through the Chinese lines.

When Battery A of the 99th Field Artillery arrived with tanks of the 70th Tank Battalion at the roadblock, the Chinese attacked. Soon the road was so clogged with vehicles that even tanks could not get through. The crews abandoned them, and most of the men took to the hills. They moved toward the sound of firing in the south, where the 9th Field Artillery Battalion at Ipsok was firing in support of the ROK 1st Division. During the hours of darkness and early morning light, men continued to infiltrate south into the American and the South Korean lines. By noon on November 2 all the men who were going to escape had done so. A nose count showed that the 1st Battalion had lost fifteen officers and two hundred and fifty enlisted men, half their mortars and machine guns.

As for Major Ormond's 3rd Battalion, it encountered a different sort of trouble. The battalion had been positioned north of the Nammyon River at the Camel's Head Bend, where the Nammyon met the Kuryong River. (See Map 3.) The command post was in a flat field, the companies were disposed along as much high ground as possible. When the orders to withdraw came, Major Ormond brought his companies together and assigned Company L to cover the withdrawal of the others. He then drove north to the junction southeast of Unsan, where he met Colonel Millikin. He started south just before enemy troops cut the road below the junction, and he returned to his command post without trouble. Since the road was now unusable, he planned

THE BATTLE OF UNSAN (NIGHT OF 1–2 NOV 1950)

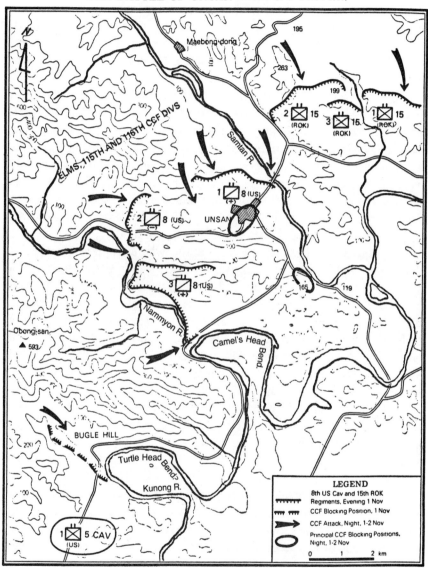

MAP 3

a cross-country retreat, and the scouts found a ford across the river. The vehicles lined up at the ford.

But the security force from Company M became careless. They were supposed to cover the ridge, but they let a large group of soldiers come up, thinking they were American. Only when the Chinese bugles began to blow did the defenders realize that they were facing the enemy. By that time it was very late. The Chinese swooped in on the command post from all sides, and the fight became general, with the Chinese throwing grenades, blowing bugles, and firing burp guns.

Major Ormond left the command post to see what was happening. Captain Filmore McAbee, the operations officer, also went out to see what was going on at the bridge. Five minutes later a bullet knocked off his helmet, and another hit him in the shoulder. He turned back toward the command post and ran into a group of Chinese soldiers. He began firing, ducked behind a jeep, and emptied his carbine. He was stopped by a group of Chinese soldiers, but they did not try to capture him. He pointed south, and they went away. That happened again, and he saved himself by the same technique, then walked into the command post, weak from loss of blood.

The dugout had become the aid station, where Captain Clarence R. Anderson, the battalion surgeon, was working. Major Veale Moriarty, the battalion executive officer, stepped outside the dugout just as Captain McAbee came up. Moriarty saw four figures wearing fur caps and knew they were Chinese. He grabbed McAbee and thrust him into the dugout. Just then he heard a cry for help and saw the battalion supply officer on the ground, wrestling with a Chinese soldier. Moriarty shot the Chinese with his .45 pistol and then shot another who was crouching there. For the next few minutes he was engaged in hand-to-hand pistol combat.

Staff Sergeant Elmer L. Miller, who was in charge of a section of tanks near the command post, found himself beset on his tank by the enemy. He fought them off with a pistol, and the tanks then engaged the enemy around the command post. The Chinese came up with satchel charges and blew up one tank. The others drove the Chinese off.

Major Moriarty saw the commotion around the tanks and went that way. He found about twenty men crouching next to Miller's tank and took them across the stream to the south. They knocked out a group of Chinese on the south bank and then proceeded down the bank to safety inside the ROK lines near Ipsok.

The fighting in the 3rd Battalion area continued until an hour after daylight. The Americans clustered in small groups in several areas and fought with machine guns, rifles, and mortars. The Chinese fought with grenades, for the most part, except in the hand-to-hand combat, which was with knife and bayonet and pistol. When the light was steady, fighter bombers began coming over the area, and this forced the Chinese into hiding and made it possible for the scattered Americans to assemble and bring in the wounded. They found Major Ormond very badly wounded and brought him in. Altogether, they picked up 170 wounded men. There remained half a dozen officers and about 200 men in fighting shape.

As the day wore on the surrounded battalion assembled its resources in the command post area and dug a trench network. An L-5 liaison plane dropped medical supplies. A helicopter came over and apparently intended to land, but the Chinese hit it with ground fire, and it went off. Another pilot informed the command post that a relief column was on the way.

This column was composed of the 1st and 2nd battalions of the 5th Cavalry. The 1st Battalion moved along the left of the road, and the 2nd Battalion along the right. General Gay sent the 1st Battalion of the 7th Cavalry off to the left on a wide flanking movement, but he had not reckoned with the difficulty of the country, and the 7th Cavalry men got bogged down and never did join the battle.

Colonel Johnson, the 5th Cavalry commander, expected his 3rd Battalion to come up as the other two battalions captured the ridge line, and then to drive through to the relief of the 8th Cavalry's 3rd Battalion.

The trouble with the attack was that it had no artillery support. The only guns in situ that could reach the area were two 155 mm howitzers, and General Milburn was so concerned about the spread of the Chinese attack that he would not allow any movement forward of the lighter 105 mm howitzers. Consequently, the two lead battalions of the 5th Cavalry failed to reach their objectives. They had air support, but the Chinese were dug in, and the air strikes did not seem to do much damage. When dusk came, the air strikes ceased, and the real fighting began.

Meanwhile, General Milburn decided to withdraw further south and ordered General Gay to bring back the 1st Cavalry Division. That meant the 5th Cavalry had to stop its attempts to reach the 3rd Battalion of the 8th Cavalry. That evening the 3rd Battalion was abandoned to its fate by General Milburn.

All day long that battalion had been beset by sniper fire. Father Emil J. Kapaun, the chaplain, had risked his life half a dozen times to save wounded; Captain Anderson, the surgeon, worked around the clock. At dusk Chaplain Kapaun joined the wounded in the dugout. By this time there were about sixty of them, and the position was no longer within the defense perimeter of the battalion. Chaplain Kapaun was walking into certain capture, and he knew it.

At dusk a liaison plane flew over and delivered the orders for the 1st Cavalry Division to withdraw. The whole corps was moving south across the Chongchon River. Specifically the 3rd Battalion was told that it was on its own and was instructed to withdraw under cover of darkness. What that meant, as everyone knew, was if they could make it without help through the enemy lines.

The officers and noncoms talked over the situation and decided to stay inside the perimeter and try to hold through the night. But as darkness fell they soon learned the folly of the decision: the Chinese had spent the day bringing up dozens of 120 mm mortars and, as night came down and the danger of air attack vanished, they began a barrage. It was directed at the center of the perimeter. The tanks moved outside, but the mortars followed them. Soon one tank was burning. One crewman was killed in putting out the fire. Sergeant Miller soon saw that if the tanks stayed put they would be destroyed, so he told them to move out and wished them good luck. The tanks moved southwest. They got down into the valley of the Kuryong, but there the tankers had to abandon them and try to make it out on foot.

The Chinese shelled the infantry positions for a time and then launched an infantry attack involving about two companies—four hundred men. The Americans fired rockets into their own abandoned vehicles on the edge of the perimeter and thus created flares that lit up the area. As the Chinese came, they were mowed down against the light of the fires. The bugles blew, and the assault ended with very heavy Chinese casualties.

Five more times the Chinese came, whistles shrieking and bugles squawking. Each time, they were repelled with heavy casualties. During the night the battalion had some welcome help—about fifty stragglers from the 2nd Battalion came down out of the hills and joined up.

Outside the perimeter, the Chinese attacked and quickly captured the old dugout. They ordered the walking wounded up and out of the dugout, and they moved them down to the Nammyon River. These included Captain McAbee and Chaplain Kapaun. The other wounded were left by the Chinese, unmolested.

The dawn of November 3 came. This day there was not even any air support. A small patrol went outside the perimeter to the old command post dugout and found the remainder of the wounded. They gave them the last rations of the battalion. All day long sniping continued, but no real fighting. The Chinese believed what the Americans had ceased to believe—that the American command would send some sort of help.

As night fell, the Chinese moved again. The scenario was the same as that of the night of November 2, but on this second night the Americans were running out of ammunition. As the Chinese came and were repelled, Americans crawled out across the perimeter and retrieved the enemy's weapons and ammunition.

When day dawned on November 4, there were still about two hundred Americans fighting, with two hundred and fifty wounded. There was no doubt at all now about their total abandonment by the I Corps. The officers and NCOs held another conference. They decided that those who could escape should. Captain Anderson volunteered to stay on with the wounded.

Lieutenant Walter L. Mayo, Jr., and Lieutenant George W. Peterson, and two enlisted men went scouting for an escape route. They crawled to the old command post and talked to the wounded and then crawled to a village up the road. They found some Chinese wounded there but no one else. All the way they had to crawl over the bodies of dead Chinese and American soldiers, many more Chinese than Americans. By midafternoon they had found a ford across the river, and the two enlisted men were sent back to bring the group out while the officers continued to scout the way.

The two enlisted men reached the perimeter and reported. Captain George F. McDonnell of the 2nd Battalion stragglers, Captain William F. McLain of E Company, and Lieutenant Paul F. Bromser of Company L led the way, and the two hundred men moved to the east side of the perimeter. They were very lucky. Just then, the Chinese launched an enormous barrage of white phosphorus shells, apparently aimed at screening a new infantry attack. Instead, the smoke screened the American escape. Within five minutes the two hundred had cleared the area.

They traveled all that night, east and northeast, and then south and southwest. They were sheltered from curious eyes by a series of rainstorms. They saw many Chinese, infantry and horse-mounted cavalry. They finally reached the area northeast of Ipsok, within sight of American artillery firing. Here the battalion was surrounded by Chinese, and the decision was made to break up and try to escape in small groups. Thus, the 3rd Battalion of the 8th Cavalry came to an end. The small groups tried to infiltrate the enemy lines toward Ipsok, but the Chinese concentration was heavy. Most of them were killed or captured. Altogether, only ten officers and two hundred men, including Major Moriarty, were left of the thousand-man battalion. The loss was more than 80 percent. Later, as other men came in, the loss was reduced to about 60 percent. But for the next two weeks, virtually all of the replacements coming up to the Eighth Army were assigned to build the new 3rd Battalion of the 8th Cavalry.

The Unsan disaster was complete. It indicated precisely what the Americans and South Koreans would be facing if the war went on: the Unsan attack had been made by the Chinese 39th Army's 115th and 116th divisions. The Chinese had taken enormous losses, but the Chinese commanders expected to take enormous losses, and they could afford them, with an army of a million men in and around North Korea.

2

The Battle of Sudong

While at the end of October and early in November the Chinese attacked in great force at Unsan, on the other side of Korea the story was somewhat different. In Wonsan, Lieutenant General Edward M. Almond was thinking about the future in a strictly MacArthurian fashion. On October 30 the general held a briefing at his command post for Major General David Barr, commander of the army's 7th Division. The division, said the commander of the X Corps, would advance northward to Hyesanjin on the Yalu River. Meanwhile, the 1st Marine Division would move up the Sangchon Valley, which runs through the coastal plain to Chinhung-ni, Koto-ri, and Hagaru. The army 3rd Infantry would remain in reserve, guarding the rear area. This movement would be brisk and swift. "When we have cleared all this out," said General Almond, "the ROKs will take over, and we will pull our divisions out of Korea."

Following this briefing, Colonel Edward H. Forney, the chief U.S. Marine Corps liaison officer on Almond's staff, arranged for one marine officer to make a reconnaissance flight over the territory where the marines would operate. He was Major Henry J. Woessner, the operations officer of the 7th Marines. What he saw below was the spacious coastal plain of the Songchon estuary. The port city of Hungnam and the town of Yonpo flank the mouth of the Songchon River. Eight miles upstream is Hamhung, which straddles the

MAP 4

road from Wonsan to Songjin. (See Map 4.) If one went far enough along the road up the coast, one would reach the Soviet border.

But if from Hamhung one turned left a few miles up the road, one would be on a narrow, dirt and gravel passage, flanked by a narrow gauge railroad, which winds its way seventy-eight miles to Yudam-ni on the western end of the Chosin Reservoir. The first half of the road, as far as Chinhung-ni, moves through flat land and rolling hills. At Chinhung-ni the terrain changes abruptly, and one moves into mountain peaks as formidable as the Colorado Rockies. The road narrows from double to single lane, and, in the eight miles of Funchilin Pass, it rises 2,500 feet, with a cliff on one side and a vertical drop on the other. Two miles south of Koto-ri the road reaches a high plateau. The road follows the Chongjin River to Hagaru, at the edge of the Chosin Reservoir. From there the road goes into the mountains again and winds up through the 4,000-foot Toktong Pass, then down through a series of gorges to the valley that leads to Yudam-ni.

Major Woessner and his army pilot flew in the T-6 over this whole area that afternoon. The scenery was rugged, but the land was apparently as peaceful as a Swiss valley. They did not see a single enemy vehicle, column, or even soldier, although there were thousands of them down there somewhere, as marine intelligence had indicated.

When Major Woessner returned to the 7th Marines that evening after the flight, Colonel Homer L. Litzenberg, commander of the regiment, held another briefing, this one for the officers and noncommissioned officers of the regiment. The colonel, like General Smith, the commander of the 1st Marine Division, did not have a great deal of faith in the judgment of General Almond or of General MacArthur. He warned that the regiment might very soon be involved in the opening battle of World War III. They would be fighting the Chinese, he said, and it was important that they win this first engagement, because of the effect it would have in Moscow and Peking.

Colonel Litzenberg and the other regimental commanders of the 1st Marine Division were no happier than General Smith with General Almond's planning or direction. They had already suffered through one example of his errors, when he had ordered a night attack against the "retreating" North Koreans in Seoul, at a time when the North Koreans were stepping out in a counterattack. Nor were the marines very pleased with the situation of X Corps, fifty miles from the right flank of the Eighth Army, with their left flank wide open. They had done what they could since Seoul to change the planning and had met with absolutely no success. The plan was MacArthur's alone, and Almond was his loyal protégé.

On November 1 the 7th Marines moved up from Hamhung to a position behind the ROK 26th Regiment south of Majon-dong. (See Map 5.) The ROK regiment had just come out of a fight in which they discovered they were attacked by troops of the Chinese 124th Division. They and the marines knew of three Chinese divisions in their immediate area, around the Chosin and Fusen reservoirs, at a time when MacArthur and his planners were talking of fewer than 30,000 Chinese in all Korea.

General Smith's intelligence officer suggested that the Chinese intervention was not, as Tokyo thought, a matter of volunteer cadres and piecemeal units, but a planned movement of at least one army group and several armies. The only question was whether or not the Chinese had yet decided on full-scale intervention. But even the marines did not recognize the real nature of the threat. They were puzzled by what reasoning would lead the Chinese to consider intervention when the North Korean army was virtually destroyed.

The next few days did nothing to unravel the puzzle. On October 31 and November 1 the ROK forces in the north withdrew, since the marines were replacing them. The ROKs were attacked by a large Chinese patrol four miles south of Sudong, but the engagement was brief and did not give any indication of what the Chinese were really up to.

The 1st Battalion of the 7th Marines moved up to Majon-dong that day, followed by the 2nd Battalion. On November 2 they were accompanied on

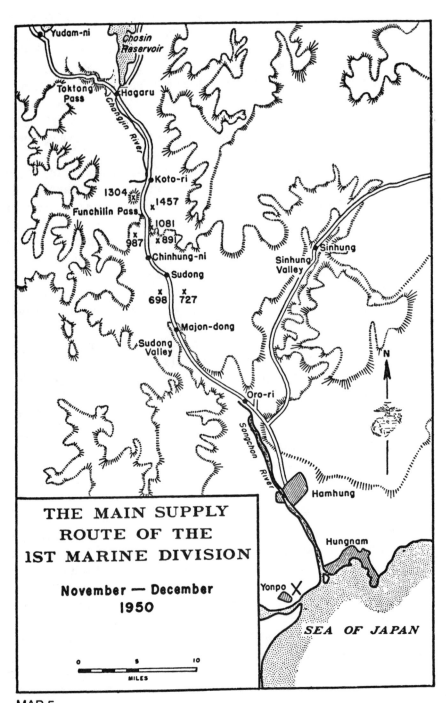

THE MAIN SUPPLY
ROUTE OF THE
1ST MARINE DIVISION

November — December
1950

MAP 5

the march by Corsairs of the marine fighter squadron VMF-312, which orbited the columns, ready to give close support if a battle developed. There was no battle, but the 1st Battalion did come under long-range fire that gave the unit a few casualties. By noon they were in position and two batteries of the 11th Marine artillery regiment were with them.

The 2nd Battalion was to replace ROK troops on Hill 698. Company D went up the hill. When the ROK troops saw the Americans coming, they fled down the hill instead of waiting. Company D moved up against light resistance. When it grew a little heavier, Captain Milton A. Hull stopped the company and called for an air strike. A few minutes later a flight of Corsairs came in and worked over the hill, but the air strike did not solve Captain Hull's problem. His assault platoons were working on a steep, unprotected slope under fire from camouflaged Chinese positions. The marines worked their way up, taking casualties, and reached the ridge line. But the Chinese were still all around them, and the marines were tiring from the climb up 1,600 feet from the valley. Hull stopped the advance and called for support fire from the artillery. For some reason it did not come. Company D, however, had relief when Company E passed through and occupied a plateau near the crest of the ridge. By this time it was dark. Company A was deployed across Hill 532 and part way up the slope of Hill 727. The company 3.5-inch bazooka squad was along the road in case tanks showed up. The 60 mm mortar section was in low ground behind the spur of the hill with the company command posts. Captain Hull was not in the command post, having decided to spend the night in an outpost with a rifle platoon.

Company C was on the northeast slope of Hill 698, and so was Company B. The battalion's 81 mm mortars were on low ground.

The 2nd Battalion was located at the foot of Hill 698 and along the slopes of Hill 727. The antitank and 4.2-inch mortar companies were down in a meadow behind Company F. South of a bend in the road was the 3rd Battalion, protecting the regiment's supply train, the artillery, and the regimental command post. Companies H and I occupied high ground along the road farther south. But south of them was a valley that bothered Colonel Litzenberg. It joined the Sudong Valley below Oro-ri. (See Map 5.) He sent a helicopter out on a reconnaissance mission in the middle of the afternoon, but absolutely nothing was seen of any enemy concentrations in the valley.

During the daylight hours planes of VMF-312 and VMF-513 had flown about twenty missions in support, thus causing the Chinese to stay under cover. As evening came, however, the Chinese began to fire 120 mm mortars and one artillery piece. One mortar round struck in the 1st Battalion's command post and wounded three men. But as night closed in, the area seemed generally quiet. What the marines did not know was that they faced the entire Chinese 124th Division, so skillfully concealed that they had no inkling of its presence. The division's 371st Regiment was on the north and west of the road, the 370th Regiment was east of the road on high ground, and the 372nd Regiment was in reserve a few miles to the Chinese rear.

That evening was very quiet, although two Chinese battalions at Sudong were preparing an attack. They would use the *haichi shiki* formation, which meant a double envelopment by an inverted V formation. This action involved sending a small unit straight forward into the teeth of the enemy, to spring the trap. Then, as the enemy surged forward, the two enveloping columns would slip around behind and surround them. This was, of course, the same technique that the North Koreans had used and for the very good reason that many of the North Koreans officers had learned their trade in the Chinese Communist armies.

At 11:00 P.M. the 1st Battalion reported an attack on Hill 727. The report was premature, the Chinese were simply probing, but it did alert the whole regiment to the fact that this was not going to be a quiet night after all.

An hour later the attack began for certain, with heavy fire on Hills 698 and 727 and the blasting of those Chinese bugles as the attackers came abreast of the marine positions, working down ridge lines on each side. At one o'clock in the morning the 1st and 2nd battalions were being hit on both flanks as the Chinese tried to envelop the regiment. (See Map 6.)

Company A and Company F on the east and Company B on the west were hit first. The initial attack knocked out a number of marines of Company A. Sergeant James Irsley Poynter saw the Chinese setting up three machine gun positions only twenty-five yards away from him. He gathered up all the grenades he could find on the fallen men and set out to take those positions. He killed the crew of the first machine gun and, then, the crew of the second. Then he went after the third. He knocked out the gun but was killed in the attempt. Posthumously he was to be awarded the Medal of Honor.

Over at the position of Company B, the men of the 3rd Platoon were nervous. During the afternoon they had seen some Chinese activity. Platoon Sergeant Archie Van Winkle had spent much of the time potting at Chinese with an old Springfield '03 with a sniper scope. Chinese bugles screamed, whistles blew, and flares shot up all around. The 7th Marines had only been organized two and a half months earlier at Camp Pendleton. They had fought very well in the drive on Seoul, but that was the limit of their experience. Platoon Sergeant Van Winkle steadied his men in their positions on the ridge. "I'll tell you when," he said. "Just sit tight."

He took a fire team up the hill and set up an observation post. He had a

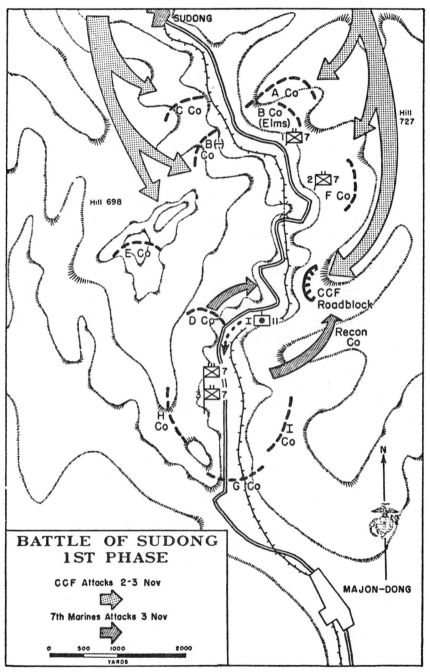

SUDONG

Hill
727

C Co

A Co

B Co
(Elms)

B(-)
Co

1 ⊠ 7

Hill 698

2 ⊠ 7

F Co

E Co

CCF
Roadblock

D Co

1 ◼ ll

Recon
Co

7
ll
7

3 ⊠ 7

H
Co

I
Co

N

G Co

MAJON-DONG

BATTLE OF SUDONG
1ST PHASE

CCF Attacks 2-3 Nov

7th Marines Attacks 3 Nov

0   500   1000   2000
YARDS

MAP 6

phone, and he kept listening on it to talk from other platoons, until the phone went dead. He realized, then, that his platoon was coming under fire, and he took the fire team back down the hill. When he reached the foxhole line, he found that the Chinese were coming from every direction. He still had that old Springfield, instead of his M-1, but he fed cartridges in one by one and began firing. He was charged by a Chinese, and he picked up the Springfield and used it as a club to put that enemy down. He did the same several times more. When he saw that the center of the platoon line had caved in under Chinese attack, he took off on a frontal assault by himself, charging across forty yards of open ground under fire to reach his left flank squad. He got there, but he was hit. His left arm was struck in the elbow and a grenade ripped open his left shoulder to the bone and knocked him down. He got up and kept fighting. He was kneeling, trying to load the Springfield with one hand, when he saw a Chinese red stick grenade come tumbling at him. It exploded directly against his chest, and he went down again.

Shortly after the battle began on the hills, marines at the command post of Company A heard the telltale clanking of a tracked vehicle coming down the road from the north. It was a T-34 tank, but in the dark the marines mistook it for one of their own bulldozers. The tank rumbled directly past the rocket section, and for some reason the bazooka men did not fire. It rolled right into the command post and stopped. Its single headlight burned into the mortar crews and the command post itself.

"Tank!" somebody shouted.

A burst of machine gun fire from the T-34 sent marines scattering for cover. Then the tank began to move again toward the 81 mm mortars. The 85 mm gun spoke up, and four shells flashed through the night. But all missed the mortars.

The bazooka men of Company C and the recoilless rifles of the 7th Antitank Company began firing on the tank. One 75 mm round hit the T-34, and it began to burn. The driver swung around and headed back north. It approached Company A's roadblock, and the bazooka men put one rocket into it. The tank replied with an 85 mm shell that knocked out most of the antitank crew; then, trailing sparks and flames, the tank moved around the bend and disappeared up the road.

Meanwhile, the fighting on Hill 698 and Hill 727 spread down to the road, the Chinese forcing the 1st and 2nd platoons of Company A into the 3rd Platoon's positions. Two platoons of Company B were forced down onto the low ground, but later they recaptured their foxholes on the hill.

The Chinese moved down to the low ground and swarmed over the valley. They overran most of the 4.2-inch mortar company and captured one mortar tube.

As dawn came on November 3, marines and Chinese seemed to be all mixed up down in the valley. The rifle companies were up on the hills and the Chinese occupied the ground between them and the 1st and 2nd battalion command posts.

Colonel Litzenberg had to do something quickly to regain the initiative from the Chinese. He ordered up the heavy weapons. The 4.2-inch mortars and the eighteen howitzers of three batteries thundered against the Chinese positions. Beginning with first light, VMF-312 began sending planes to bomb and strafe the enemy positions on the ridges and to seek out and destroy enemy artillery and vehicles on the road to the north.

On the ground, the marines set about evicting the Chinese from the valley floor and the hillsides. They found Sergeant Van Winkle, hunched down on the ground at his position, half conscious.

He was hurried back to an aid station. It was remarkable that he was still alive since the Chinese grenade had broken every one of his ribs.

With the assistance of artillery, their own mortars, and the air strikes, the 1st Battalion cleared the low ground of enemy troops by noon. The Chinese tried to escape north along the road but were annihilated by the heavy machine guns of the weapons company. Nearly seven hundred Chinese dead were counted in the 1st Battalion's zone of operations.

That day the Chinese held stubbornly to positions on Hill 727. Early on November 3 an air drop brought supplies to the beleaguered 2nd Battalion. D and E Companies moved out to clear the Chinese away. Company D circled to the left along the incline of Hill 698, and Company E moved up Hill 698. At eight o'clock in the morning, Lieutenant John Yancey's 2nd Platoon moved onto a small plateau below the crest. Lieutenant Robert T. Bey's 3rd Platoon then moved through to assault the peak but was thrown back by a tremendous barrage of grenades. Another air strike was called, and after the Corsairs had worked over the ridge line, Company E secured the crest of the hill. They found forty dead Chinese there.

All this activity occupied every rifle company, so Colonel Litzenberg called up headquarters troops to assault the Chinese roadblock on the north end of the perimeter. Lieutenant Earl R. Delong of the antitank company led the men with a 75 mm recoilless rifle. Under the cover of an air strike and artillery, Delong moved up to within five hundred yards of the enemy block point. Meanwhile, the division's reconnaissance company ascended the ridge east of the regimental command post and advanced north to envelop the roadblock. From a hillside they took the rear of the Chinese position under fire.

Delong began firing 75 mm high explosive and white phosphorus shells in the front of the Chinese position. The recon company fired on the rear. Company D, having cleaned up Hill 698, came down to help and prepared to make an infantry assault. The airmen brought their planes down and flamed the position with napalm, blasted it with bombs, and strafed it. The Chinese began an orderly withdrawal into the hills to the east of the road, and shortly after 6:00 P.M. they were gone, leaving twenty-eight dead.

So, by nightfall of November 3 the road was again open, the Chinese counterattack in strength had been defeated, and the marines had the situation in hand. Trucks came up to deliver supplies to the forward battalions and to evacuate Sergeant Van Winkle and about a hundred other wounded marines back to Hungnam. For his valor during that long night of November 2 Van Winkle won the Medal of Honor and was given a battlefield commission.

The coming of darkness brought some apprehension but no repeat of the Chinese infantry attack. Those two Chinese regiments had been very badly hurt in their encounter with the marines, and they moved back three miles north of Sudong to join the third reserve regiment of the Chinese 124th Division. The 370th and 371st regiments had lost the equivalent of five companies, or more than a thousand men. The marines had learned something in their first major encounter with the Chinese army, a bit of knowledge that was to become doctrine: when the Chinese staged a night attack, its effect could be nullified by holding fast in position until dawn and then bringing in the aircraft and artillery to break down the Chinese force.

That single T-34 tank that had attacked down the road on the night of November 2 was one of five North Korean tanks that represented all that was left of the NK 344th Tank Regiment. The tank had rattled off northward after its unsuccessful attack and was found abandoned the next day. The other four tanks moved up to Chinhung-ni and took up defensive positions there. (See Map 5.)

On the morning of November 4 Colonel Litzenberg sent out patrols along the road and the hills toward the Chosin Reservoir. He expected more trouble because air observers had reported sighting some three hundred enemy vehicles along the road the day before.

When the patrols returned early in the morning with the word that no enemy were in sight as far as Sudong, the regiment prepared to move out, leaving the 2nd Battalion on Hill 698 and Hill 727 to guard the regimental flanks.

As they moved north, the reconnaissance company took the lead. In the middle of Sudong they surprised a group of Chinese soldiers and captured twenty of them. They took the high ground above Sudong without opposition and moved on. They moved on toward Chinhung-ni, followed closely by the 1st Battalion.

At Chinhung-ni the highway runs east of the river, while the railroad and the station sit on the west side. The station, called Samgo, was also the railhead for the cable car system that ran up Funchilin Pass. (See Map 7.)

The recon company approached the town with the 2nd Platoon in the lead. Behind came a section of recoilless rifles. A little over a mile outside the town they saw fresh tank tracks and stopped. Lieutenant Colonel Raymond G. Davis, commander of the 1st Battalion, told them to move on, so they did. At the highway entrance to the town they moved in, and, when they reached a point opposite Samgo station, they saw a large number of Chinese soldiers in and around the station. The marines opened fire on the Chinese, and they scattered. Suddenly, Lieutenant Donald W. Sharon spotted a T-34 tank, concealed under a pile of brush on the right hand side of the road. He climbed up on top of the tank and so did Staff Sergeant Richard B. Twohey and Corporal Joseph E. McDermott. As they boarded the tank, the periscope began to revolve. McDermott smashed the glass of the hatch, and Twohey dropped in a grenade. They jumped down as the grenade exploded inside. The tank lurched forward toward the marines, Twohey jumped back on and dropped another grenade. It exploded, and the tank stopped and began to smoke.

Now, Staff Sergeant William L. Vick came up with a 75 mm gun and a bazooka crew. They blasted the T-34. Just then, Sharon saw a thatched hut down the road come apart and another tank appear from the wreckage, its 85 mm gun turning toward the marines in the valley. Lieutenant Dan C. Holland, the battalion air controller, called for an air strike. Up above, a Corsair peeled off and came down into the valley.

The 75 mm guns began firing and so did the bazookas. The T-34 took several hits but was not stopped. It came on menacingly toward the road that was filled with troops and vehicles. The Corsair was screaming in at this point, and the pilot let go two 5-inch rockets. He scored two direct hits, and the T-34 blew up on the road.

Lieutenant Sharon's platoon continued to advance. They saw another tank camouflaged against a hillside. Just at that moment marines behind them,

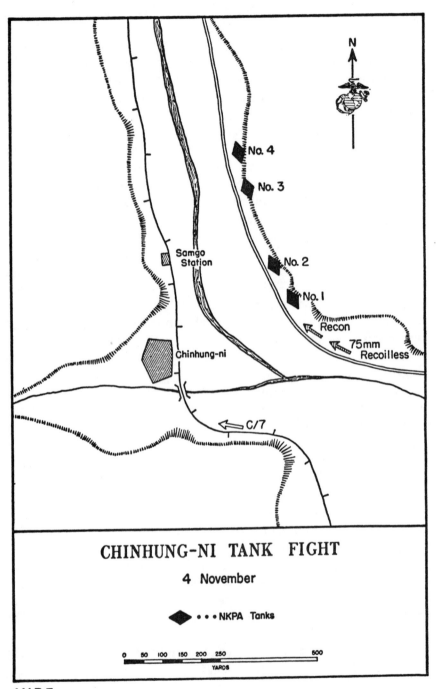

N

No. 4

No. 3

Samgo
Station

No. 2

No. I

Recon

75mm
Recoilless

Chinhung-ni

C/7

CHINHUNG-NI TANK FIGHT

4 November

●●● NKPA Tanks

0   50 100 150 200 250   500
YARDS

MAP 7

opposite Chinhung-ni, stumbled on a tank that Sharon and his men had not even seen as they passed. The bazookas and the recoilless rifles opened up, and the tank crew came out and surrendered. Seeing this, the crew of the last tank also surrendered without a fight, and the tank was destroyed.

Colonel Litzenberg ordered the 7th Marines to stop and set up their perimeter around Chinhung-ni. The rest of the afternoon would be spent bringing all the regiment's elements up and consolidating positions.

Colonel Litzenberg knew that the Chinese occupied the top of Funchilin Pass, but that was about all he did know about their positions. To find the enemy, at four o'clock in the afternoon he ordered the reconnaissance company to patrol a little over a mile into Funchilin Pass and establish an outpost on the southern tip of Hill 891. (See Map 8.)

Lieutenant Charles R. Puckett's 3rd Platoon led the way in a motorized column. When they were about a mile into the pass, they followed a hairpin turn in the road, where the highway veered east for a thousand yards. As they moved around the turn, they came under fire from three directions. Chinese troops occupied Hill 987 on the left, Hill 891 in front, and a patrol had moved up on the road on the right.

Puckett and his men were pinned down. He called for an air strike and got it, which relieved the pressure somewhat. As darkness lowered, the column retreated to the marine lines with two killed and five wounded. The first two jeeps in the column had been destroyed.

That night Colonel Litzenberg was ready for another night assault by the Chinese but it did not develop. On the morning of November 5 the marines set out again. This day the 1st Platoon of the recon company led. It set out along the road, and when it reached the hairpin curve, it was pinned down, just as the marines had been the day before. The results, however, were slightly different: Colonel Litzenberg had planned for this, and from positions south of Sudong the howitzers and the 4.2-inch mortars began high-angle fire on the Chinese positions ahead. On the move was the 3rd Battalion, passing on both sides of Chinhung-ni, Company I moving on Hill 987, and Company G on Hill 891. As they came up to positions abreast of the bend in the road, the Chinese began firing on them, and for the rest of the day Chinese and Americans exchanged fire. The Chinese fired their 122 mm mortars, and the marines fired their howitzers. The marines won that artillery battle by destroying an ammunition dump on the Chinese side and by destroying one mortar and damaging two others badly enough to put them out of action. The airmen came in and worked over the Chinese-held ridges, and the Chinese suffered heavy losses. When night fell they still held their positions, but they did not try a night attack.

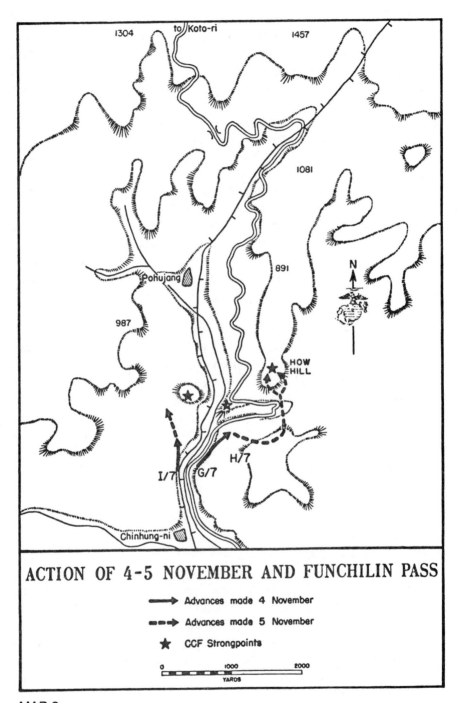

1304

to Koto-ri

1457

1081

891

N

Pohujang

987

HOW HILL

H/7

I/7 G/7

Chinhung-ni

ACTION OF 4-5 NOVEMBER AND FUNCHILIN PASS

→ Advances made 4 November

-→ Advances made 5 November

★ CCF Strongpoints

0   1000   2000
YARDS

MAP 8

The marine objective was the village of Koto-ri. On the morning of November 6, Company H of the marines moved up to begin an attack toward Hill 891. The approach was to outflank the Chinese from the southeast. The company waited until four o'clock in the afternoon for air support; following the air strike on the hill, the American artillery and mortars began firing on the Chinese positions. Two assault platoons started up separate draws. Lieutenant Minard Newton's platoon began receiving fire about a hundred yards up the hill. The going was hard because the slope was steep and the powdery soil crumbled underfoot. On the right, Lieutenant Robert Reem's platoon met no opposition. The plan to envelop the Chinese encountered an unexpected obstacle when the two draws joined near the top of the hill and so did the marine platoons. Lieutenant Howard H. Harris, the commander of Company H, sent Newton's platoon to the top, with Reem's platoon behind it. Up there Newton was to swing to the right, and Reem was to envelop on the left. As the marines moved, the Chinese met them with a hail of grenades and counterattacked Newton on the left. For a time it appeared that the marines would be thrown back, but Sergeant Charlie Foster made a one-man charge to the top and drove the Chinese back. He was killed in the attempt, but his heroic action saved the moment.

In the fighting on the left Lieutenant Reem gathered his squad leaders to instruct them on the final assault. An enemy grenade came lobbing into the middle of the group, and Reem fell on it to save the others. He was killed, and Sergeant Anthony J. Riccardi took command of the platoon.

It was growing late and dark, and the marines were tired out. Lieutenant Harris radioed battalion that he was sending for his reserve platoon since the Chinese still held the crest of the hill. Company H had suffered only eight casualties, but their ammunition was low. When Colonel Litzenberg received the report, he ordered Company H to disengage for the night and come down the hill. They went back down the hill, carrying the wounded and the body of Lieutenant Reem, and secured within the marine lines at eight o'clock that night.

The next morning when the assault was renewed, there was no opposition. The Chinese had vanished during the night. It was November 7, the day the Chinese withdrew from their engagement with the Eighth Army on the other side of the peninsula. The marines speculated that the Chinese had withdrawn because of heavy losses. It was true that their 124th Division had been made ineffective in the last few days, but that was not the real reason for the Chinese withdrawal. They had plenty of other divisions to throw into the battle. They were awaiting the turn of events.

3

The War Changes

Who were these Chinese who had so suddenly entered the Korean War? Peking Radio said they were "volunteers." In fact, they were nothing of the sort, but regular Chinese army soldiers assigned to Korea.

One reason the Americans were confused was that the first few Chinese prisoners captured wore North Korean uniforms. The first unit to come in contact with the Americans consisted of about 2,000 soldiers who had come down from Tangshan, Manchuria, and ridden by train to Antung on the Yalu River. They had been issued North Korean uniforms and had then crossed the river on October 19. They had been part of a force of five Chinese armies that had moved into the North Korean mountains between October 13 and October 20. Each army consisted of three infantry divisions, plus supporting troops. Each division was set at 10,000 men, although sometimes they were smaller. But the Chinese troops who came into Korea in the last half of October were told that Peking was sending 600,000 men in, to destroy the American army.

The first Chinese were identified on October 25, and in the next week General MacArthur exhibited enormous contempt for them. They wore brown padded uniforms over their summer uniforms and rubber shoes. They had no weapons heavier than light mortars and machine guns. Most of them carried old Japanese .25 caliber rifles left over from the Kwantung Army of

1945. About 20 percent of them had no weapons at all. Their training was minimal. So the appraisal of the American intelligence officers had some basis in fact, although it was hasty and, in the final analysis, made the mistake of initially underrating the enemy.

When it became apparent on November 1 that the Eighth Army faced a strong enemy force in the Unsan area, General Walker had to reappraise his whole operational plan. From Tokyo were still coming the demands for "attack! attack! attack!" But Walker's supply line was attenuated, and his forces also strung out. By November 2, the day the 3rd Battalion was abandoned to its fate, he had ordered the withdrawal from the north and concentration along the Chongchon and Taeryong rivers in the Anju–Pakchon area. (See Map 2.) The 27th British Commonwealth Brigade and the U.S. 19th Infantry Regiment were told to remain on the north bank of the rivers to protect the bridges and fords. General Walker still had enough confidence in the future to look to resuming his attack.

By the evening of November 3 the 27th Brigade was in position around Pakchon, having moved down from Taechon in the face of a Chinese attack.

That same day the 19th Infantry moved to its new assigned position, north of the Chongchon River, east of Anju. The ROK 1st Division then moved through the 19th Infantry and retreated across the river to join the rest of I Corps.

In Tokyo and in Washington there was a good deal of confusion about the situation of the Eighth Army. The wheels were already in motion to stop the buildup of supplies and troops in the Far East; one division in Japan was scheduled to be moved to bolster European defenses. United Nations members who had earlier pledged to send troops to join the common effort were canceling the pledges with great relief since their help no longer seemed to be necessary in view of General MacArthur's claims that victory was on the horizon.

Major General Charles L. Bolté, the G-3 (operations) officer of the Department of the Army, had flown in to Tokyo at the end of October to discuss all these reductions in force. Even as he was talking them over with MacArthur's staff, the Chinese struck. Bolté could make no sense of the optimism that hung over Tokyo, so he flew to Pyongyang to discuss the matter with General Walker. He talked to Eighth Army staff, to the corps commanders, and to some of the division commanders. He was exposed to the sense of confusion and panic that had overtaken the command and had brought about the general retreat below the Chongchon. No matter what they were saying in Tokyo, Bolté cabled Washington, there must be no withdrawal of forces. The

Eighth Army needed all the help it could get. What they were saying in Tokyo was enormously confusing to Washington. Besides the Chinese troops operating against the Eighth Army, Chinese elements were captured at the end of October in the Hamhung area of the east coast where X Corps was operating independently. MacArthur's attitude toward that development was that it represented nothing serious. "Not alarming," said the general. But the next day, November 1, he said he did not know what the Chinese were doing or thinking. The following day he had a still newer appraisal of the military situation from General Willoughby, his intelligence officer. Willoughby announced that there were 16,500 Chinese soldiers in Korea. They were "The Volunteer Corps for the Protection of the Hydroelectric Zone." This report changed MacArthur's mind, at least for that day, and on November 2 he told the Pentagon that the Chinese intervention was "a serious proximate threat."

On November 1, at the State Department, Deputy Secretary Robert A. Lovett had expressed serious concern over the intelligence report that the Chinese intended to establish a *cordon sanitaire* south of the Yalu border to protect the reservoirs and power plants. That action would certainly change the nature of the war from the simple roundup that MacArthur had been discussing in recent weeks.

Lovett spoke to several important Pentagon officers, and they agreed that the rollback of forces had to be stopped immediately. Instead of calling on the UN members for less, the Americans would have to call on them for much more. So, on November 3, despite MacArthur's backing and filling, the process of rollback in Korea was stopped. The Department of the Army had taken action to send 40,000 replacements to Korea in November and December, and the orders stood.

Along the Eighth Army front on November 3 General Walker faced three Chinese armies, although he had no knowledge of that enormous strength. The Chinese 40th Army had engaged and virtually destroyed the ROK 6th Division at Onjong. It had been joined by the Chinese 38th Army, and the two armies had then pushed what was left of the ROK II Corps back southwest along the valley of the Chongchon to the edge of Kunu-ri. On November 3 the Chinese attacked again and moved down to a point two and a half miles from Kunu-ri. (See Map 2.)

The Chinese 39th Army had attacked the ROK 1st Division at Unsan and, then, the 8th Cavalry positions and had surrounded the 8th Cavalry's 3rd Battalion and decimated it.

Over on the X Corps eastern side of Korea, the Chinese 42nd Army had marched to the Changjin Reservoir and on October 25 had fought the ROK

26th Regiment there. Some troops of the 124th Division engaged the 1st Marine Division, but most of this Chinese army took up position south of the reservoir to await events, blocking the roads to Kanggye.

On November 4 the Chinese drove toward Kunu-ri. The key to the whole area defense was the point on the map called Hill 622. It stood three miles from Kunu-ri and dominated the valley of the Chongchon as well as the rail and road lines passing down the valley. It was held by the 3rd and 5th regiments of the ROK 7th Division. Backing them up was the 5th Regimental Combat Team of the U.S. 24th Division and the ROK 8th Division in reserve.

The attack began in the morning. The Chinese broke the 3rd Regiment's position, and the troops began retreating down the mountain. But when they hit the lines of the 5th RCT, Captain Hubert H. Ellis, commander of Company C, ordered them to go back and fight, and they did. Soon the ROK 8th Regiment was also committed to the hill. Several times during the day the position changed hands, but by nightfall the South Koreans had it back again.

Another element of Chinese attacked the 5th RCT itself and forced it to withdraw about a thousand yards from its position at Kunu-ri. This attack was conducted by what the Americans in the field believed to be a full division. There were many acts of heroism that day, including that of Lieutenant Morgan B. Hansel of Company C, who charged single-handedly into several Chinese machine gun positions. He knocked out a number of them but finally was killed. By such actions on the part of Americans and South Koreans the positions were saved, and at the end of the day the Chinese had been repulsed.

But if there was one thing the Chinese had in plenty, it was manpower. While the attacks were occurring during the day in the Kunu-ri area, equal forces were attacking the bridgehead on the northern bank of the Chongchon.

It began with the movement of about a battalion (a thousand men) across the Kuryong River at the position of the 1st Battalion of the 19th Infantry. Aerial observers spotted the troops moving south, trying to outflank the American positions. They did so with ridiculous ease; the Americans abandoned their heavy equipment and infiltrated across the Kuryong and the Chongchon rivers to friendly territory. Most of the men escaped, but they had lost their part of the bridgehead.

While the 1st Battalion was putting up its desultory battle and then running, the 3rd Battalion tried to fight through to help, but it was repelled by a strong Chinese force on the road.

By this time it was apparent that what was needed was some command north of the river. Major General John H. Church, the 24th Division commander, ordered Brigadier General Garrison H. Davidson, his assistant, to go north and take over command of all division troops and to coordinate their efforts with those of the 27th British Commonwealth Brigade. The command up there would be known as Task Force Davidson.

By one o'clock on the afternoon of November 4, General Davidson was on the north bank of the Chongchon. Things went badly from the beginning. The Americans were being driven back. It did not seem likely that they could hold the bridgehead unassisted. General Walker wanted that bridgehead for the future, so General Church committed the U.S. 21st Infantry to the battle. That night they crossed the river.

During the night the Chinese made one of their night attacks and penetrated the 19th Infantry's lines, but next morning the 21st Infantry attacked and restored the lines.

By November 5 the Korean civilians were making a voiceless comment on the state of the war: they were moving south in droves. In two days the Americans counted twenty thousand civilians who moved south across the Chongchon.

The UN position on the north bank of the Chongchon was most insecure. A large mountain mass lay in a five-mile gap between the 19th Infantry and the British brigade. This was no-man's-land, and the Chinese could move around it freely. The 19th Infantry's extreme left flank was at Hill 123, which overlooked this gap and the valley village of Chonghyon, four miles north of the Chongchon River.

On the night of November 5 the Chinese began an attack all along the bridgehead. They found the field telephone lines of Company E and Company G and followed them up to the positions. On Hill 123 Company G and Company E were completely surprised, and many of the men were shot in their sleeping bags. In a few minutes the entire position was overrun. Why this should have happened is a mystery explicable only by pointing fingers at the officers on the scene. The 19th Infantry had been engaged in Korea since July 4 and had participated in many engagements. It should have been tougher and more "battle-wise" than it was showing itself to be. Perhaps part of the failure was overconfidence. If so, the regiment, known as "The Rock of Chickamauga," was paying dearly for the fault.

Even in the rout, there were, as so often happened, singular instances of great valor. Corporal Michael Red Cloud had been trained as a BAR man, and he knew his job. His position was at a point on the ridge where a trail climbed up to the Company E command post. Suddenly out of the night a large group of Chinese attacked him. He swung up his BAR and began firing.

He was wounded. He dragged himself to his feet and supported himself with one arm around a small tree and continued to fire his Browning Automatic Rifle, until he was killed.

Another BAR man also distinguished himself that night. He was Private First Class Joseph W. Balboni. He was also attacked by Chinese soldiers who had sneaked up to within seventy-five feet of his position. He, too, began firing and fired, until he fell.

Nevertheless, the position was soon overrun, and the battalion quickly withdrew half a mile from the line. There the Chinese moved so fast and so competently that the battalion was barely able to hold. All that saved them was the coming of daylight. The Chinese withdrew.

On the south side of the Changchon, the battered remnants of the 1st Battalion of the 19th Infantry were reequipped and reinforced and sent back to fight on the north side of the river. They counterattacked on the morning of November 6 and closed up the gaps. Soon the position of the Americans along the bridgehead was restored.

When patrols moved in to reoccupy Hill 123, they found Red Cloud and Balboni, each with a pile of dead Chinese around his position, attesting to the bravery of their single-handed fighting.

The Chinese had surprised the Americans, and they had driven them back temporarily, but at a cost no American commander would have liked to have paid. The Americans counted 474 dead Chinese around Hill 123, and some had already been buried by their fellows. There must have been an equal number of wounded. Most of these were victims of artillery fire, for during the long night the artillery on the south side of the Chongchon had fired constantly to protect the American positions. The scouts also found a number of dead North Koreans. Prisoner interrogation showed that the enemy had attacked with no less than three regiments to try to take the east side of the 19th Infantry's position next to the mountains.

On the morning of November 3 elements of the Chinese 39th Army and of the Chinese 66th Army attacked the British and Australian positions on the western side of the Chongchon. (The British knew a good deal more about their enemy than the Americans did even now. Their representation in Peking had paid off: they knew the units involved and their armament—the 1942 British Bren gun, the U.S. Thompson submachine gun, the rifle, stick grenade, and 7.62 mm light machine gun.)

The British and Australians withdrew to the north bank of the Chongchon, covering Sinanju, but on the morning of November 5, after the hard fight against the U.S. 19th Infantry the night before, the Chinese attacked on the other side of the mountain mass against the British and Australians.

The Australian 3rd Battalion and the Argyll 1st Battalion were occupying defense lines on the west side of the Taeryong River, opposite Pakchon. Company A of the Argylls was on the east side of the river, south of Pakchon, and the U.S. 61st Artillery Battalion was firing in support, from a position two and a half miles south of the town. During the night, as their fellows attacked the 19th Infantry positions, the Chinese moved east around Pakchon, and by daylight they were in position to start their attack, to cut off the brigade by cutting the road behind them. The object of the Chinese attack here was to blow a bridge on the Taeryong River, which, if it could be done, would prevent the British and Australian withdrawal.

To begin, a Chinese demolition party was killed by gunners within fifty feet of the bridge. (See Map 2.) The immediate Chinese target was the U.S. 61st Field Artillery Battalion. A battalion of Chinese began the attack at dawn with mortars and small arms. The battery commanders placed their men in tight rings around the gunners and manned their automatic weapons. They sent word to the British that they were being hit. Company A of the Argylls started down to relieve them. It was hard going because the Chinese had the river crossing ford under fire, and the men had to move across in single file. This was not only slow, but it cost the battalion a number of wounded.

As they came, the Americans were under heavy attack. Battery C was taking it worst of all. Captain Howard M. Moore moved one 105 mm howitzer around so that it could fire point-blank into the Chinese in the paddy field to the east. Forty-five minutes later another howitzer was turned around to do the same. The firing range averaged about three hundred yards, although some shells were fired at fifty yards.

The battery fired 1,400 rounds that morning. The Chinese just kept coming. At nine o'clock a pair of U.S. tanks arrived at the Battery C perimeter to help. They came just about in time, for the battery was nearly out of ammunition. They had lost two men killed and eighteen wounded. Then the Argylls arrived with two more tanks. They saw dead Chinese piled up within thirty yards of the artillerymen's gun muzzles.

With the help of the tanks, the Argylls moved against a nearby hill. They had air support, but a counterattack by superior Chinese forces forced them to withdraw from the hill.

In the daylight the observation planes were out. So were the air support fighter bombers, both American and those from the Australian 77th Squadron, a P-51 unit. The pilots reported that the Chinese, with their enormous skill in concealing large bodies of troops from air attack, had moved a whole division around the British brigade. The air attacks of the day helped break up the concentration. Brigadier Basil A. Coad ordered the Australian 3rd Battalion, which was still west of the Taeryong, to cross over to the east side. They passed through the Argylls and in the early afternoon attacked north toward Pakchon. Staging one of their famous bayonet charges, they regained the ground lost earlier, but at a cost of twelve men dead and sixty-four wounded.

By late afternoon it was apparent that there were just too many Chinese. The British brigade could hardly be expected to hold the northern salient, so the Middlesex 1st Battalion cleared the road south, and the troops moved out toward the Chongchon. That evening the Australians, the Middlesex and the Argylls set up a perimeter astride the Pakchon road, on the line of hills four miles north of the river. The night was quiet except for the constant racket of Chinese bugles and whistles. Next day the British made a count. The Chinese had lost about 1,300 men the day before.

On November 6 the Chinese milled around but did not make any attacks other than the predawn strike against the Kunu-ri area. That day they withdrew. Nor did the Chinese on the east side of the peninsula launch any attacks. There were signs of their drawback all along the line. They were obviously sending a message to the United Nations forces: do not advance, and we will not advance. They also gave a number of signals to the Americans. The common practice of the North Koreans in dealing with seriously wounded enemy soldiers was to shoot them immediately. In several cases the Chinese brought the wounded Americans by stretcher to neutral territory where they could be picked up, and they suspended attacks so that wounded in the battlefield could be saved. They also released a number of prisoners, asking them to tell their friends that they had been treated well and that the Chinese did not wish to fight. All this indicated that it was not yet too late for the Americans to heed Chou En-lai's warnings and that if they simply did not advance further, some accommodation might be reached. The question now was what attitude the American high command would adopt toward the new situation.

4

The Wrong Moves

From the middle of October onward, there was another indication of trouble, which was almost totally ignored in the American authorities's planning and consideration of the future of the Korean War:

When the UN forces began moving above the 38th parallel, the airmen, as ordered by the high command, had been careful not to come within fifty miles of the Soviet and Manchurian borders.

On October 17 General Stratemeyer, the commander of the Far East Air Force, had set up a new "chop line," beyond which UN aircraft were not to operate. Essentially it ran twenty miles south of the Manchurian and Soviet borders. Later that month, as General MacArthur had urged the drive speeded to the Yalu, Stratemeyer had authorized close support air missions as near the border as necessary. Inevitably, on occasions airmen violated Soviet and Manchurian airspace. As of mid-October the Chinese were firing on UN aircraft that approached the border, and they shot several down.

Then on November 1, fifteen miles south of Sinuiju, three Yak fighters attacked two American aircraft. One of them, a B-26 bomber, shot down one of the Yaks. Later that day a pilot saw fifteen Yaks parked on the Sinuiju airstrip. American fighter bombers were summoned, and they strafed the field; on approaching the Yalu, one was shot down. And that day, for the first time, the Americans encountered a swept-wing jet fighter, a MIG-15, in

Korean airspace. The question was immediately raised as to whether these were Chinese or Soviet planes, but that point really did not make any difference. What the Americans were being told was that in the air, as well as on the ground, the northern neighbors of the North Koreans were prepared to take a hand if the American advance continued. Here was another unmistakeable warning, which General MacArthur chose to ignore, and so, unfortunately, did the Joint Chiefs of Staff.

On November 4 the Joint Chiefs found themselves so confused by the conflicting messages sent in recent days from Tokyo that they asked General MacArthur for a new appraisal of the situation.

MacArthur gave them four choices:

1. The Chinese intended to intervene with full force when they found it appropriate.

2. The Chinese would give "covert" military assistance, but for political reasons would conceal their assistance.

3. The Chinese would really permit and aid volunteers to flow into North Korea but not commit their own troops.

4. The Chinese had made an error in intervening, on the belief that only South Korean forces were coming north. They would withdraw.

This estimate was made despite the fact that prisoner interrogation a week earlier had shown that the Chinese in Korea were disciplined troops, sent in as units, and that most of them on the west side of Korea were regular army, many of them having fought for the Nationalists, until their generals surrendered the whole armies to the Communists. In other words, the Chinese were professionals, and many of them had trained under American advisors and were armed with American weapons.

MacArthur concluded his estimate with bland advice to the Joint Chiefs: "I recommend against hasty conclusions which might be premature and believe that a final appraisement should await a more complete accumulation of facts."

This November 4 estimate by General MacArthur flew in the face of other estimates by his own staff. For example, General Beiderlinden, MacArthur's personnel officer, had been demanding replacements in increasingly urgent tones. He was under no illusions about the decision of the Chinese to enter the war. On November 5 in a message to the Joint Chiefs of Staff he predicted increasing casualties as the UN forces fought the Chinese. He accepted Chinese intervention as a fact and expected the worst. He pointed out that battle casualties had risen from 40 a day in October to 326 a day in the first week of November. This was no flash in the pan, he said. This was what the UN could expect if the war continued.

Indeed, unlike his chief, General Beiderlinden gave the Joint Chiefs all the ammunition they needed for some vital reconsiderations. His conclusions were as follows:

1. The casualties would continue to mount.
2. The Chinese armies were well trained and highly disciplined.
3. The danger now faced was as great as that at the Pusan Perimeter.
4. The winter weather would make the fighting far more difficult for the UN.
5. This Chinese intervention was no "flash in the pan."

On November 4 the Peking government issued an official statement charging that the Americans were bent on conquering Korea and China and said that Chinese military forces had to assist North Korea.

But then the Chinese withdrew from contact with the Americans, British, and South Koreans. Signals again. They should not have been too hard to read. But how were these signals received in Washington and Tokyo?

Washington was understandably confused by the inconsistent messages from General MacArthur in Tokyo that week. One day it was business as usual and continue the drive to the Yalu; the next day it was plaintive wailing that the Chinese threatened his whole operation with their unfair entry into the war; the next day it was business as usual again. On November 3 General Willoughby decided there might be 34,000 Chinese in North Korea, rather than the 16,000 he had discussed a few days before. A full week earlier Hanson W. Baldwin, the military editor of the *New York Times,* had written that there were 200,000 Chinese soldiers inside Korea, and his estimate was just about correct. Why was Reporter Baldwin's intelligence so far superior to the American army's?

It was not until November 5 that Willoughby decided the Chinese had the strength to launch a major offensive—after they had already done so and smashed the ROK II Corps and forced General Walker to retreat. General Willoughby was not providing intelligence, he was stating history.

When the Chinese drew back, the fact was duly noted at the State Department, but no particular inferences were drawn. Harry Truman was a canny man with a strong intuition, and he might have drawn the proper inference if the congressional elections of 1950 had not gotten in the way. Politics is everything to a president, and the election was only one day off.

The failure of the Pentagon is not so hard to understand. The Joint Chiefs of Staff had already persuaded themselves that MacArthur could win the war against the Chinese if they did enter. They had not gone a step further and considered whether it was in the best interest of the United States to become bogged down in North Korea. And bogged down, the nation would have to be, because the Chinese could throw a million men into the conflict if they wished.

General MacArthur was not interested in reappraisal. He was a man possessed—his mania was that he had won this war with his stroke at Inchon, and that now the Chinese were unfairly trying to take the victory away from him. As biographer William Manchester put it, MacArthur was suffering from paranoia. His messages to Washington often indicated that he considered the U.S. military and political establishments to be as much his enemy as the North Koreans and Chinese. This is hardly a healthy attitude in a field commander.

On November 5 MacArthur pulled one of his little tricks, aimed at accomplishing a change in strategy without the permission of the Joint Chiefs of Staff, by creating a confusion of messages. He had done this before—sent a message and then ridden off into the night before the Joint Chiefs could answer.

On November 5 MacArthur received reports from aerial observers that a steady stream of Chinese was crossing the Yalu bridges. He panicked and ordered General Stratemeyer to send his B-29s up to bomb the bridges. "Combat crews are to be flown to exhaustion if necessary," he said. Except for the dams and hydroelectric plants, "every installation, factory and village" was to be destroyed.

The airmen agreed. They had been unhappy for months with the restrictions imposed on their activities. They had been told to stay clear of the Soviet and Manchurian borders. They had wanted to destroy Sinuiju early in October but had been refused by the Joint Chiefs. Early in November General Earle Partridge, commander of the Fifth Air Force, had again asked for permission to burn the city of Sinuiju in retaliation for the death of an aviator who had been shot down by flak over that city. Partridge also asked for permission for his pilots to fly "in hot pursuit" over Manchurian territory after enemy planes that attacked his aircraft and then skidded over the border. He wanted to go after them in the air, and, if they landed on airfields in Manchuria, to then attack the airfields. There could not possibly have been a more clear violation of airspace than that, and General Partridge's request was twice refused.

Yet, without any specific directive from Washington, by November 3 the air war was geared up. There was no specific reason that it could not be, since the Joint Chiefs's directive to MacArthur was fuzzy about the extent of his operations. As of November 3 the military was taking advantage of every bit of latitude in the directive. Kanggye was to be attacked by B-29s on

November 4, Sakchu and Pukchin on November 5, Sinuiju was to be hit on November 7. All were to be bombed with incendiaries; the announced purpose was to burn these cities to the ground (taking care to avoid only hospitals).

The first of the big new Korean raids was held up by weather until November 5. On that day twenty-one B-29s headed for Sakchu and Pukchin, but were diverted by bad weather and attacked Kanggye instead. They dropped 170 tons of incendiary bombs and claimed to have destroyed 65 percent of the city. This action was justified by the U.S. Air Force—as with these other cities—because each was claimed to be a "virtual arsenal and important communications center."

That series of attacks General Stratemeyer's airmen conceived for themselves. General MacArthur's demands were far broader. He wanted two weeks of maximum air effort to destroy the Korean end of all the international bridges across the Yalu River.

These orders were given to General Stratemeyer on November 6 and were to be carried out at dawn the next day. Stratemeyer was to be careful not to impinge on Manchurian territory but to bomb from the Korean side.

MacArthur would not have dared take such stringent action without at least pretending to inform the Joint Chiefs of Staff, but he had a method of making sure that the information arrived after the fact. This was the routine teleconference program between the Pentagon and Tokyo, a sort of open line that both sides used to convey nonurgent material. Under normal circumstances, because of the difference in time between Tokyo and Washington, nearly a day would pass before Washington would have dealt with this message, and, in the interim, the first raid would have been carried out.

General Stratemeyer smelled a rat; until this time he had been constrained from operations so close to Manchuria. Further, Stratemeyer was not at all sure that any effective bombing could be carried out without violating Manchurian territory, and in the preliminary discussions he had told MacArthur that. MacArthur was insistent. Furthermore, he wanted the Far East Air Force to begin working back south and to destroy "every means of communication, every installation, factory, city and village."

So Stratemeyer sent a fast message to the U.S. Air Force chiefs at the Pentagon, and they had it in time. Under Secretary of Defense Lovett feared that the bombing of the bridges would invariably lead to violations of Chinese territory. He took the matter up with Secretary of State Acheson and Assistant Secretary Rusk. The latter added a new element to the discussion: the United States had promised the British that the American command would not make attacks that might involve Manchuria without consultation. And there was always the Sino-Soviet mutual assistance treaty to consider. Further, the United States was just then trying to secure UN condemnation of the Chinese for entering the war. Failure to get it would weaken the position of the United States in calling for military participation by other UN members.

These American officials agreed among themselves that MacArthur should not be allowed to bomb the bridges; then they called Secretary of Defense Marshall. His position was more that of the military man. He agreed with them . . . But. The but referred to the possibility of mass movement of the Chinese across the Yalu, which might threaten MacArthur's forces. And, of course, that is precisely what was happening.

Marshall's position changed the focus of the argument in a manner that militated toward the MacArthur position. The President, who was at home in Missouri to vote in the next day's elections, was consulted on that basis, and he decided that the bombing should not be carried out unless the threat to the military was immediate.

The Joint Chiefs of Staff told MacArthur to lay off the bombing, pending consultation with the British and a more careful survey of events.

MacArthur came back immediately with a protest in which he indicated the situation in Korea was worse than at any time since July. And he was right, although, in view of the general's yawing back and forth, the Joint Chiefs tended to believe he was playacting again.

MacArthur demanded that the President be informed. He told the Joint Chiefs: "I believe that your instructions may well result in a calamity of major proportion for which I cannot accept the responsibility without his [Truman's] personal and direct understanding of the situation."

The buck was passed in a manner that had to both annoy and worry the President. Nothing that MacArthur had said at the October conference at Wake Island had prepared him for this. Indeed, MacArthur had assured all concerned that he was prepared to handle the situation if the Chinese did intervene. Nothing had been mentioned about Yalu bridges, Sino–Soviet pacts, or consultation with Allies by any of the parties involved. So, the President was now faced with another crisis decision for which no preparations had been made, and for which he still had the most inadequate of information. In such an atmosphere it had to be all but impossible for the American administration to take a long-range view, a problem from which it had suffered since the beginning of the Korean War.

The violent manner in which General MacArthur presented his case for disaster without the bombing of the Yalu bridges startled the Joint Chiefs of Staff and seemed to meet General Marshall's criterion of emergency. MacArthur had his way. The Joint Chiefs reversed themselves within a matter of hours, with the President's acceptance. There were restrictions: he was to bomb no power plants or dams, and he was not to violate Manchurian airspace. The Joint Chiefs added the proviso that he was to inform them of any hostile action from Manchuria. Why they did so seems again inexplicable; they already had evidence that each time the UN planes came near the border rivers they were bounced by fighters and that recently these fighters had become MIG-15s. Could anyone have believed that the Chinese and the Russians would take any less severe a view of the bombing of Yalu bridges? In this crisis the level of thought at the Joint Chiefs of Staff seemed to have descended to confusion.

Matters were not helped at all by a new estimate prepared by the American intelligence agencies in Washington for the Joint Chiefs of Staff and the President. It indicated that there were no more than 40,000 Chinese in North Korea. The report also stated that there were perhaps 400,000 Chinese in Manchuria, ready to move in. The intelligence was absolutely inadequate. There were at that moment between 150,000 and 200,000 Chinese troops in North Korea and 600,000 in Manchuria who could be committed. *And the Chinese had said so!*

The Washington intelligence estimate concluded with the following appraisal:

"At any point the danger is present that the situation may get out of control and lead to a general war."

This danger was inherent in the situation in which the UN forces found themselves in November. It did not take a Napoleonic genius to estimate the dangers.

On November 7 the airmen faced a new problem, as the tale of Captain Howard Tanner of the Fifth Air Force's 36th Fighter Bomber Squadron indicates:

Tanner was flying a combat air patrol in a P-51 propeller-driven fighter plane along the south side of the Yalu River with several other fighters. On November 6 a similar patrol had been jumped by several MIG-15 jets, which had taken off from Antung, climbed to high altitude, crossed the border at 30,000 feet, and dived down in single firing passes at the American planes, then scurried back to the safety of the Manchurian side of the Yalu. The attacks had come so fast that the Americans had had no time to retaliate.

Captain Tanner and the other American pilots had been briefed on this development before they took off at one o'clock in the afternoon. They flew north from Kimpo air base to Sinuiju, then turned along the Yalu, and flew to Uiju. They reversed course at Uiju and started back down toward Sinuiju. They saw four aircraft take off from the Antung airfield and climb high into the sun. They lost the planes then and continued their mission, flying at 10,000 feet.

Suddenly one of the pilots opened up on his radio:

"Bogies at 1:30 . . ."

Captain Tanner looked up. There they were—four MIG-15s—peeling off to attack.

The first enemy pilot came in firing his 37 mm cannon. The next two followed him, doing the same. As each plane came across the sights of the P-51s, the American pilots squeezed off a burst from their six .50 caliber guns.

This counterattack seemed to dent the ardor of the fourth pilot, who began firing long before he was in range and then made a sharp right turn. Captain Tanner turned with him and got inside, then let off a two-second burst, all he had time for because of the great disparity in speed between the propeller-driven P-51 and the enemy jet. But he made several hits with his armor-piercing ammunition. The MIG climbed away in a hurry. Captain Tanner then joined up with the other American fighters.

He was flying "tail end Charlie" when the next pass came. The MIG leader and one other started a head-on attack. What they got for their pains was a lot of lead, as the two lead American P-51s both scored hits. The enemy planes then headed back across the Yalu, and the Americans completed their mission. When they landed they found that none of their planes had been scratched, but that was not due to the superiority of their aircraft; the MIGs had it all over the propeller-driven P-51s. It was a tribute to the training of the Americans and the lack of skill of the MIG pilots, whoever they were.

By this time, MacArthur knew that the Chinese strength had to be greater than anyone in the U.S. command had estimated. General Walker was stopped cold on the west and was on the defensive. On the east, General Almond's forces had been halted. The impact of the withdrawal of the Chinese from battle had not yet reached MacArthur. But, typically, he rushed from depression to euphoria now that once more he had his own way with Washington. Two days earlier he had expressed the fear that he would be overwhelmed; now he proposed to continue the advance northward as though nothing had happened! To settle the growing doubts of the Joint Chiefs of Staff in his operations, he called this new move a "reconnaissance in force." Whatever it was called, if the Chinese had the resources indicated, as well as the will to fight, then the Americans were going to be in serious trouble.

There was another problem: if Manchurian sovereignty was not to be violated in the bombing of the Yalu bridges, then the bombers under no conditions could move past the center of the river on approach or getaway.

That meant they had no more than 180 degrees of the navigational circle with which to play, and sometimes they would have much less. Their runs would be into heavy antiaircraft fire; there was no getting away from that. The situation was reminiscent of that of the German Rhine dams and other installations on the border of Swiss territory in World War II. How effective could the bombing be? And what would happen if the Chinese or the Soviets sent up more of the MIG-15s that had already been interdicting UN planes along the border?

These matters bothered General Stratemeyer, and he went to MacArthur to complain. MacArthur asked Washington for permission to follow the "hot pursuit" theory. He was informed that it was going to take some time to get the authorization for this because the Allies of the United States had to be consulted. Meanwhile, General Stratemeyer continued his operations under the restrictions laid down.

On October 8 a major raid was scheduled against Sinuiju. This city on the southern shore of the Yalu was across from the Manchurian steel city of Antung. Two big bridges connected the cities. Each bridge was more than half a mile long. The highway bridge had been constructed by the American Bridge Company in 1909, its foundations were laid in bedrock, and it was as strong as any bridge in the world, withstanding flood currents and the thick ice of the Manchurian winter. The other bridge was a two-track rail bridge built by the Japanese in 1934. These were two of the twelve bridges across the Yalu and the Tumen rivers over which the airmen had seen the Chinese pouring into Korea.

Sinuiju was not only the temporary capital of the North Korean government, but its warehouses were full of supplies, and it was believed that Chinese troops were concentrated here. So the attack was to be major.

P-51 fighters and F-80 jets were sent in to hit the antiaircraft guns with strafing and napalm. They were met by MIG-15s from the Antung side in what turned out to be the first confrontation between American and Soviet-built jet aircraft. The American F-80s of the 51st Fighter Interceptor Wing flew top cover for other jets and the P-51s as they went in to attack ground positions. The MIG-15s were clearly superior to the American F-80Cs, more heavily armed and lighter and faster. But, once again, skill and experience counted for more; one MIG pilot made the mistake of trying to dive away from the heavier F-80 of Lieutenant Russell Brown, and Brown caught up with him and poured a stream of .50 calibre fire into the MIG. The enemy plane flipped over and crashed to the ground.

This event seemed to exercise a salutary effect on the Antung airfield, for when the seventy-nine B-29s arrived to attack the city and the bridges, no

MIGs appeared. Antiaircraft guns on the Manchurian side sent up a heavy volume of fire, but no planes were shot down. Although nine of the B-29s dropped 1000-pound bombs on the approaches and abutments of the two bridges, neither bridge was knocked out. Sinuiju was about 60 percent burned, but the bridges still stood.

General Stratemeyer ordered the destruction of six of the international bridges and of ten cities. The air force employed heavy bombers, medium bombers, and the carrier bombers of the navy. But the problems were enormous, as Stratemeyer had known they would be. For example, the railroad bridge at Namsan-ni was located in a bend in the Yalu, and there was no way a plane could get at it without flying over Manchurian territory. Nor, given the intense flak that came up from the Manchurian side, which could not be put out of action, was it possible to bomb from low altitude. The B-29s came in at 18,000 feet and above. Below them were layers of crosswinds which they could not measure. Consequently, their bombing was inaccurate.

After the B-29s failed to destroy the bridges at Sinuiju, the navy took a crack at them. For three days, beginning on November 9, planes from the *Valley Forge, Philippine Sea,* and *Leyte* struck the bridges. They did destroy the southern ends of the highway bridge at Sinuiju and two smaller bridges at Hyesanjin. They were unable to destroy the railroad bridge at Sinuiju.

On November 14 the B-29s were back, but again they failed to destroy that bridge, and two of the big bombers were badly shot up.

In the next two weeks, while ground activity was at a standstill, the air force continued its efforts. But by midmonth it was apparent that the whole idea of bombing the Yalu River bridges was a failure. Half the bridges still stood, the Chinese had built new pontoon bridges, and the Yalu was frozen by this time, which meant men could move directly across the ice.

General MacArthur had created an enormous issue with Washington, had been given his way, and the result was tactical failure. Far worse was the strategic and political result of the bombing of the Yalu bridges. Every bomb that fell helped to convince the Chinese that the Americans were intent on destroying their government.

Furthermore, the bombing created new tensions within the United Nations. The French proposed a resolution in the General Assembly, calling on the United Nations command to declare the Yalu border "inviolate." The Joint Chiefs of Staff objected to that wording because it would give the Chinese the feeling that they were safe from attack no matter what they did. The Joint Chiefs need not have worried. The Chinese had no such feeling of safety. They were feeling very threatened and were determined to resist further military action toward their border. Their feeling was certainly borne out by the attitude of the Joint Chiefs of Staff, who considered it quite possible that the Americans would be invading Manchuria soon in force.

This was far from the attitude of President Truman. On November 16 at a press conference he pledged that he would "take every honorable step to prevent any extension of the hostilities in the Far East." That same day Truman made a public statement that the United States "never at any time entertained any intention to carry hostilities into China."

It was now very late, and the Chinese reply accused the United States in particular of aggression against China and, of course, brought up that old sore point of Taiwan once more.

By mid-November the answers to the questions that had been asked the UN Allies were coming in; unanimously they spoke against extending the air war into Manchuria. In the field, commanders spoke of having their hands tied behind their backs. It was true that the interdiction of "hot pursuit" made the offensive task of the airmen virtually impossible.

The Joint Chiefs of Staff were in a dilemma. As military men they were trained to fight for victory. In Korea they were beginning to see new sorts of problems, and credit must be given the Joint Chiefs at this point for suggesting that it was time to reconsider the strategic policy in Korea. They, however, went at it the wrong way; they approached General MacArthur as though the decision were his. Up to that point, all the decisions actually had been his; MacArthur had bulled his way through from the beginning, and the policy of the destruction of the North Korean People's Republic had been essentially announced by him in July.

Even in mid-November, the war could yet have been wound down. On November 9 the President's National Security Council began considering the options. One, suggested by Secretary of State Acheson, was the establishment of a buffer zone, ten miles on each side of the Yalu River. But in these Council discussions, no real decision was made. Everyone fell back on his ignorance of Chinese intentions, although the Chinese had made those intentions clear in their public statements and by their actions. All that had happened so far was a warning, but, because the American military and political leaders were conditioned not to believe anything a Communist said, they did not take the warning at face value. This attitude was, in its way, the first of a new set of values in America: "There are no easy answers," a truism which solved no problems at all. A more realistic attitude would have been "there are no pleasant answers" and the realization that the unpleasant had to be accepted in a Korean War that had suddenly changed completely in character.

The major factor determining the course of events in the middle of November was General MacArthur. Having panicked at the thought of

Chinese hordes rushing across the Yalu, then having seen that the Chinese withdrew from their assault on the Eighth Army, MacArthur recovered his ego. He ignored the fact that the Chinese had destroyed the ROK II Corps and the 8th Cavalry Regimental Combat Team. He made plans in the second week of November for business as usual—the advance to the Yalu would continue. Barring some change in policy in Washington, the Far East Command would forge ahead. There was no soul-searching here; MacArthur gave the orders. His subordinates obeyed them, which was as it had to be. General Walker was bringing up the IX Corps to reinforce the badly mauled I Corps. The South Koreans were rebuilding their II Corps. On November 15 these three army corps would advance side by side up the west to the northern border of Korea. Walker had not solved his logistics problem, his army was being supplied largely by air, and the Korean airfields did not have the capacity to do much more than they were already doing. I Corps had only one day's firepower. Even a day of bad weather plus an enemy attack could put it in a crucial position. What was needed was a port of supply; Chinnampo was the logical one—but it would be weeks before that port could be readied for the purpose. At the eleventh hour General Walker realized that his supply position was impossible, and he postponed the attack date. By straining the resources of Inchon, Chinnampo, and Kimpo, Walker managed to begin the movement of 4,000 tons of supply per day toward the Eighth Army, and that was what he had set as minimal. He rescheduled the attack for November 24.

5

The Big Push

The Chinese had no fear of the American troops they had faced in their first limited offensive. They did respect American firepower, artillery, heavy mortars, tanks, air support, and the volume and range of infantry weapons. But they did not respect the American soldier's character. Based on what they had seen at Unsan, the Chinese propagandists published a pamphlet, which was distributed to the Chinese troops. It spoke of the tendency of American troops to panic when surrounded and to abandon their heavy weapons.

"Their infantrymen are weak, afraid to die, and haven't the courage to attack or defend. They depend on their planes, tanks, and artillery. At the same time they are afraid of our firepower. They will cringe, when if on the advance, they hear firing. . . . They are not familiar with night fighting or hand-to-hand combat . . . if defeated they have no orderly formation . . . they become dazed and completely demoralized . . . at Unsan they were surrounded for several days and yet they did nothing. They are afraid when the rear is cut off."

For the future, the Chinese high command set forth several principles: First, surround the enemy and cut off his retreat. Second, avoid highways and flat ground to keep losses from tanks, artillery, and aircraft to a minimum. Third, conduct night attacks, to avoid American air power. Fourth, coordinate units in attack down to the platoon level. Fifth, attacks should be led by patrols, which would then sound their bugles, whereupon the main forces would attack.

In essence, these were the methods followed by the North Koreans in the first savage weeks of the war when they had so nearly driven the Americans out of Korea altogether, until the 5th Marines had stopped the North Koreans at the Naktong Bulge.

It is significant that the Chinese troop instruction pamphlet had nothing to say about the fighting on the east side of the Korean peninsula, where the Chinese had engaged the marines. For none of the deficiencies attributed to the Americans had appeared there, and the marines had severely beaten the Chinese in all encounters until the Chinese withdrawal of November 7.

For the following two weeks, the eastern front was also quiet. On November 7 the marines sent a patrol to the Chosin Reservoir plateau near Koto-ri. The land over which they traveled was, as they said, mostly "perpendicular." It was also populated by bears, and at least one marine swore that one tried to climb into his sleeping bag. But he also swore that the bear was wearing a hammer and sickle. The bear was more startled than the marine and disappeared into the night. The patrol was twenty-six hours in traveling twenty-five miles, but the patrol was worth the effort; it reported back that Koto-ri was clear of enemy.

On the morning of November 10 the 7th Marines moved out of Funchilin Pass onto the plateau and occupied Koto-ri. (See Map 9.) Here, for the first time, they encountered the intensive cold of Korea. The phrase "windchill factor" had not been adopted yet, but the actual temperature was made far more severe by winds that swept across the treeless plain. The marines fought the intense cold by setting up warming tents that were heated by camp stoves and buckets of hot water to warm the C rations. The marines had come up to the north in summer uniform and had just recently received their cold weather gear. They had much to learn about the operation of weapons and men in subzero climates.

Another factor that now haunted the UN forces was the existence of guerilla bands throughout the peninsula, the heritage of MacArthur's rush to the north at the expense of the orderly routing out of enemy strong points. The U.S. IX Corps was entrusted with establishment of security, operating out of Taejon, with the ROK 11th Division. Its area of operation extended down to the southern tip of Korea. The North Koreans had planned shrewdly for guerilla warfare. Kim Chaek, the commander of the North Korean front headquarters, was the coordinator of the guerilas. In November an estimated 20,000 of them were operating in the southwest corner of Korea. They managed to create inestimable mischief: one night they opened the Hwachon

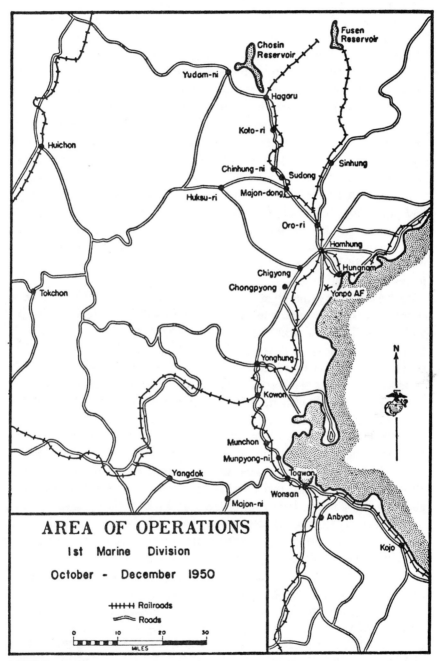

AREA OF OPERATIONS

1st Marine Division

October - December 1950

+H+H Railroads

Roads

0   10   20   30
MILES

Chosin Reservoir
Fusen Reservoir
Yudam-ni
Hagaru
Huichon
Koto-ri
Chinhung-ni
Sinhung
Sudong
Huksu-ri
Majon-dong
Oro-ri
Homhung
Hungnam
Chigyong
Yonpo AF
Chongpyong
Tokchon
Yonghung
Kowon
Munchon
Munpyong-ni
Yangdok
Togwon
Wonsan
Majon-ni
Anbyon
Kojo

MAP 9

Dam north of Wonju, and the Pukhan River rose four feet and demolished a railroad bridge. When the ROK forces came in, they found the control panels of the dam wrecked. And early in November guerillas captured the town of Chunchon, only forty-five miles southwest of Seoul.

In the south the U.S. 25th Division had the biggest job in antiguerilla warfare with 6,500 square miles to cover, most of it mountainous. In one day the 3rd Battalion of the 35th Infantry captured 549 prisoners.

In the rugged Taebaek Mountains 4,000 guerillas operated against roads and ROK troops. There were even guerillas working in the middle of Seoul, and on October 15 they attacked and destroyed a radio relay station less than five miles from the capitol building.

In the north the guerillas posed a menace to the marines. The fight at Kojo had been only one of such incidents. There was a continuing series of skirmishes along the rail and road lines between Hungnam and Wonsan. On the night of November 6 guerillas ambushed a convoy south of Kowon, thirty miles north of Wonsan, and burned three jeeps and twenty trucks the UN forces could ill afford to lose.

In Kowon that same night the guerillas attacked a northbound marine supply train, which was guarded by thirty marines. The train had stopped at a water tank. The night was black and the visibility was hampered by snow flurries. Suddenly, a North Korean soldier flung open the door to the front coach. A marine shot him dead. Enemy burp guns began to blurt their deadly pellets. The guerillas blew up the track ahead of the train, shot the engineer of the train as he tried to back up, attacked the coaches, and killed every marine they saw. Two marines escaped by feigning death.

Later that same night five hundred guerillas attacked a battalion of the 65th Infantry of the U.S. 3rd Division, newly arrived and not yet hardened to battle. Just the day before, this unit had occupied Yonghung, between Wonsan and Hungnam. The guerillas cost them forty men that night. The guerillas also got into the camp of the 96th Field Artillery Battalion and destroyed six 155 mm howitzers and the whole battalion supply train, including all the ammunition. Another forty Americans fell there. When day came and air activity could begin, the airmen saw about two thousand enemy troops on the roads around the area. These were parts of the North Korean 5th Division, which had been cut off but not cleaned out.

The Majon-ni ambushes continued against Lieutenant Colonel Ridge's 3rd Battalion of the 1st Marines, until they were relieved by the army's 15th Infantry and ROK troops. The ambushes, however, did not stop then; on the night of November 20 there was another try by about two hundred guerillas, apparently left over from the NK 15th Division. And at Tongdyang, the Korean marines were besieged, their roads mined and cut, and they had to be supplied by airdrop during this period. Several battles were fought, and in the last week of November the roads were opened, but the Majon-ni area was never safe. As long as UN forces continued in the area they were harried by guerillas from the mountains. After the 3rd Division got its land-legs, the intelligence organization estimated that about 25,000 guerillas operated within a ten-mile radius of Paeksan. A survey of 110 enemy prisoners taken in one twenty-four-hour period in the X Corps rear areas showed that they represented no fewer than sixty-two different North Korean units.

On the west the guerillas were not as powerful, probably because the Eighth Army had driven most units north before it, along the routes to Pyongyang and above. Nonetheless, there were guerillas and plans for guerilla activity. Troops of the U.S. 23rd Infantry discovered Arsenal No. 65, a full-fledged munitions plant, operating in an old lead mine nine miles northeast of Kangdon. It had four hundred lathes, located in nineteen different rooms, and was capable of building 120 mm mortars and burp guns.

The guerillas were merciless to prisoners. On November 6 between Kumchon and Siyon-ni, a large guerilla force ambushed two platoons of the U.S. 27th Infantry. They captured fifteen men, and when the Americans refused to give any information but name, rank, and serial number, they killed them all and buried them in a shallow, common grave. Another guerilla band murdered all the hospital patients and personnel at an ROK field hospital at Ichon.

The greatest enemy activity in the northwest was in the Iron Triangle in central North Korea. The UN forces were trying to open the rail line that ran from Seoul through the Iron Triangle to Wonsan. The guerillas attacked them constantly, usually just north of Pyonggang, the northern apex of the triangle. ROK troops rode all trains as guards, and nearly every trip brought a fight along the road. On November 2 a thousand guerillas ambushed a work train near Pyonggang. About two hundred ROK troops were riding the train, and they fought off the attackers. Prisoners told them there were at least four thousand guerillas in the area and that they had promised to attack every train moving toward Wonsan, since those trains would be carrying supplies to the eastern front. Attacks at Chorwon and Yonchon were also common, and at one point Pyonggang was surrounded, until ROK troops broke through.

This was the legacy of MacArthur's haste in September and October.

During this November lull the enemy of the troops in the north was the cold. They saw many Chinese but almost always at a distance. On November 11 Company C encountered a good-sized Chinese force and lost four men killed and four wounded, while inflicting about forty casualties on the Chinese. On November 13 the regiment moved up toward Hagaru. At the same time the 5th Marines approached the Fusen Reservoir to the east. (See

Map 9.) The army 7th Infantry Division advanced to Paeksan and other points to the northeast, and farthest north and east of all were elements of the ROK Army, moving toward Nanam and Chongjin.

It was all very quiet, eerily quiet, with the exception of a fight here and there, which seemed to come about almost by accident. The marines had indications that the quiet was not to last. Marine airmen making strikes against Sinuiju in the first ten days of November reported a steady stream of Chinese trucks and other vehicles crossing the Yalu bridges from Antung into northwest Korea. Chinese prisoners spoke of very large forces coming into Korea. One said that the Peking government was committing twenty-four divisions—240,000 men—to drive the UN forces out of Korea.

All this should have been known to General MacArthur in the second and third weeks of November, but he seemed peculiarly insensitive to the intelligence reports from the field forces. In mid-November General MacArthur was totally confident that his was the course of victory. In response to the Chiefs of Staff's suggestion that it seemed to be the time to reexamine the U.S. Korea policy, MacArthur was adamant.

"There were but three possible courses," he wrote in his *Reminiscences*. "I could go forward, remain immobile, or withdraw."

If he went forward, he thought there was a chance that the Chinese might not intervene in force and the war would be over. "A chance," he wrote. What sort of chance? On the face of things it could not be very good, given the punishment the Chinese had already inflicted in one week of operations.

If he decided to remain immobile, he would have to choose a defense line and dig in. He claimed there was no natural defense line. That was not true. There were defense lines: the Chongchon River line was one of them. It was occupied by General Walker's forces. It had to be built up, but it could have been. A better defense line could have been laid across the narrow neck of the peninsula from the Kuryong River to the Hamhung area. That way, MacArthur could have avoided what he feared: the Chinese sending in enough divisions to surround his armies, which would have meant "the ultimate annihilation of our entire command."

The third alternative was to withdraw to the 38th parallel. This, wrote MacArthur, would be in contradiction to his orders and "would destroy any opportunity to bring the Korean War to a successful end."

MacArthur never gave any real consideration to two of the alternatives or to the Joint Chiefs's suggestion that it might be time to rethink the military objectives of the war. Forge on, he insisted.

His rationale was that if the Chinese attacked in force, he would break contact and withdraw rapidly, to lengthen the enemy supply lines. This, he said, would make it possible for the airmen to destroy the Chinese as they came south. On the east X Corps would be withdrawn by sea *when it had completed its covering of the right flank of the Eighth Army.* It was a modernized version of the Russian defense against Napoleon, withdraw, let the enemy commit himself, starve him out, and wait. As MacArthur put it, it all sounded very sensible and logical. The flaw, hardly noticeable in Washington, was that X corps was not covering the right flank of the Eighth Army. A huge mountain mass lay between the two UN forces.

The one problem, from MacArthur's point of view, was the order prohibiting him from bombing the Yalu bridges all the way. It was, he wrote, "the most indefensible and ill-conceived decision ever forced on a field commander in our nation's history."

Perhaps it was. If MacArthur had thought so at the time, he could have either resigned his command or taken the advice of the Joint Chiefs and adjusted his military sights to the political situation that had developed. He said in his memoirs that he had decided to resign, had written the letter, and allowed himself to be persuaded otherwise by General Doyle Hickey, his acting chief of staff. Certainly, he must have done just that. The tale is of a piece with another related by Joseph C. Goulden in the introduction to his *Korea, The Untold Story of the War.* According to that story, when MacArthur was chief of staff of the army in the 1930s, he kept an apartment in Washington, in addition to the big house the government alloted him at Fort Myer. He liked to go to the apartment for relaxation with his aide Lieutenant Thomas Jefferson Davis Smith. He had even then all the signs of paranoia. Sometimes he would sit in the apartment with a loaded revolver in hand and threaten to commit suicide, until Lieutenant Smith talked him out of it. This went on time after time, until one night, on a train bound south, MacArthur banged on the door of Smith's compartment and announced that he was going to jump off the train as it crossed the Tennessee River. At that point, Lieutenant Smith rebelled:

"General," he replied, "would you hurry up and get it over with so I can get back to sleep?"

In retrospect, General Hickey lost a chance to be invaluable to his country when he followed the code of the aide and persuaded the general not to quit. For if MacArthur had truly resigned, the resulting furore in Washington would have forced a reconsideration of the U.S. Korean War policy, and either the war would have been prosecuted with every weapon (possibly short of atomic), or the UN forces would have dug in and waited. The one possibility would have pleased the military, although it might have brought on World War III. The other would certainly have brought a speedy end to hostilities with an armistice line far north of the 38th parallel.

What could not be seen in Washington could be seen in London, Paris, and

Canberra. The British, in particular, had been with President Truman all the way thus far and were the first UN Allies to send a force to fight. But now Foreign Minister Ernest Bevin counseled caution. He pressed for the establishment of a *cordon sanitaire* south of the Yalu River. The very thought made MacArthur furious. He compared it with the cession of the Sudetenland to Germany in 1938. "... this so called buffer zone," he said, "would be a signal to further aggression on the part of the Chinese, and perhaps more important, would bankrupt our political, military, and psychological position in the Far East."

What this statement meant is impossible to understand, unless one accepts the MacArthur premise that the Communist government of China had to be destroyed. History has shown that the American Far East policy was then already bankrupt, and the result was going to be not one, but two, major wars. Some in Washington saw that MacArthur was demanding an extension of the war into China, but no one did anything about it. The reason, according to Secretary of State Acheson, was morale, the morale of the troops in Korea and the morale of Americans at home. That is a fair reading and also proof that government all too often follows the people instead of leading them. The China Lobby and other hysterically anti-Communist elements in America had set a climate by 1950 in which it would have been very difficult for any administration to make an accommodation with the Chinese government. So, in that sense, MacArthur's wrongheadedness represented a national failing. Like the U.S. Supreme Court justices, according to Mr. Dooley, the Joint Chiefs of Staff read the election returns. The 81st Congress, just returning to Washington, was solidly Democratic in both houses. But in the election just past the Americans had changed the character of the 82nd Congress: when it arrived in January it would have only forty-eight Democratic Senators, forty-seven Republicans, and one independent. And not all those Democrats, by far, were Fair Deal Democrats of the Truman variety. Thus, it was conceivable that only the vice-president could save administration policy by casting a tie-breaking vote on some issues. The elections had shown that the American people were not pleased with the way things were going, and the Korean War was a part of the cause of their discontent.

As MacArthur had always done, he played American public opinion to the hilt. He was completely confident of victory, and he exerted the enormous force of his personality and reputation to have his own way. It is remarkable how successful he was, considering what the others on the scene knew or suspected about the future.

6

MacArthur's Blunder

The marines were worried.

In the first place, no one seemed to be able to agree on what the Chinese were doing or how many of them were doing it. Were there 30,000, or 100,000, Chinese in North Korea? By mid-November MacArthur had recovered his courage and estimated the former. Any larger number than that, he told Ambassador John J. Muccio, would have been detected from the air. That MacArthur could have held such a view was remarkable; his Eighth Army command put the number of Chinese at 100,000. The fate of the ROK II Corps and the 8th Cavalry and the difficulties of the marines in the East certainly indicated forces far greater than 30,000, even if the intelligence officers simply ignored the testimony of the Chinese prisoners of war who spoke of forty-five divisions of 10,000 men each. The Americans discounted that information because of the source: non-commissioned officers and private soldiers. It was unthinkable in the American army for low-ranking soldiers to possess such vital information. The U.S. intelligence officers fell into error because they did not understand the enemy: ever since the days of the war against the Japanese, the Chinese Communist commanders had shared basic information about forces and war aims with the common soldiers. It was part of the *gung ho* (work together) technique of instilling loyalty and inspiring effort.

The U.S. officials in Washington also had received all sorts of warnings about Chinese strength. Washington, however, was in a state of indecision. President Truman and his political advisors were working on the diplomatic aspects. Truman did not want to get involved in a long, costly war in Asia, and so the United States was trying, through the United Nations, to create a dialogue with China. To do so, Truman accepted a French resolution which held the Yalu River border inviolate. In mid-November a clear statement came from the Netherlands ambassador to Peking: Chinese activity in Korea was motivated by fear of U.S. aggression against Manchuria. If the UN forces would stop and hold fifty miles south of the Yalu, the Chinese would not advance farther.

That being the case, the next step ought to have been a sharp curtailment of military actions. As had already been seen in the first Chinese offensive and the first bombing of the Yalu bridges, the Chinese could put enormous manpower into the field by simply crossing a river, and it would be futile to continue the war if the enemy was to have a safe haven.

Somehow, official Washington failed to understand this fundamental problem. MacArthur did not explain it, because he expected to bomb the Yalu River bridges and the Manchuria bases to carry the war against China, and, if necessary, to fight the Soviets there and then. He so told his political advisor, William Sebald.

Most military men in Washington now backed MacArthur's view that the UN forces should continue the drive to the Yalu. The army planning section proposed the bombing of Manchuria if the Chinese did not withdraw from North Korea. It also proposed the use of the atomic bomb. The Joint Chiefs of Staff did not go so far. In conference with the political men they evolved a complicated view that would allow MacArthur to continue to the Yalu, but with diminished forces, so as not to frighten the Chinese. General J. Lawton Collins, the army chief of staff, suggested that MacArthur march to the Yalu, then pull back his forces, and send ROK forces up to hold the line. Only if it were a "military necessity" would the Americans destroy the hydroelectric facilities on the Korean side of the Yalu. Assuming they did not, once the battle was won, the United Nations organization would decide on the "equitable distribution" of power from the hydroelectric installations. The unconscious arrogance of this view was totally unperceived in Washington; the military and political men were saying "Since we are reasonable and honest people, China and the world must believe in our good intentions." But China did not believe American intentions were good, and, undoubtedly, at this time, due to the activities of those busy Soviet agents Guy Burgess and Donald MacLean, the USSR and China had a clear insight into the MacArthur attitude and the MacArthur plans.

MacArthur rejected the Joint Chiefs's proposals. Even without the espionage, MacArthur had made his views on Red China so well known that Peking could hardly have been in error about them. By this time Peking must have perceived that MacArthur, and not Washington, was running the show.

Years later, when asked how the situation in Korea came about, President Truman took full responsibility for allowing MacArthur to have his way. He had been convinced—undoubtedly by General Marshall—that in war the theater commander on the scene must be given the authority to handle the military situation.

MacArthur was in charge. The drive to the Yalu would continue.

In the third week of November 1950 MacArthur's planners revised the war plan, giving at least lip service to the thought of closing the gap between the X Corps and the Eighth Army. That army was to advance to the Yalu with the main effort in the center, parallel to the Huichon–Kanggye line. The X Corps was to start an attack westward from the Chosin Reservoir area to Mupyong-ni and Manpojin. (See Map 10.)

General Smith did not like this plan. MacArthur was still speaking glibly of finishing the war before the Yalu River froze over, which was expected around December 1. If the UN forces reached the Yalu by then, the Chinese would be stymied, but if they did not, the Chinese could cross the river readily and MacArthur would have to attack Manchuria. General Smith did not believe it was possible for the UN forces to reach the Yalu all along the line before "winter" set in. Already they faced subzero temperatures, and Smith was making plans for a midwinter campaign in the mountains, which meant building airstrips along the single road that led north and rebuilding the road to carry tanks. Such projects would require time and material, both in short supply in North Korea.

What General Smith saw was a strong buildup of Chinese forces throughout North Korea and the absence of a reasonable goal by the MacArthur command. Smith did not believe the American soldiers and marines should be asked to fight a winter campaign in the mountains of North Korea. The way to stop it, obviously, was to stop. But Smith was a good soldier, and, although his heart was not in it, he planned within the framework of MacArthur's war.

The 7th Marines occupied Hagaru. The temperature was four degrees below zero, Fahrenheit, and it was only November 15. General Smith wrote all this to General Clifton B. Cates, commandant of the U.S. Marine Corps. And he prepared for a major Chinese offensive.

Work started on an airstrip. The engineers began rebuilding the road from Chinhung-ni to Koto-ri. Supplies began to come up to Hagaru and were stored in dumps. They came via the narrow gauge railroad to Chinhung-ni

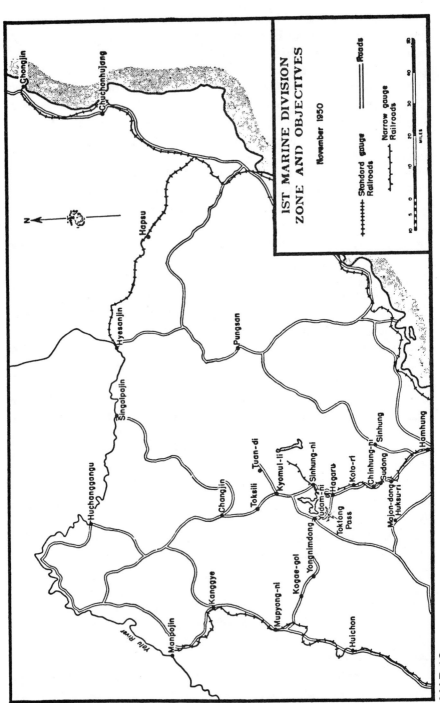

1ST MARINE DIVISION
ZONE AND OBJECTIVES

November 1950

Standard gauge Railroads
Narrow gauge Railroads
Roads

MILES

MAP 10

and were then trucked to Hagaru over the narrow, winding road. This route the marines called the MSR—Main Supply Route. It was soon to become almost a household word in America.

At about this time more soldiers were arriving in Korea from many lands, truly changing the nature of the war from an East–West struggle to a UN operation. The British 29th Brigade arrived, bringing in the new British Centurion tanks. The soldiers were from the Northumberland Fusiliers, the Gloucesters, the Royal Ulster Rifles, the 8th Hussars, the 4th Field Artillery, and the 55th Squadron of engineers. The 29th Brigade moved up to North Korea and went into reserve. The 41st Independent Commando of the British Royal Marines had requested service with the U.S. marines and was assigned to the 1st Marine Division. General Smith would use them in reconnaissance.

A Turkish brigade under Brigadier General Taksin Yazici had come into Korea in mid-October and been assigned to the IX Corps on the west. In November it was attached to the U.S. 25th Division and moved to Kunu-ri, on the right flank of the Eighth Army, along with its artillery unit.

A battalion of the 21st Thai Infantry and three Thai warships arrived early in November, too. The troops went to Taegu for integration with the UN forces, and the ships joined the UN navy.

The No. 2 South African Air Force Squadron of fighter planes moved into K-9 airfield near Pusan to join the UN air force. The 10th Battalion Combat Team of the Philippines had arrived in September to be attached to the U.S. 25th Division, which was fighting guerillas in the southwest, and the Filipinos had fought several actions there. The battalion was brought north to provide security for installations at Kunu-ri, Sinanju, and Sukchon. The Netherlands Infantry Battalion was on its way from Rotterdam, a flight of Greek air transports was coming in from Athens, and the Greek infantry battalion was also on its way. So was the French battalion.

Three Canadian destroyers had been operating with the UN navy since July. The Indians sent an ambulance team, and other nations were gearing up to help, now that the warning signals had been sent to the UN headquarters that, perhaps, all was not as well as had earlier been presumed. In most instances these military units were far more than tokens—another reason it was important for the U.S. leaders to preserve the unity of the United Nations action in Korea.

It was apparent in mid-November that General MacArthur's impatience with General Walker was coloring Tokyo's views. The Eighth Army intelligence organization warned of a new buildup of Chinese forces in North Korea, on both sides of the Yalu. MacArthur did not believe. Blandly he continued his planning for "The End-The-War Offensive," as if it were going to be a cakewalk into occupation. That is how MacArthur's attitude looked to the marines in the field, but MacArthur's confidence was so complete and persuasive that in Tokyo and in America Thanksgiving Day was celebrated on November 23 in an atmosphere of rejoicing over the expected immediate end of the Korean War. Even in the frozen wastes of North Korea, the soldiers and marines fed on shrimp cocktail, roast turkey, with sweet potatoes, stuffed olives, cranberry sauce, fruit salad, fruit cake, and mince pie. For a few minutes they might as well have been at home.

That day the U.S. 7th Infantry Division troops reached Hyesanjin on the Yalu and MacArthur's glory was complete. The eastern pincer had moved into position to crush the Chinese. General Almond flew up to the area and had his picture taken looking across the Yalu. The photograph appeared in the American newspapers and confirmed the worst fears of the Chinese.

The next day the great offensive began with a stirring communiqué from General MacArthur:

> The United Nations massive compression envelopment in North Korea against the new Red Armies operating there is now approaching its decisive effort. The isolating component of the pincer, our air forces of all types, have for the past three weeks, in a sustained attack of model coordination and effectiveness, successfully interdicted enemy lines of support from the north so that further reinforcement therefrom has been sharply curtailed and essential supplies markedly limited. The eastern sector of the pincer, with noteworthy and effective naval support, has now reached commanding enveloping position, cutting in two the northern reaches of the enemy's geographical potential. This morning the western sector of the pincer moves forward in general assault in an effort to complete the compression and close the vise. If successful, this should for all practical purposes end the war, restore peace and unity to Korea, enable the prompt withdrawal of the United Nations military forces, and permit the complete assumption by the Korean people and nation of full sovereignty and international equality. It is that for which we fight.

For three days General Walker on the west and General Almond on the east had been moving into position to jump off on the morning of November 24. General Walker was a chastened man, and he ordered caution to his commanders. He had gut feelings that something might be developing. And, for a change, so did General Almond over on the east coast.

Back in Tokyo, MacArthur's intelligence wizard, General Willoughby, estimated that the UN forces faced about 80,000 remaining North Korean soldiers, plus perhaps 70,000 Chinese. There were an estimated 300,000 Chinese on the north side of the Yalu. But, intelligence assured Washington, the Chinese were having a lot of supply problems. Many of the Chinese units, Willoughby said, had embarked on the Korean adventure with only three days' rations. It seemed apparent that they could not sustain an effort. American planes flying day and night along the Yalu had seen nothing of supply trains, nor had they observed any activity in the gap between the Eighth Army and the X Corps on the right.

The Willoughby estimate said nothing about General Barr's fears for his 7th Division, for such was not within his intelligence purview. But General Barr told General Smith privately on Thanksgiving Day that he was seriously concerned about the future, largely because all his division had on hand was *one* day's supply. His 17th Infantry was also stuck out on a long limb with its flanks wide open.

The confidence in Tokyo made for a certain carelessness. American reporters were told some of the details of the coming operation, and they sent their dispatches back to the United States. Soviet spies Burgess and MacLean were sending out their reports, too, but they might not even have been necessary, except to confirm what the Soviets and Chinese learned from the American newspapers. The London *Times* suggested that it seemed strange to fight a war in the glare of an advance publicity campaign that gave the enemy a good insight into the UN military operation.

On the morning of the great assault, General MacArthur flew up to Eighth Army headquarters on the Chongchon River for a briefing and a tour of the front. He was talking of "getting the boys home by Christmas." After a five-hour tour he boarded his transport plane again and ordered the pilot to fly up the east coast to the Yalu River so the general could see what was happening. They flew at 5,000 feet over Sinuiju and the important bridges that crossed over to Antung in Manchuria. Below they could look across into the mountains of Manchuria and look down on the roads and mountains of North Korea. None of the roads showed signs of heavy use, the snow was thick and white down there. MacArthur's fondest hopes were confirmed: there was no indication of heavy Chinese military activity.

Had General MacArthur seen some activity and gone back to Tokyo to look at his situation map, he might have had some qualms. (See Map 11.) But having none, he paid no further attention to the troublesome gap that existed between the Eighth Army and the X Corps. The corps was like a thumb penetrating to the Yalu. At no place was the northern right flank of the Eighth Army closer than twenty air miles to X Corps. The space increased as it went south, and along a line east of Pyongyang and west of Wonsan it was

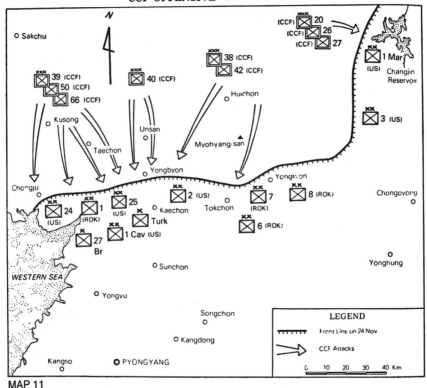

MAP 11

thirty-five air miles. The road mile distance, over twisting trails, was twice as far. On a line projected westward from Hungnam there were no Eighth Army units opposite X Corps units. All the land from the X Corps boundary west to the Yellow Sea was unknown territory. In the south, the right flank of the Eighth Army was protected by the rebuilt ROK II Corps, still regarded by the Eighth Army staff as a weak link. In this enormous gap no one really knew what existed. The terrain was so difficult that very few patrols went out at all.

On the morning of November 24 the Eighth Army attacked on a three-corps front, the I Corps on the left, IX Corps in the center, and ROK II Corps on the right. The attack started toward a line on the edges of Taechon, Unsan, and Huichon, eighty miles wide from right to left.

The movement began at ten o'clock. All along the broad front the soldiers moved quickly, meeting virtually no opposition. By the end of the day the advances ranged from six to ten miles. On the west the I Corps had advanced past Chongju. In the center the IX Corps had moved ten miles north. On the right the ROK II Corps had moved six to eight miles.

On the morning of November 25 the Chinese launched some strong probes against the ROK 1st Division on the western front of I Corps and against the ROK 8th Division on the eastern end of ROK II Corps. Thus, the Chinese discovered the UN weak point: the twenty-five mile gap between the right flank of the Eighth Army line and the left flank of X Corps on the east.

On that second day the ROK II Corps moved out from Tokchon but began to encounter heavy resistance. The South Koreans fell behind the U.S. 2nd Division, on its flank, which made the American division vulnerable to attack. The fighting that day was indeterminate.

Night fell, and with it came the Chinese. They hit the western end of the line savagely, driving the ROK 1st Division back. If the Americans and South Koreans had been impressed earlier with the orchestral accompaniment to battle that the Chinese provided, they now saw that the enemy had improved on his technique. Bugles croaked, whistles screamed, flutes screeched, cymbals clanged, and drums rattled as the Chinese came down upon the weak points of the Eighth Army by the thousands. General Lin Piao, the commander of Chinese armies in Manchuria, had completely fooled General MacArthur's intelligence apparatus.

There were not 34,000 Chinese in North Korea, or 80,000, or 100,000. There were 300,000 Chinese across the Yalu. Lin Piao's Fourth Field Army alone numbered 600,000 men. A hundred and twenty thousand of them had been in North Korea since mid-October. Night after night new divisions had streamed across the Yalu and taken refuge in the deep valleys of the mountains, so artfully concealed that the Americans had no idea they were there. When Chinese soldiers were captured, they gave the unit names they had been told to give, another trick from the war against Japan. Armies became divisions and divisions, regiments. That was one of the reasons the Americans believed that they faced about one-tenth as many Chinese as they did.

How had the Chinese accomplished this enormous buildup without being detected by the day and night observation of the Americans from the air?

Shortly after the Americans crossed the 38th parallel and Chou En-lai issued his first warning, part of the Chinese Fourth Field Army crossed the Yalu River. Then the 39th and 41st armies crossed over from Antung to Sinuiju. The 38th and 40th armies crossed from China to Manpojin. Artillery and horse cavalry accompanied them. When they were inside North Korea in mid-October, General Lin Piao placed them under the field command of the XIII Army Group. All this was accomplished by October 15, the day General MacArthur met President Truman at Wake Island and said of the Chinese:

"We are no longer fearful of their intervention. We no longer stand hat in hand. The Chinese have 300,000 men in Manchuria. Of these probably not more than 100,000 to 200,000 are distributed along the Yalu River. Only 50,000 to 60,000 could have gotten across the Yalu. They have no air force.

Now that we have bases for our air force in Korea, if the Chinese tried to get down to Pyongyang there would be the greatest slaughter."

At the moment of the general's peroration, three Chinese armies moved down in front of the U.S. Eighth Army, and one moved in front of the Changjin Reservoir. There were 120,000 Chinese troops—all seasoned veterans—ready to fight the UN forces. Ten days later two more Chinese armies moved down to the Eighth Army front.

In the third week of November the American estimate of Chinese in Korea ranged from 50,000 to 70,000. Actually, by this time the IX Army group had moved up from Shantung Province to the Changjin Reservoir area, and, in total, 180,000 Chinese soldiers faced the Eighth Army, and 120,000 stood on the flank of the U.S. X Corps. General Peng Teh-huai, Lin Piao's deputy, arrived in Korea to take control.

The Chinese managed to march three hundred miles from the Yalu to the assembly area opposite the Eighth Army without giving the slightest clue to the Americans. There were two basic reasons for the success of this secret movement. First, the Chinese did not confide in the North Koreans. Thus, there was no chance of an espionage slip up. Second, the Chinese moved entirely by night, starting after nine o'clock and marching until 3:00 A.M. Each day they covered eighteen miles. By the time day dawned every man, vehicle, and animal was hidden from sight in the mountain forests. Small patrols were sent ahead to scout the next day's march. If aircraft were heard, every man was under orders to freeze until the noise went away. In camp no man was allowed to show himself for any reason, on penalty of instant death. So successful was this movement that even aerial photography revealed nothing to the Americans. The Chinese had come like ghosts.

Peng Teh-huai's intention on November 25 was quickly made clear to General Walker. The Chinese were trying to slip down the gap between the Eighth Army and X Corps and drive to the Yellow Sea. If they did this, the Eighth Army was cut off.

One of the early indications of the Chinese intention was discovered by the U.S. 17th Field Artillery Battalion, a unit equipped with 8-inch (200 mm) howitzers. Battery A of the battalion was installed in the bleak little town of Kujang-dong, a handful of dirt-colored huts on a single road and the narrow gauge railroad, not far from Kaechon.

Battery A was seriously under strength on November 24. Its organization called for a hundred and thirty-five men, but only seventy-four were manning the weapons. The battery had been rushed to Korea in the difficult days of August, and there had been no time to bring it up to strength. When it arrived in Korea its strength had been augmented by fifty ROK soldiers. But late in October these ROK troops had been released because everyone thought the war was winding down. The decision was perfectly acceptable—until November 25.

That morning an aerial observer was registering the No. 2 howitzer on its base point when he saw below about two hundred soldiers. He assumed that these were North Koreans, the greatest number he had seen in the weeks of the march north. The discovery was noted as a bit of trivia.

For weeks the routine had been to set up, fire a few rounds, then receive orders to move the front north again, pull up stakes, set up and fire a few rounds, and pull out again. On November 24 the "front" was two miles north of Kujang-dong.

On the morning of November 25 Lieutenant Colonel Elmer A. Harrelson went forward to select positions two miles farther north. So did the commander of the 61st Field Artillery that fired 105 mm howitzers. That afternoon the 61st moved up, but the roads were so crowded that Lieutenant Colonel Harrelson held the 17th Artillery back for the night.

That night the Chinese waded the Chongchon River and attacked the U.S. 23rd Infantry. They overran the 61st Field Artillery, killed many men and captured many others. At about eleven o'clock a handful of stragglers made their way back to the position of the 17th Artillery. They had abandoned every vehicle and every weapon, even their personal equipment. One man was barefoot, having been surprised in his bedroll.

The morning of November 26 was the turning point. The ROK divisions on the right of the Eighth Army line began to collapse under Chinese pressure. The U.S. 38th Infantry of the 2nd Division reported that whole regiments of ROK soldiers were fleeing through their lines. To stem the tide, General Walker ordered the Turkish brigade into action on the right. At the IX Corps command post General Yazici was briefed on the problem: about four thousand Chinese had smashed the ROK II Corps at Tokchon and were pressing on Kaechon. The Turks were to stop them, moving up the Kunu-ri road to Tokchon. They would have the support of one platoon of tanks.

The Turks moved out that afternoon toward Wawon, eleven miles northeast of Kunu-ri. They had been in Korea only a few weeks, and it was hard for them to tell one oriental soldier from another. Consequently, their first action here involved fleeing ROK troops, whom the Turks mistook for the enemy. They killed many and "captured" more before the error could be corrected. But on November 27 there was no error. They set out in the morning from Wawon, but at two thirty in the afternoon the Turks were ordered back to Wawon to link up with the U.S. 38th Regiment and secure a retreat route to the west. They turned around and headed back. It was midnight when they began moving into Wawon. The Chinese were there before them, and they attacked. The Turks fought back. The Chinese tried to outflank them and overran the 9th Company. The 2nd Battalion rushed up in a bayonet attack and saved the moment. The Chinese withdrew.

Elsewhere along the 2nd Division line affairs were going very badly. The story of the 2nd Division's Company B tells what happened. On September 25 the company mustered 129 men. About a third of the officers and men were black, the result of the new Korean War policy of mixing the races instead of segregating them. They were a mixture of veterans and raw recruits. The confidence in immediate victory that radiated down from MacArthur's headquarters had made them careless. Many men had thrown away their heavy steel helmets and wore stocking caps instead. They carried very little ammunition for their M-1s and carbines because bullets were heavy. They carried few grenades because they were cumbersome. They had long since discarded their entrenching tools. Many of them did not carry C rations. Like a colonial army of the past, they relied on native porters to bring up their food and bedrolls at the end of the day. They were sure that the war would be over very soon.

After the Chinese forced the wedge through the ROK II Corps on the morning of November 26, Company B was ordered to capture Hill 219 on the east bank of the Chongchon River.

Company B moved up Hill 219 easily until the men neared the top. There they were greeted by a surprise—a shower of grenades. Nothing like this had occurred for weeks. Colonel Charles C. Sloane, Jr., the regimental commander, was watching the assault. He radioed division that something new had been added; the war seemed to be heating up. The division command post pooh-poohed the idea.

All day long they fought for Hill 219 but did not take it. By the end of the day the company was reduced to fewer than sixty men, who were holding two small high points on the side of Hill 219 about a hundred yards apart. Lieutenant Ellison C. Wynn, a black officer, was in command of one position, manned by about fifteen men. Lieutenant Theodore J. Weathered was in command of the other, with about forty men.

After dark the Chinese counterattacked the 9th Infantry. They overran the 3rd Battalion and surrounded the 2nd Battalion. The remnants of Company B faced a battalion of Chinese, who attacked time and again. The Americans drove them back several times with showers of grenades, but then Lieutenant Wynn's group ran out of ammunition. He told the men to fall back to

Weathered's position, and he would cover them. He had no ammunition, so he picked up rocks and threw them at the Chinese. One soldier stood with him with his M-1. The soldier had no bullets, so he used the rifle as a club. When the men had made it to the Weathered group, Wynn and the soldier started their retreat. An enemy grenade exploded just then, tearing off the side of Lieutenant Wynn's face. Somehow he made it back to Weathered, and then he continued to fight, refusing evacuation or even morphine so that others who were down on the ground might have it. Finally Lieutenant Wynn collapsed and was evacuated. Eventually he was awarded the Silver Star. Many in the regiment thought it should have been the Medal of Honor, but the 2nd Division lost so many men in the next few days that there were not enough to testify to his gallantry to meet the requirements. What he had proved was that men were men, no matter their color, and that the new army racial policy in Korea, dictated by need, was the only sensible policy.

At daybreak on November 26 Major General Lawrence B. Keiser, commander of the 2nd Division, ordered Colonel Harrelson to pull back several miles. But the road was so jammed that it was nearly midnight before the battalion began to move south.

Captain Allen L. Myers of Battery A had moved his men into position in a streambed near the road to Kunu-ri. November 27 was quiet for Battery A, although not for others, but it was cold, too cold for the men to sleep. When they had no fire missions, they sat huddled around gasoline stoves or went out in all the clothing they could find to move ammunition from Kunu-ri, twenty-five miles away. The main route of supply was still jammed with vehicles.

The Chinese were still attacking, and the 2nd Division was falling back. At seven forty-five on the morning of November 28 Company A retreated again, and now the sound of infantry small arms fire was close. Three ROK divisions had collapsed under the Chinese pressure, and the division's right flank was wide open.

Myers moved to five miles south, but as soon as he got set up again, he was ordered to retreat farther, and Battery A went into position southwest of Kunu-ri in a large field beside the road.

The Chinese were pouring down through the gap left by the ROK II Corps collapse. At eight o'clock on the night of November 28 the Turkish brigade reached the village of Sillim-ni and set up defensive positions on the road to Kaechon. At midnight the Chinese attacked the village and tried to encircle the 1st Battalion. The 3rd Battalion came to the rescue, and as the sun rose American aircraft gave an assist with air strikes. The Chinese encircling pattern was broken, and the Kaechon–Tokchon road was held. The Turks moved into Kaechon. The four thousand-man brigade had suffered 25 percent losses in this heroic action.

At six o'clock that evening the Turkish brigade was ordered to take over the right flank of the U.S. 38th Infantry northeast of Kuni-ri. They moved out of Kaechon, slowed by the retreating American troops and the litter of abandoned trucks and tanks. Four American planes dropped flares to light the road for them as night came down. At four o'clock on the morning of November 29 the Turks arrived at Kunu-ri.

Before dawn on November 29 Battery A of the 17th Field Artillery was firing missions. The confusion of disaster was beginning. Colonel Harrelson had been told to move south toward Sunchon, but he learned that the Chinese had established a roadblock on the route to Sunchon. Then came orders to get all the ammunition he needed from Kunu-ri because the dump was about to be blown up. As the ammunition carriers moved up, they passed the three 105 mm howitzer battalions and the 155 mm howitzer battalion of the division, all moving south of them.

Colonel Harrelson and Captain Myers drove south to reconnoiter a new position on the Sunchon road. They did not get far. The road was again jammed with vehicles. The 2nd Division reconnaissance company had been sent down to knock out the Chinese roadblock but had not succeeded. The situation on the line of retreat was becoming critical.

Colonel Harrelson went to the division artillery command post for a briefing. He was told that division would open the road. He was to move out on the morning of November 29 at the head of the artillery column since the 8-inch howitzers were considered the most valuable of all. If the road was not cleared, he was to take the road to Anju and then to Pyongyang.

On the morning of November 29 the direction of the battalion's fire told the story. It had been to the north. It shifted abruptly to the east, as the Chinese flanked the division. By evening the firing was at a range of ten miles. By the morning of November 30 the range was down to less than a mile.

Soon after daylight a tank stopped at Battery A's position, and the commander told Captain Myers that all infantry units to the north had withdrawn.

That morning General Keiser ordered the 9th Infantry to attack on the Sunchon road and destroy the Chinese roadblock. But the division had taken such heavy casualties in the past five days that it could muster only five hundred assault troops.

At seven o'clock in the morning the Turkish brigade split, with the brigade command post and the artillery taking the Anju road, while the infantry went south to do what the U.S. 9th Infantry had been unable to do—break the Chinese roadblock. By noon the Turks had reached the pass. General Keiser ordered tanks to lead the way, and the Turks to give infantry support. The Turks fixed their long bayonets to their rifles and charged up the ridges on the left of the road. A mile-long column of vehicles began moving down the road. Suddenly it came up against a stalled tank, a half-track, and a truck blocking the road. As the column screeched to a halt, automatic weapons and rifle fire laced out from both sides of the road. Vehicles began to blaze and some exploded. Men died on the road and in the ditches. The Turks charged again and drove the Chinese back. Dead vehicles were pushed off the road, and the column began to move. The Chinese attacked farther down, and again a roadblock stopped the column. The Turks attacked. The Chinese fell back, following Mao Tse-tung's dictum on strategy:

> Enemy advances, we retreat.
> Enemy halts, we harass.
> Enemy tires, we attack.
> Enemy retreats, we pursue.

The Turks were indeed growing tired. The subzero weather was enervating. The Chinese attacked. The airmen came in to help and saved the moment this time, strafing, bombing, rocketing, splashing napalm on the Chinese on the hills. The fight for control of the escape route went on.

At nine thirty on the morning of November 30 the 17th Artillery pulled out to join the retreating column on the Sunchon road. The column moved along at five miles an hour. At noon it stopped for two hours. Down south the Turks were attacking again. The men of Battery A were lucky enough to find themselves near a deserted supply dump of the 25th Division. They loaded up on supplies, particularly overcoats.

At two o'clock in the afternoon the column began moving again. It moved through low hills on both sides of the road. Straggling Korean and American infantrymen loaded up on the vehicles to ride. After two miles the column ran between two hills and came under fire from Chinese machine guns on both sides. The battalion was entering the seven-mile-long section of the road that was under attack. An air strike was summoned and silenced the guns while the column moved through. This same pattern occurred again and again. The column moved south, the Chinese fired on them from positions two to three hundred yards from the road, the planes came in and the Chinese stopped firing. The column moved a little farther along the road. Late in the afternoon came a long pause. It was dusk before the vehicles moved again. The road was wide enough for two vehicles, and a half-track came along, patroling beside Battery A, firing with its twin 40 mm guns at all signs of enemy activity.

The greatest danger lay at the southern end of the Chinese roadblock. There a two-lane concrete bridge had been blown by the enemy, which forced the retreating column to use a ford that led into a rice paddy on the other side. Vehicles stalled in the paddies and blocked the way for others. They had to be pulled out or moved aside, and tractors had to pull the vehicles out. In the dark the lights were turned on, and this brought Chinese rifle and mortar fire. One Chinese infantryman was firing from a point thirty feet away from the American vehicles. The artillerymen picked up their rifles and fought back. Finally all the vehicles of the 17th Field Artillery were pulled through the bypass, and this proved to be the end of the troublesome area. Battery A had eight men wounded in running the roadblock and none killed. It lost four 2½-ton trucks, three ¾-ton trucks, and the kitchen trailer. The battalion lost twenty-six vehicles in all and one howitzer, which overturned and killed eight ROK infantrymen who were riding on it.

The rest of the division was not so lucky. Shortly after one Turkish battalion cleared the ford, a tractor pulling a 155 mm howitzer stalled in the middle, blocking the route of withdrawal. All vehicles north of the ford had to be abandoned, and the rest of the men who came through the Chinese roadblock came out on foot.

The Turks took a dreadful beating in their attacks and lost another four hundred men. Altogether, seven thousand men ran the roadblock, and three thousand of them did not make it.

By December 1 the Eighth Army had retreated back to a line that ran from Sukchon to Sunchon to Songchon to Yangdok, roughly forty miles south of the positions occupied on the day "The End-the-War Offensive" started. It was called the "Pyongyang Defense Line," an indication of what had happened to the war in the last week of November. The belief of the men of the 2nd Division that the fighting was over for them was in a sense vindicated. The division, which had taken five thousand casualties, was withdrawn from action on December 2.

The Turkish brigade marched down to Pyongyang, then to Kaesong, and it finally went into reserve at Sosa, halfway between Seoul and Inchon. The ROK II Corps had again been decimated. The Chinese had suffered extremely heavy losses—in the thousands—largely from air attack and artillery bombardment, but Lin Piao had expected such a result and was prepared to lose tens of thousands more men.

7

General Smith
Escapes a Trap

On the evening of November 24 General Smith learned that General Almond had switched the role of the 1st Marine Division and the army 7th Infantry Division in the X Corps operation plan on the eastern side of North Korea. The marines were to be the northern arm of the pincers in the envelopment of the enemy. The 7th Division was to take over the mission previously assigned the marines, to advance to the Yalu River east of the Chosin Reservoir.

The marines were to march across Korea north of the Eighth Army, from Yudam-ni, fifty-five miles west to Mupyong-ni, and then to Manpojin on the Yalu River. (See Map 10.) The rear boundary would be Hagaru. South of Hagaru the army 3rd Infantry Division had the responsibility for defense. But General Smith asked for, and received, permission to keep garrisons at Koto-ri and Chinhung-ni to protect the main supply route. He was nervous when he contemplated that narrow, winding road that would be his only link with the sea and supply. The change in plan was welcome because it gave General Smith a chance to concentrate his marines. The 5th Marines would advance east of the Chosin Reservoir and the 7th Marines would move on to Yudam-ni, with the 1st Marines in reserve.

By November 24 the 1st Marines were in position: the 1st Battalion at Chinhung-ni, the 2nd Battalion and regimental headquarters at Koto-ri, and the 3rd Battalion at Hagaru. The 5th Marines were working east of the Chosin Reservoir. The 7th Marines were moving to Yudam-ni; they had been in motion on Thanksgiving and celebrated belatedly on November 24. The next day they took Yudam-ni.

On November 26 General Smith flew along the twisting road he liked so little and looked down on his marines. He was pleased with the concentration, with most of the marines south of Chinhung-ni. He had not felt easy in those days when the marines were stuck out like a handful of fingers reaching into enemy territory.

At Hagaru the airstrip was nearly complete, which should help with the supply problem, so difficult over the twisting road and the narrow gauge railroad. The units at Hagaru and Yudam-ni had two days' supply of food and fuel, but only one day's ammunition at Hagaru, plus the one-half day's ammunition carried by the troops.

That day the 7th Marines captured three soldiers of the Chinese 60th Division. The prisoners said that three Chinese divisions had reached the Yudam-ni area on November 20. According to intelligence estimates, that move brought the total to six Chinese divisions in northeast Korea. The prisoners said the Chinese plan called for them to cut the road north after two marine regiments had passed, and to seal them off.

Late on the afternoon of November 26 General Smith's helicopter brought him back to Hungnam, to receive the distressing news that on the west the ROK II Corps had disintegrated and the Eighth Army offensive had come to a standstill. So what was the northern arm of the pincer to pinch?

That evening of November 26 the 2nd Battalion of the 5th Marines completed the move into Yudam-ni and set up a perimeter. Lieutenant Colonel Harold Roise laid plans for the attack the next day. The 7th Marines were in position around Yudam-ni on the ridges. (See Map 12.) The 5th Marines would attack west of Yudam-ni, and the 7th Marines would protect their advance.

On the night of November 26 the wind howled and the temperature dropped to zero. At eleven o'clock that night the company commanders of Roises's battalion gathered in his tent to get orders for the coming attack. They would have support the next day, from marine air, and recoilless rifles, and the regiment's 4.2-inch mortars. The same sort of meeting was going on in the 7th Marine tents. The key points the next day would be the northwest ridge, which they would seize, the north ridge, and the west coast of the reservoir. And above all, they had to protect the valley that ran through the hill masses and the narrow road that wended its way back to Hagaru.

The night was quiet. At dawn the marines began to stir, and fires came alive

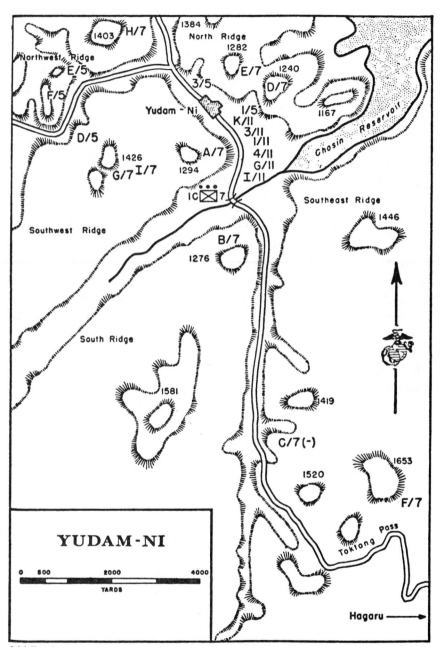

1403 H/7
Northwest Ridge
E/5
F/5
D/5
Yudam-Ni
3/5
G/7 I/7
1426
1294
A/7

1384
North Ridge
1282
E/7
1240
D/7
1167
I/5
K/11
3/11
I/11
4/11
G/11
I/11

Chosin Reservoir

IC 7

Southwest Ridge

B/7
1276

Southeast Ridge
1446

South Ridge

1581

1419

C/7 (-)

1653

1520

F/7

Toktong Pass

YUDAM-NI

0   800   2000   4000
YARDS

Hagaru ⟶

MAP 12

to thaw out the men and their weapons. In the extreme cold organization took time, so it was eight fifteen that morning before the marines moved to attack. The 3rd Battalion of the 7th Marines led off to take Hill 1403, the high point of Northwest Ridge, and Hill 1426, the peak of Southwest Ridge. (See Map 13.) Both high points were captured by midmorning.

The main attack was that of the 5th Marines, up the road from Yudam-ni. Soon, from long-range fire, the marines discovered the enemy. A liaison pilot informed them that the Chinese were entrenched on high ground on both sides of the road, on the lower slopes of Northwest Ridge, and on Sakkat Mountain. The artillery was brought into action to bombard the hills, and Company F left the road to scramble along the slopes of Hill 1403. Company D kept on along the road, until, at the curve at the mouth of the craw between the two Chinese positions, it was met with heavy small arms fire. Mortars and the 75 mm recoilless rifles were brought up, and Corsairs of VMF-312 came down to strafe and bomb the Chinese positions. The marines advanced steadily on the right but were stopped by heavy machine gun fire in midafternoon. The marines of Company D on the road could not move farther than the valley junction, where they came under fire from several tiers of Chinese entrenched on Sakkat Mountain. General Smith had been counseling caution for weeks, and Lieutenant Colonel Roise exercised caution. He broke off the attack at two thirty in the afternoon and set up his perimeter.

So on November 27 the day's advance stopped with about a mile gained. The marines now found themselves facing a semicircle of Chinese positions that ranged from Sakkat Mountain around the western side of Northwest Ridge, then across the north road, and along North Ridge. The marines held those two important hilltops, and down below in the valley of Yudam-ni were part of the 5th Marines and part of the 7th Marines, with forty-eight howitzers of the 11th Marine artillery. The strength was impressive, but the supply situation was not.

Colonel Litzenberg sent down to Hagaru for help, and five truckloads of food and ammunition came up that night, and the trucks went back down to Hagaru.

By six thirty that night Yudam-ni was silent, and the night was pitch black. The temperature had dropped to twenty degrees below zero. On their hills and in their valleys the marines shivered and ached with the cold. And all around them, unseen, the hills came alive with thousands of Chinese soldiers. These were troops of the Chinese 9th Army Group, led by General Sung Shin-lun. The 79th and 89th divisions were massing in a semicircle around Yudam-ni. The 59th Division had made a wide circle between South Ridge and Toktong Pass and had already taken positions on both sides of the single

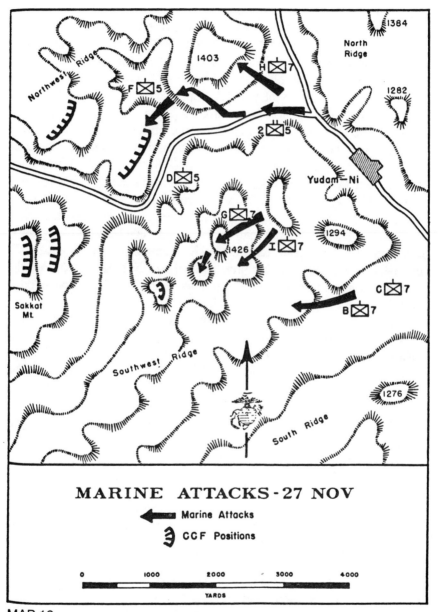

MARINE ATTACKS · 27 NOV

← Marine Attacks

Ɔ CCF Positions

0   1000   2000   3000   4000

YARDS

MAP 13

road south before the marine trucks returned empty to Hagaru that afternoon. They had let the trucks through to avoid giving away the surprise saved for the night attack.

By nine o'clock that night of November 27 the Chinese were sneaking up Northwest Ridge in their rubber shoes. To divert the marines on the ridges, the Chinese commander staged a small raid against the marines on the road between the heights. Chinese came up, and the marines killed two of them; the rest dropped back into the blackness. Chinese patrols probed around the edges of the marine positions on the hills but dropped back when they came under fire. Infiltrators came up to within yards of the marine perimeter. Then the attack began. First the bugles shrieked, and the infiltrators hurled a shower of grenades into the marine positions. The submachine gunners let loose an enormous racket—all this aimed at unnerving the Americans. Mortars poofed and machine guns rattled, and, finally, the Chinese infantry came in a great assault wave on a very narrow front. The marines mowed them down by the dozens, but others came charging past the bodies. The piles of bodies stacked up, but still the Chinese came, and they broke through between Company E and Company F. Captain Samuel Jaskilka, commander of Company E, immediately sent a light machine gun to the edge of the breakthrough, and the 2nd Battalion's 81 mm mortars concentrated there. The Chinese were foiled in their attempt to get behind Company E.

Other units attacked with the intention of getting behind Company F, but the marines never faltered. They set fire to a Korean hut in the draw, and its light exposed the Chinese on the slopes and in the narrow defile. For the marines it was "turkey shoot" for the next hour and a half. At the end of it, the Chinese force had been decimated by mortars, machine guns, Browning Automatic Rifles, and M-1s.

The Chinese, however, still held that salient between Company E and Company F. Lieutenant Colonel Roise brought up reinforcements to the rear of the Company F side, and this action made the salient into a trap for the Chinese. After a few tentative efforts ended in disaster, they did not try to use that route again.

Over on Hill 1403 to the north the Chinese surrounded Company H of the 7th Marines. The fighting was fierce, the Chinese were held back by artillery and mortar fire, but Captain Leroy Cooke was killed in leading an assault on the right flank to bolster his line. Lieutenant H. H. Harris was sent in to take over the company, and he found all but one of his officers wounded. The platoons were badly shot up but they had held.

After this attack, for two hours the Chinese reorganized and planned. They called up new battalions to replace those decimated. At three o'clock in the morning the waves started coming again. Three hundred Chinese tried to advance along the draw in the center, and Captain Jaskilka's men mowed them down. The next wave saw the piles of bodies and stopped to take cover. They did not advance again.

On Company F's hill about a company of Chinese attacked time and again. They overran two machine gun positions but got no further.

Over on Hill 1403 Lieutenant Harris's men were in the most exposed position of all, still hemmed in on all sides by Chinese. The Chinese attacked for an hour, and the marines shot them down. But Lieutenant Colonel William F. Harris decided that the position was much too exposed, and, finally, the commander of the battalion ordered the company to withdraw. The Chinese took Hill 1403, which put them in a position to command the valley floor and split the 2nd Battalion of the 5th Marines away from the rest. (See Map 14.)

Meanwhile, the Chinese 79th Division was moved across North Ridge, three whole regiments, to assault the marines from the north side—complete the encirclement, and close the trap at Yudam-ni. Fortunately for the marines, one battalion got lost and failed to arrive for the attack. The Chinese had also failed to account for Hill 1282 in the middle of their battle approach route, and as they descended on the hills and valleys around the village, the marines on Hill 1282 blunted their attack. The assault began at 11:00 P.M. and continued until 2:00 A.M. on November 28. The northeastern slope of Hill 1282 was covered with quilted bodies. The marines still held the hill.

Down in the valley of Yudam-ni the marines were prepared for an attack. Lieutenant Colonel Robert D. Taplett of the 3rd Battalion of the 5th Marines took advantage of as much high ground as he could find and waited, listening to the sounds of battle around the hills above. The Chinese came at about one thirty in the morning, aiming to cut the road. They managed to isolate the battalion command post, and for an hour Taplett sat in his blackout tent, issuing orders over a field telephone, with Chinese all around him. They could have attacked the tent at any time, but apparently they believed it was deserted. Major John J. Canney, the battalion executive officer, left the tent to try to find and bring back the headquarters company and was killed approaching the road. But Taplett sat calmly and waited.

Lieutenant Colonel Raymond Murray, commander of the 5th Marines, brought most of the 1st Battalion up to the village area to await the next attack.

Lieutenant Nicholas Trapnell's 1st Platoon of Company A started up Hill 1282 at one o'clock in the morning to reinforce the marines there. The going was very hard, the temperature was –20 degrees, the ice was slippery, the air

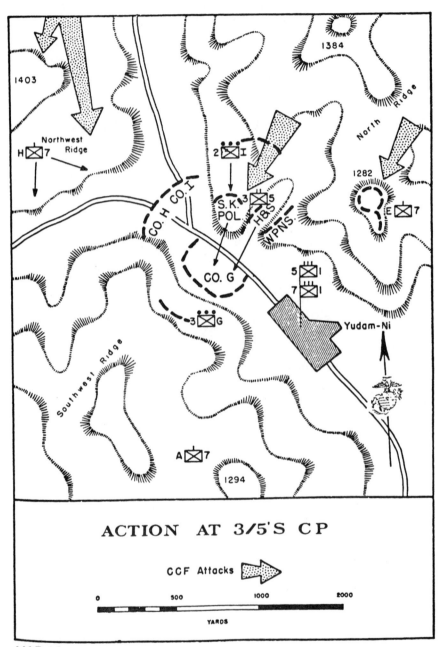

ACTION AT 3/5'S CP

CCF Attacks

0   500   1000   2000

YARDS

MAP 14

was thin (Yudam-ni itself was above 3,000 feet). The troops did not arrive at the top until three o'clock. Behind them came Lieutenant Robert Snyder's 3rd Platoon of Company A. And behind it came the Chinese.

In the hand-to-hand fighting that ensued, the Chinese finally broke through between the marines on the top and the others. On top the officers of Company E fell one by one. Lieutenant Yancey was wounded as he tried to organize the survivors for a last stand. Lieutenant Leonard Clements was wounded. So was Lieutenant William Schreier. So was Lieutenant Robert Snyder. Captain W. D. Phillips, the company commander, was killed as he was throwing grenades at the Chinese. Lieutenant Raymond O. Ball took command of the company then, but he was down with two wounds already. About all he could do was shout and encourage the men. He was hit again and again, and, finally, he fell unconscious. Lieutenant Snyder took command.

At five o'clock the Chinese occupied the summit of Hill 1282. The marines were driven into two enclaves on the reverse slope on the west and on the southeast ridge. Company E had been reduced to about the strength of a rifle platoon.

The Chinese now held a height overlooking Yudam-ni, and they wanted more. Captain Hull's Company D on Hill 1240 came under heavy attack. The command post was overrun at about three o'clock, but Captain Hull led a counterattack that surprised the Chinese, and the marines won a foothold on the hill again. But as dawn came, Captain Hull had only sixteen effective men left to fight, and the enemy was on his front, his right and left, and on the slope to his rear.

Two Chinese divisions were attacking Yudam-ni, and the third division of that army completed its wide flanking move and prepared to strike the road that led back to Hagaru, in order to cut the marines off completely. Captain John F. Morris's Company C of the 7th Marines was given the task of holding Hill 1419, which controlled a vital stretch of the road above Toktong Pass. (See Map 12.) The awaited attack came at two thirty on the morning of November 28. Several companies of Chinese assaulted the hill from right and left. Captain Morris shifted his marines from one side to the other and barely managed to fight off the enemy in an action that lasted until after dawn. Then, as was their custom, the Chinese retreated rather than face the aircraft they knew would be coming in.

Although the Chinese retreated, they did not cease to fight. They went to prepared positions, dug in against air attack, and peppered the marines and the road all day long. They controlled the road back to Hagaru that day.

Captain Morris's Company C was in bad shape that morning. It had suffered forty casualties. This number was extremely high; it left them with greatly reduced fire power. Morris had with him only two of his three rifle platoons, the other having been sent elsewhere. His radio had been blown away by enemy fire, so he could not get direct help from the Corsairs that ranged above that morning.

His 60 mm mortars had only a few rounds of ammunition left. One squad had been sent to an outpost on the highest ground, and this squad was cut off. Corporal Curtis J. Kielsing volunteered to go for the squad but was killed by a Chinese machine gunner as he tried to scale the height. Others came under fire as they pulled the wounded down a draw toward the road. The company was surrounded, and the only possible help could come from Yudam-ni. Captain Morris pulled in his perimeter to a tight circle east of the road and watched as the Chinese closed in.

Further south at Toktong Pass Captain William E. Barber was in much better shape to begin with. His company F was reinforced by heavy machine guns and mortars from the weapons company. Altogether, he had 240 men. He had taken position on an isolated hill north of the road, one platoon on the summit, one on the right, and one on the left with the machine guns. The mortars were down at the base of the hill, and the rocket squad was on the reverse slope.

At one fifteen on the morning of November 28 Lieutenant McCarthy inspected his 3rd Platoon perimeter on top of Fox Hill. The moon was bright, too bright, yet he moved to the top without challenge. The night was stunningly cold, and the marines were half numb. McCarthy admonished his squad leaders: they had to be more alert. As he left he heard the challenges ringing out loud and clear.

McCarthy's caution had been well placed. At two thirty the Chinese attacked from the north, west, and south. On the top of the hill McCarthy's platoon was hit hard, and, of a total of thirty-five men in two squads, fifteen were killed, three were missing, and nine were wounded. The other eight men fell back, and the Chinese took over the top of Fox Hill.

On the left side of the hill the Chinese tried to drive between the 2nd and 3rd platoons. They failed because of three men: Private First Class Robert F. Benson, Private Hector A. Cafferatta, and Private First Class Gerald J. Smith. These three marines wiped out two platoons of Chinese.

At the rear a platoon of Chinese stumbled on the Company F command post, and, when they had recovered from their surprise, drove the company commander and the mortar crews to move up the hill to a line of trees. The Chinese tried to climb over an embankment to get at them, but the marines shot those that reached the crest and rolled grenades down the hill to blow away those below.

Fighting continued in a 270-degree arc until dawn. At the end the Chinese were completely disorganized, and although individual soldiers came crawling along the hillside, in the light the marines picked them off with their rifles. The enemy dead were estimated at four hundred and fifty, while the marines of Company F had lost twenty men killed and fifty-four wounded. They had also held their position.

At Yudam-ni the problem was to get the Chinese off the high ground of North Ridge. Lieutenant Colonel Taplett was still isolated in his blackout tent in no-man's -land at the base of the ridge. At three o'clock in the morning of November 28 he ordered Company G to counterattack Hill 1384. (See Map 14.) Two platoons moved out, drove the Chinese away from the command post, and cleared the area. Headquarters and supply company came back to their old positions. The two platoons then moved up Hill 1384 and routed the Chinese on the spur. They halted there until daylight. Then Lieutenant Dana B. Cashion's platoon attacked, and Lieutenant John J. Cahill's platoon gave fire support. They moved fast and went too far. They were about to take the crest of the hill when Lieutenant Colonel Taplett drew them back to hold the ridge line overlooking Yudam-ni. They were not to advance beyond until given further orders.

Captain Jack R. Jones of Company C of the 5th Marines took his men up a draw to help the marines surrounded on Hill 1240. It took them two hours of slogging, stopping to help and talk to wounded men coming down, but learning little from these numbed casualties who were suffering as much from shock as anything else.

At four thirty the column stopped. The head of the column had come under fire. Captain Jones led the fight up the hill. He found Company E of the 7th Marines up there, a handful now, along with another handful from Company A of the 5th Marines.

Jones moved his men right and left to attack the Chinese. Down in the valley the 81 mm mortars were called up to give support. Shortly after daybreak the marines assaulted the Chinese in a frontal attack, Jones in the van. They charged forward against a hail of grenades and burp gun fire, engaged them hand-to-hand, and overran them.

Here is the official Chinese account of the fighting:

> ... At that time the enemy counterattacked very violently. Accordingly the assistant company commander ordered the 1st Platoon to strike the enemy immediately and determinedly. Before the 1st Platoon's troops had been deployed, Lee Feng Hsi, the Platoon leader, shouted, "Charge!" So both the 1st and 2nd squads pressed forward in swarms side by side.

When they were within a little more than ten meters of the top of the hill they suffered casualties from enemy hand grenades and short-range fire. Consequently, they were absolutely unable to advance any farther. At that time the assistant company commander and the majority of the platoon and squad leaders were either killed or wounded.

While the 1st and 2nd squads were encountering the enemy counterattack, the 3rd Squad also deployed and joined them in an effort to drive the enemy to the back of the hill. As a result more than half of the 3rd Squad were either killed or wounded. When the second assistant platoon leader attempted to reorganize, his troops suffered again from enemy flanking fire and hand grenades. Thus, after having fought for no more than ten minutes, the entire platoon lost its attacking strength and was forced to retreat. . . .

The marines had bridged the gap between the two surviving marine outposts and had thus stopped any chance of enemy reinforcements coming up. When the fight was over, they had wrecked the 3rd Company of the 1st Battalion of the Chinese 235th Regiment. Only half a dozen men survived, including the political officer, who had retired from the fighting.

By the end of the fighting the battalion had lost four hundred men, including nearly all the company commanders, platoon leaders, and non-commissioned officers. But the marines had not gotten off lightly. Their casualties here were over two hundred men.

As dawn came on November 28 Captain Jones directed the rescue of a number of wounded marines trapped in their foxholes on the hill. The evacuation had to be carried out under fire from Chinese on the lower slopes. That day, also, the marines reinforced Hill 1240 and held it against determined Chinese attack.

On the left of North Ridge that morning of November 28 marines and Chinese were mixed up together. The Chinese had taken the top of Hill 1403, but the marines were on the slopes around them. The fighting was hard, and the Chinese losses were staggering. Companies E and F of the 5th Marines counted five hundred dead Chinese in front of their positions.

At dawn on the 28th Colonel Litzenberg and Colonel Murray met and agreed to go on the defensive. General Smith concurred. He wanted concentration on the reopening of the road between Yudam-ni and Hagaru, where Company C and Company F of the 7th Marines were encircled. That night Company C was rescued by a column of marines. But Company F could not be reached before dark.

The men of Company F had spent the day at the top of Toktong Pass preparing for an enemy night attack. They collected weapons and ammunition from dead marines and dead Chinese, including, from the latter, Thompson submachine guns and Springfield 1903 type rifles—bits of the Peking government's inheritance from U.S. aid to Chiang Kai-shek. The marine wounded were sheltered in two tents on the hillside and cared for by navy medical corpsmen. But there was a limit to what the corpsmen could do: the blood plasma that so often saved wounded men from death by shock was frozen solid and could not be used. The worst of the wounded died that day.

In midmorning Australian P-51s hit the Chinese positions around Toktong Pass. Under that cover, Captain Barber sent out patrols. They came back to confirm what he feared: they were completely surrounded by Chinese. He called for an airdrop, and one came, hitting at the base of the hill. Men went down and brought the supplies back, suffering two wounded on the way.

As darkness came the marines prepared for another night of siege. Their morale was high, although their ranks were thin. They felt they could hold out through the night.

At two fifteen on the morning of November 29 the Chinese attacked, having found the 3rd Platoon area most to their liking. They penetrated the line, but a machine gunner turned his gun on the massed Chinese and wiped them out. The marines followed the new dictum: hold position. The next morning Staff Sergeant John D. Audas led a counterattack that restored the original positions. The marines had lost five more men killed and twenty-nine wounded in the night's fighting. Captain Barber and Lieutenant McCarthy were both wounded, but they fought on.

On the morning of November 29 colored parachute material was spread out to mark the airdrop zone, and this time the airmen hit it. Ammunition and supplies came right into the marine lines. Lieutenant Floyd Englehardt brought his helicopter down to deliver batteries for the radios and took off again. His helicopter was hit by ground fire but made it back to base safely.

At eight o'clock on the morning of November 29 a relief column began to move out of Yudam-ni. It consisted of bits and pieces of various units under the command of Major Warren Morris of the 7th Marines. The column moved down the road three hundred yards and then ran into intense machine gun fire from the hills on both sides of the road. Morris called for air strikes, and they came in, but one of the planes dropped messages telling him that the Chinese were formidably entrenched all along the road.

So the mission was changed: the column was only to rescue Company F and then return to Yudam-ni. Even that could not be accomplished. Airmen warned that the Chinese were moving around the flanks of the column and threatening to envelop it, and so the column was called back to Yudam-ni.

Company F was still on its lonely hill. At five o'clock that night Captain Barber called his platoon leaders together and told them they could not expect any help until the next day at least. The Chinese would attack again, and the marines had to expect the attacks to be tougher than ever. They had to hold.

Fortunately, the airdrops of the day had brought them plenty of ammunition and grenades. The night was quiet until about two in the morning of November 30, when the Chinese began again. This time a Chinese voice called out:

"Fox Company, you are surrounded. I am a lieutenant from the 11th Marines. The Chinese will give you warm clothes and good treatment. Surrender now!"

The marines replied to that ruse with a barrage of 81 mm illuminating mortar shells, which revealed the Chinese advance across the valley from the south, and the American machine guns mowed them down. They cut up three companies.

At sunrise the Corsairs came in again, and the Chinese vanished. The marines were jubilant. They had the feeling that they had blunted the enemy attack. Now it was about time for something positive to happen.

While the marines were struggling to survive against a whole Chinese army at Yudam-ni, the base at Hagaru was having its problems. In order to give greatest strength to the forward push toward the Yalu River, General Smith had allocated most of his troops to the forward area, leaving only a reinforced infantry battalion and two battalions of artillery to hold this important base on the main supply route.

Lieutenant Colonel Thomas C. Ridge, commander of the 3rd Battalion of the 1st Marines, moved his troops onto a straggling four-mile perimeter. But, with the shortage of men, he could not defend everything properly. Thus, the Chinese had two open avenues of approach to Hagaru and the airstrip that was under construction there. (See Map 15.) One possible attack route could be through the hills east of town; the other was along a draw on the southwest side.

The division command post was located in the northeast corner of the town, near the Changjin River, in a Japanese-style house. On November 27 division intelligence officers questioned Korean civilians as they moved into the town, to discover what they could about the movements of the Chinese. Counterintelligence Corps agents went into the countryside and mingled with the Chinese troops. They were told that the enemy expected to occupy Hagaru on the night of November 28. On that day headquarters learned that the Chinese were all around the city, not more than five miles away, and that they had cut off Yudam-ni, Fox Hill, and Koto-ri, as well as Hagaru.

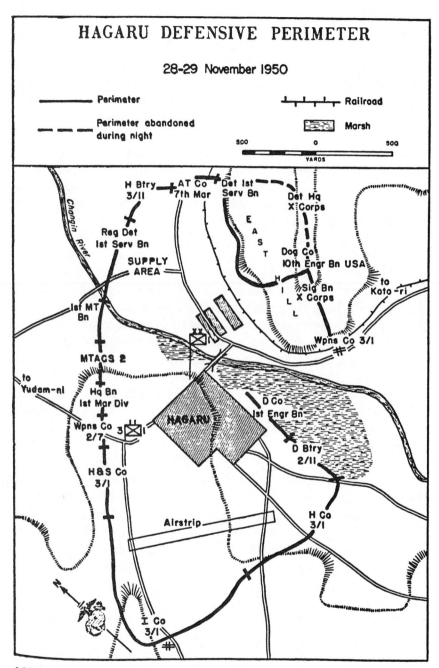

HAGARU DEFENSIVE PERIMETER

28-29 November 1950

——— Perimeter

- - - Perimeter abandoned during night

⊥⊥⊥⊥⊥ Railroad

Marsh

500 — 0 — 500
YARDS

Changin River

H Btry 3/11

AT Co 7th Mar

Det 1st Serv Bn

Det Hq X Corps

Reg Det 1st Serv Bn

SUPPLY AREA

E A S T

Dog Co 10th Engr Bn USA

to Koto-ri

1st MT Bn

H I L L

Sig Bn X Corps

Wpns Co 3/1

MTACS 2

to Yudam-ni

Hq Bn 1st Mar Div

D Co 1st Engr Bn

Wpns Co 2/7

3 ⊠ 1

HAGARU

D Btry 2/11

H&S Co 3/1

Airstrip

H Co 3/1

N

I Co 3/1

MAP 15

All this information greeted General Smith when he arrived by helicopter at eleven o'clock that morning and looked over the frozen town, with the frozen river running alongside below the frozen hills. He had scarcely gotten his feet warm in the command post when General Almond appeared to confer, making one quick visit before hurrying to confer with a stunned General MacArthur in Tokyo. Almond reported on the debacle that had befallen the Eighth Army to the west, which came as small surprise to the marines.

The enemy's activity began at three o'clock in the afternoon, with the firing of a single 76 mm shell into the 1st Battalion command post area just north of the road to Yudam-ni. The explosion killed Captain Paul E. Storaasli, the battalion supply officer. Marines jumped and scattered, but there was no more activity during the daylight hours.

In midafternoon the unit commanders assembled to plan the night's defenses. Platoons were moved to key locations around the perimeter; then, at five o'clock in the afternoon the commanders returned to prepare their officers and noncoms for the battle they knew would begin after dark. The digging in was hard, the ground beneath the snow and ice was frozen ten inches down. The marines stuffed C-ration cans with explosive and blasted their foxholes. The loose dirt was gathered and stuffed into sandbags to make emplacements around the machine gun and mortar positions. The perimeters of Company H and Company I were lined with barbed wire entanglements, trip flares, booby traps, and five-gallon cans of gasoline to which were attached thermite bombs that could be exploded to make long-burning flares. Fields of fire were established, and the artillery was sighted in on the possible routes of attack.

Night fell quietly, the loudest sounds being the crunch of men's boots in the frozen snow and an occasional far-off rifle shot. The sky had the grayish look that presaged snow, and just before eight o'clock the snow began to fall. The marines waited. An hour passed, and another, with no sign of the enemy. Then, at 10:30, three red flares went up to the east, and a whistle blew shrilly. It was not long before the booby traps began to explode, and the trip flares went up. The Chinese patrols were moving along the marine lines, probing. A few minutes passed, then the Chinese fired white phosphorus mortar shells into the marine line, and the Chinese platoons moved forward. The marine fire was devastating, but the Chinese kept coming, stumbling across the bodies of the dead and wounded. Three Chinese soldiers came toward Lieutenant Wayne Hill's foxhole. His carbine failed (not unusual in the cold), and he shot them at close range with his .45 caliber pistol. The third shot was point-blank, and the Chinese soldier fell dead inside Hall's foxhole.

The attack continued, concentrated on an 800-yard front in the center of the marine line, more or less equally against H and I companies. The Chinese came in waves, each wave preceded by heavy mortaring. Shortly after midnight the Chinese broke through the marine line in the Company H sector and in two attacks swept back toward the airstrip, so close that some of them fired at the engineers working the bulldozers under floodlights. Lieutenant Colonel Ridge rounded up all the service troops he could find and sent them up to help Company H.

But inside the marine lines the Chinese troops seemed more interested in looting than in shooting. One wounded marine saved his life by playing dead while a Chinese soldier stripped him of his parka. More marines were rushed in, and little by little the Chinese were killed or forced out of the gap.

One key defense area was East Hill. (See Map 15.) The defense lines here were manned almost entirely by service and engineer troops, with part of the weapons company. The largest unit was Company D of the 10th Engineer Combat Battalion, composed of seventy-seven Americans and ninety South Koreans. Aside from infantry weapons, they had four heavy machine guns, five light machine guns, six 3.5-inch bazookas.

They had been late getting into position, and not all of the men had dug their foxholes by the time the Chinese began attacking. And when the attack began, the deficiencies of the ROK Army training showed up fast. The ROK troops quickly became demoralized and retreated in virtual panic. Many of them did not even stop to fire their weapons. The Americans fell back 250 yards in a tight knot, and the Chinese held a good part of East Hill. They could have taken it all against the thin marine defense, but they did not. They did, however, impose heavy casualties on the marines and the ROK troops. The Americans lost almost 50 percent of their men killed or wounded, and the ROKs lost more than half of theirs, most of them missing in action, which could mean they were captured, but more likely that they deserted in the field.

What saved East Hill and Hagaru that night was the artillery. The howitzers banged away for hours, shifting fire as directed by well-placed observers. Captain Andrew J. Strohmenger, commander of Battery D fired 1,200 rounds of 105 mm ammunition that night, consistently breaking up Chinese troop concentrations before they could become effective. But his neatest maneuver was to trick the Chinese artillery into defeat.

Four Chinese guns were firing from the hills down on the marines in Hagaru, and Captain Strohmenger feared that they would soon hit an ammunition dump, which could start a chain reaction that would blow up half the town. He ordered the six weapons to cease fire and then moved one howitzer out 150 yards toward the line as a decoy. That howitzer opened up on the hills, and the Chinese guns all began firing at its flashes. Battery D's other five howitzers then ranged on the gun flashes of the Chinese artillery and gave the coordinates to the sixth. All began rapid fire. The enemy guns suddenly went silent. Later the artillerymen learned they had destroyed two of the four enemy guns and forced the Chinese to move the other two.

The 60 mm mortars and the heavy machine guns also helped enormously. The marines set fire to two Korean houses, and in that glare two tanks at the base of East Hill made mincemeat of several units of Chinese soldiers. By four o'clock in the morning the assault on the perimeter had ended, and it only remained to clean up the Chinese who had penetrated the line. This took until six o'clock in the morning. Company H took the heaviest casualties, with sixteen men killed and thirty-nine wounded. As for the Chinese, no one counted bodies, they counted heaps of dead, hundreds of still figures lying in the snow, and ragged bloody trails that led back to the hills where the wounded had dragged themselves.

The Chinese attack had failed. Still, the occupation of East Hill posed a threat, so Lieutenant Colonel Ridge ordered a counterattack that morning by a column of about two hundred reserves, who would be led by Major Reginald R. Myers, the battalion executive officer.

Myers assigned Lieutenant Robert E. Jochum's pickup platoon the task of flankers. They climbed the left side of the hill, while Myers led the main body up the front. Marine air came on the scene at about nine thirty that morning, the fighter bombers plastering the Chinese positions with napalm and bombs. Chinese fire shot down one Corsair, but the pilot managed to crash-land within the marine perimeter and was saved.

After one or two false starts the reserves moved up the hill, led by Lieutenant Nicholas Canzona. (See Map 16.) At the top they were pinned down. They managed to bring up a machine gun, only to find it would not fire. The cold again. Another machine gun came up. This one worked and kept the marines from being pushed back down the hill. But what was needed was firepower to take the hill, and the machine guns and mortars were not forthcoming, so in midafternoon the marines retreated halfway down. The howitzers were finally assigned to fire on the hill, and they hit the Chinese on the hill hard. By the end of the day marine intelligence had learned more about who and what they faced. The enemy was the 58th Division, with three infantry regiments and some horse-drawn artillery. The Chinese 172nd Infantry, having carried the attack on the night of November 28, had suffered 90 percent casualties. But there were two more regiments to be heard from.

Meanwhile, farther south the marines were also having trouble. The next town down the snaky road to Hamhung and safety was Koto-ri, which was

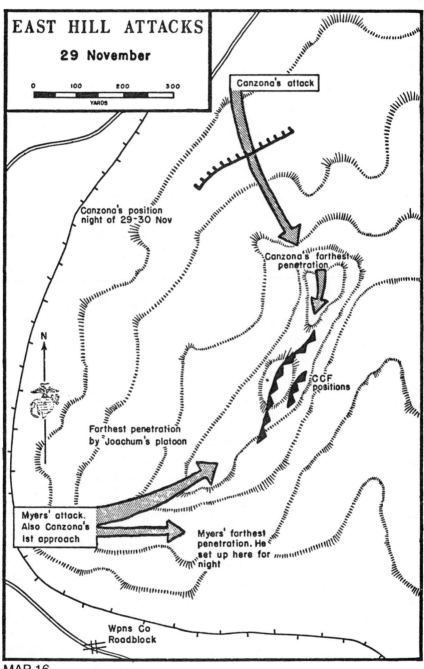

EAST HILL ATTACKS

29 November

0   100   200   300
YARDS

Canzona's attack

Canzona's position
night of 29-30 Nov

Canzona's farthest
penetration

N

CCF
positions

Farthest penetration
by Joachum's platoon

Myers' attack.
Also Canzona's
1st approach

Myers' farthest
penetration. He
set up here for
night

Wpns Co
Roadblock

MAP 16

held by Lieutenant Colonel Allan Sutter's 2nd Battalion of the 1st Marines. The Chinese first skirmished in this area on November 27. On the twenty-eighth General Smith called the marines to march north from Koto-ri and relieve the pressure on Hagaru, and they tried, but they were stalled by a large force of Chinese dug in on both sides of the road, and late in the afternoon they had to go back to Koto-ri.

That evening Company G of the 3rd Battalion, the 41st Commando (British), and Company B of the army 31st Infantry moved up to Koto-ri from the south. Their task was to open the road. These units were organized under Lieutenant Colonel Douglas B. Drysdale of the 41st Commando. Task Force Drysdale they called it. The orders were to fight their way up to Hagaru on November 30.

At 9:45 in the morning of November 30 Task Force Drysdale moved north, under supporting fire from howitzers and mortars. Almost immediately they hit Chinese strength. (See Map. 17.) By noon they had penetrated about a mile and a half north of Koto-ri. They then headed for Hill 1182, where mortars and heavy Chinese fire stopped them, and they waited for tank support. The tanks showed up, and the advance continued. Progress was slow because there were so many Chinese in pockets, houses, gulleys, all along the road, and each pocket of enemy had to be cleaned out while the column waited. The Chinese had good mortar protection, too. One round hit a personnel carrier of Company G, wounding every man in the truck.

By the end of the fighting day, at four fifteen in the afternoon, the column stopped in the valley four miles out of Koto-ri. As night fell there were some difficult decisions to be made. It was apparent to Colonel Drysdale that the Chinese resistance was going to be heavy, and this meant new dangers for the trucks and other vehicles on the narrow road. He suggested that General Smith would have to make the decisions: should the convoy continue under these conditions or not? General Smith had no real alternative. The road to Yudam-ni had to be opened; otherwise, his marines were trapped in the reservoir country. So he told Drysdale to go on. And from Koto-ri a new contingent of tanks set out to join the task force.

The column resumed its advance and made a point about halfway to Hagaru, where a long, deep valley spread out ahead. On the right of the road and railroad the high ground rose steeply. On the left lay the frozen Changjin River, and between wound a little stream, which made its way across a plain several hundred yards wide. Caparo Stream it was called. From the hills came powerful fire, so the men piled out of the vehicles and prepared to fight back.

A mortar shell hit one of the trucks at the far end of the valley, and the resulting fire created a roadblock that split the column in two. The Chinese

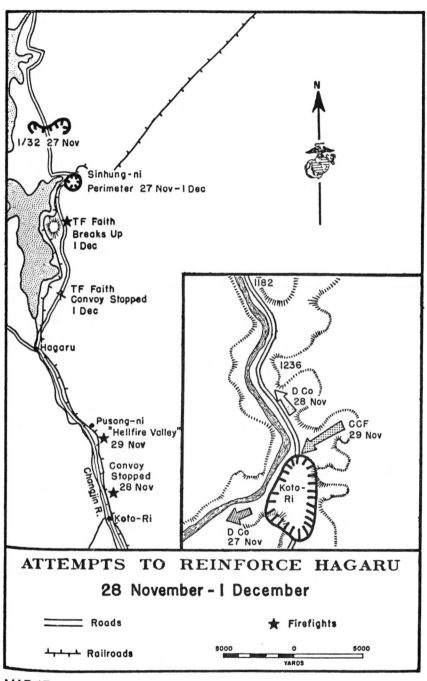

N

1/32 27 Nov

Sinhung-ni
Perimeter 27 Nov-1 Dec

★TF Faith
Breaks Up
1 Dec

TF Faith
Convoy Stopped
1 Dec

Hagaru

Pusong-ni
"Hellfire Valley"
29 Nov ★

Convoy
Stopped
★ 28 Nov

Changjin R.

★ Koto-Ri

1182

1236

D Co
28 Nov

CCF
29 Nov

Koto-
Ri

D Co
27 Nov

ATTEMPTS TO REINFORCE HAGARU

28 November - 1 December

Roads

★ Firefights

Railroads

5000   0   5000
YARDS

MAP 17

saw what they had done and poured in mortar and machine gun fire to prevent the Americans and British from moving the burned-out truck.

Ahead of that truck, the column continued to advance, led by tanks, for Colonel Drysdale had orders to get to Hagaru as quickly as possible, at all costs. So behind was left the second half of the convoy, sixty-one of the British commandos, much of Company B of the 21st Infantry, and a large number of marine division headquarters and service troops.

Lieutenant Colonel Arthur A. Chidester, senior officer with that half of the convoy, tried to turn it around and head back for Koto-ri, but the Chinese attacked and severed the convoy again, and a Chinese unit cut off the road to Koto-ri. Colonel Chidester was captured.

The troops of the convoy spilled into the shallow ditches and dug in. Air strikes protected them as long as the day lasted. When daylight ceased, the Chinese firing grew heavier, but initially no attacks were mounted. The marines strengthened their positions for the night, and so did the army. They clustered in four perimeters, the largest on the north near a village, under army Major John N. McLaughlin. He had about 140 men. The three other perimeters were the result of the Chinese splitting attacks. Two army platoons were crowded in a drainage ditch, along with several marines. Further down the ditch was Captain Michael J. Capraro, with about 20 men. South of them was Major Henry J. Seeley with just a handful of men.

The tanks coming up from the south ran into heavy opposition on the road and did not reach the convoy.

The men of the convoy waited in the valley. Until midnight no Chinese attacks were launched. Then the Chinese began the usual probes to discover the nature of the enemy positions. McLaughlin's position was hit by a grenade attack and then by another. The marines fought back, and so did the commandos. But by 2:00 A.M. they were out of grenades. An army crew had a 75 mm recoilless rifle, which they managed with great skill, until all the men were killed or wounded and the gun was put out of action. Some of the commandos slipped out of camp to try to make it to Koto-ri and get help. At four thirty in the morning the Chinese sent some prisoners to the perimeter with a demand that the Americans surrender. Colonel McLaughlin replied with a demand that the Chinese surrender. But that was pure bluff, and the Chinese knew it. McLaughlin was virtually out of ammunition, the most in one man's hands was eight rounds. Forty men were able to fight. He talked to them, and they agreed that surrender was the only answer. They surrendered on the promise that all the seriously wounded would be evacuated. And while McLaughlin stalled and talked, the word went out to the other perimeters, and most of the men managed to slip away. The Chinese did not evacuate the wounded, but they did let the Americans move them to a Korean house where they were found the next day and taken to Koto-ri.

So the battle that the marines would call Hell Fire Valley came to an end. The task force had lost seventy-five vehicles, and 321 men. About 100 men of the tank company along with 300 infantrymen managed to reach Hagaru and strengthen those defenses. Colonel Drysdale was wounded on the way. Another 300 troops made it back to Koto-ri to help in that defense. Task Force Drysdale had been knocked to pieces in the attempt to clear the road. The road to Yudam-ni was still closed, but the Chinese had failed to take any one of the three positions. The trap was still open, but the Chinese had not been able to spring it.

8

The Army Trapped

On the night of November 29 all the UN troops in the Chosin Reservoir area were placed under the command of General Smith and the 1st Marine Division. The army 7th Division, operating to the east of the marines, had been badly mauled by the Chinese and needed all the help it could get. That help was going to have to come from the marines.

The 31st Infantry had relieved the marines on the drive to the east shore of the Chosin Reservoir on November 25. The soldiers were cold. They wore long woollen underwear, two pairs of socks, a woollen shirt, woollen trousers with cotton fatigues on top, shoe pacs, pile jacket, parka with hood, and trigger-finger mittens. If they had scarves they wore them around their heads to keep their ears from freezing under the steel helmets.

That day Lieutenant Colonel Don C. Faith moved his 1st Battalion up from Hamhung. Just before the men left the nice warm barrack town, they had heard a news broadcast from Tokyo describing the new UN offensive that was to end the war. The announcer had predicted that the soldiers would all be back in Tokyo for Christmas. Everybody cheered.

When the column had reached Hagaru that day, it had taken the road to the right, the one that led along the east side of the Chosin Reservoir. By late afternoon the men reached the defensive positions they would hold, a mile or so north of the town. They went out to the posts, but half the men were sent back to warm-up tents, and the two groups of soldiers alternated during the rest of the day. Nonetheless, one or two men from each company reported in that night as frostbite victims.

Colonel Allen D. MacLean, commander of the 31st Infantry, was on his way north to take command of all the troops on the east side of the reservoir. His task force included the 3rd Battalion of the regiment, an artillery battalion, medics, and an antiaircraft artillery outfit with half-tracks mounted with quadruple .50 caliber machine guns and dual 40 mm guns. MacLean's task was to secure the single road that looped along the east side of the reservoir to the Manchurian border.

On the morning of November 27 Colonel Faith moved his battalion north, and that afternoon Colonel MacLean's men arrived and took up positions a few miles south of Faith's men. The marines, who were pulling out to the west, gave the army a few hints: three divisions of Chinese had just moved into the army side of the reservoir, and their mission was to cut the road.

So Colonel Faith and Colonel MacLean had the idea that life was not going to be exactly idyllic for the next few days. They ordered their men to dig in defensively and cut fields of fire through the scrub brush on the hills. Colonel Faith set up his command post in a farm compound in a valley half a mile from the front line. (See Map 17.)

That night Colonel Faith called his company commanders to a meeting. While the officers were assembled, the Chinese attacked. It was the usual probe, and the army fell for it. Lieutenant Cecil Smith, the executive officer of Company A, suspected what the Chinese were doing and went up and down the line telling his men not to fire, but they fired anyhow and thus gave the Chinese patrol the information they wanted. By midnight the Chinese commander had a good picture of the American positions, and he ordered his attack.

One Chinese unit struck south along the road, another tried to break through the two companies east of the road. They were very persistent and by midnight they had seized the high ground on the ridge lines east of the road. Several platoons were forced out of position.

Very early in the attack the Chinese cut the telephone wires that linked Faith's battalion with MacLean's task force. Radio communication was not very satisfactory, but it established the fact that MacLean was also under attack and that the artillery were defending his position and Faith would have to shift for himself.

At dawn on November 28 Colonel Faith took stock. His battalion was still in position, but there were gaps in the line. He was ordered to attack, but that was out of the question. A high number of officers and noncoms had been wounded. Company A was an example:

A platoon commander, Lieutenant Raymond C. Denchfield, was wounded in the knee. Captain Edward B. Scullion, the company commander, set out to take over that platoon temporarily. He was killed by a grenade. Colonel Faith then sent Captain Robert F. Haynes, his assistant operations officer, to take over Company A. Haynes was killed before he could get into action. So Lieutenant Smith took over the company.

Company morale suffered from these successive shocks, but the cold was even harder on the men. They sat huddled half in their sleeping bags in their foxholes, waiting for enemy attack. The light machine guns, the BARs, and the carbines did not work well. No warming tents had been set up, so there was no relief from the cold for anyone in the line. And it was morning before the Chinese withdrew in their usual fashion.

All day long on November 28 Colonel Faith tried to reestablish his line, and he did recover all but one important knob on high ground east of the road. The battalion that day suffered sixty men wounded, and about twenty men were killed.

During the day General Almond had come up to the front by helicopter with his pocket full of Silver Star medals. When he arrived at the battalion command post, he still had three. He pinned one on Colonel Faith and asked the colonel who else should have them. The colonel spotted Lieutenant Everett F. Smalley, Jr., sitting on a jerry can outside the aid station, waiting to be evacuated. He had been wounded in the night's fighting. He got one. The other one went to Sergeant George A. Stanley, the mess sergeant for headquarters company, who happened to be walking by at the moment. General Almond then made a little speech to all the men Faith could assemble on short notice:

"The enemy who is delaying you for the moment is nothing more than remnants of Chinese divisions fleeing north. We're still attacking and we're going all the way to the Yalu. Don't let a bunch of Chinese laundrymen stop you."

And with the satisfaction of a job well done, General Almond got back into his helicopter and flew to a nice warm room at Hungnam. Colonel Faith watched the whirlybird ascending and then ripped off the medal and threw it in the snow.

"I got me a Silver Star," said Lieutenant Smalley as he went back to sit on his jerry can and wait for an evacuation helicopter. "But I don't know what the hell for."

That afternoon Colonel MacLean came up to see Faith. When he started back, he was stopped by a Chinese roadblock. Those "remnants of Chinese divisions fleeing north" had stopped long enough to surround Colonel MacLean's task force. The colonel stayed with Faith's battalion.

By midafternoon it was certain that the night ahead would see bitter fighting. The Chinese laundrymen had managed to harry the battalion all day, so that no food was brought up. When food did come up after dark, it consisted of frozen C ration cans.

In midafternoon an air unit attacked a battalion of enemy troops marching down from the north.

The Chinese attacked the area east of the road and after an hour or so were driven back. While the soldiers were fighting, General Almond was answering a summons to hurry to Tokyo for a meeting with General MacArthur. At that command conference, MacArthur announced that the UN forces must retreat. That word was radioed to Eighth Army and X Corps and filtered down to Colonel MacLean and then to Colonel Faith. The battalion was to abandon all unnecessary vehicles and supplies, load up the wounded, and break through the roadblock to the south to join MacLean's force. It was not quite as simple as it sounded, because when the laundrymen sensed that the Americans were pulling out, they grew bolder. Colonel Faith sent two companies ahead on the sides of the road to provide security for the column. All went well until they reached the roadblock, which was located at the end of a long finger of the Chosin Reservoir, now frozen solid. The road here made a 180-degree turn around the finger, crossing a bridge, and there was the roadblock.

Colonel Faith sent two companies onto high ground east of the roadblock to outflank the enemy. He set up his heavy weapons on a hill overlooking the roadblock. From their hill the weapons company men could see the perimeter of Colonel MacLean's force, less than a mile past the roadblock on the other side of the ice. They could also see Chinese all around.

Colonel MacLean was out ahead. He saw Faith's column coming. It stopped suddenly when it began taking fire. Colonel MacLean believed the fire was coming from his troops, so he started across the finger of ice to call a halt to it. But the fire was Chinese, and Faith's men watched as the colonel was hit four times—they could see his body jerk as each slug jolted him. He managed to reach the other side of the ice but then disappeared and was not seen again.

Colonel Faith led his men against the Chinese on the finger and thus broke up an attack that was assembling to hit the 57th Field Artillery. At the same time, the two companies surrounded the Chinese roadblock and broke it up, too. The Chinese troops melted into the hills, and the column of vehicles joined up with MacLean's task force.

When it was certain that Colonel MacLean had disappeared—killed or captured—Lieutenant Colonel Faith assumed command of the task force. Their position was better than it had been, but hardly enviable. Chinese occupied the ridges all around them, and they were on low ground, squeezed into an area about a mile long and a third of a mile wide. They were short of food and ammunition and gasoline, and it was so cold they had to fire their weapons every fifteen minutes to be sure they were working.

During the day three air drops came in. One landed squarely in Chinese territory, one landed in no-man's-land, and the Americans fought for, and got, most of it. The third came inside the perimeter, and the Americans had all of it. The marine Corsairs also kept the enemy off balance all day long, and the night fighters came out to continue the job at night. They dropped napalm and bombs and fired rockets and machine guns. And Task Force MacLean waited for rescue from the south.

The rescue had been planned. Brigadier General Henry I. Hodes, the assistant division commander of the 7th Division, had started north with a task force but was stopped just north of Hudong-ni. The 2nd Battalion of the 31st Infantry was also told to move to the rescue, but so disorganized was X Corps headquarters that no transportation was provided for the battalion. The men sat and waited, as did Task Force MacLean. When the 2nd Battalion did get going, it had to be diverted to protect the withdrawal route at Koto-ri, and so Task Force MacLean was still on its own.

On the night of November 29 the Chinese attacked, but were repelled. Next morning the task force waited hopefully for rescue. It did not come. Helicopters came to evacuate the seriously wounded, fighter bombers came to harry the enemy, but no column came.

On the night of November 30 the Chinese attacked again. Five times they penetrated the lines, and five times they were thrown back. Just before dawn they seized a hill in the middle of the perimeter. Lieutenant Robert D. Wilson volunteered to counterattack and take the hill. He assembled about thirty men and waited for dawn. They were very short of ammunition; they had only rifle clips and three hand grenades among them. Wilson led the men up the hill in the growing light. He was hit three times and killed. Sergeant First Class Fred Sugua took over, and he was killed a few minutes later. Nevertheless, the volunteers drove the Chinese off the hill and the enemy fled from the perimeter.

The situation of the task force was desperate. Most of the men were out of ammunition. Most of their medical supplies were gone. So many men were dead or wounded that the perimeter was dreadfully thin. They had been under attack for eighty hours, frostbite was so common no one talked about it, and the end seemed near. When a friendly fighter plane reported that there was no column in sight, no friendly forces nearer than Hagaru, Colonel Faith decided he had to make a break for Hagaru. An air strike was promised for one o'clock in the afternoon. Faith ordered the artillerymen to shoot off all their ammunition and then destroy the weapons. The vehicles were lined up, most of them carrying some of the several hundred wounded men. Company C of the 32nd Infantry would take the lead as advance guard. Lieutenant Mortrude's platoon would have the point, supported by a half-track with 40 mm guns. Mortrude, who had been wounded in the knee, would ride the half-track.

When friendly planes appeared overhead at one o'clock that afternoon, the column began to move. The friendly planes zoomed down in support. They dropped napalm and bombs—unfortunately on the head of the column. One napalm container fell squarely on the half-track. Several men were burned to death inside. Others fled in all directions, clothes streaming fire. The column was immediately thrown into confusion. Chinese fire was coming in, and it did not help matters. The column dissolved into disorganized clots of men, all trying to escape, to keep on moving south.

Lieutenant Mortrude gathered ten men and tried to carry out his orders. He moved down the road, scattering Chinese before his group. They reached a blown bridge two miles south of the starting point. There they were joined by Lieutenant Herbert Marshburn of Company A and a number of men. They crossed under the broken bridge and moved east and south. They came under fire from the high ground to the northeast. Lieutenant Mortrude was hit in the head and knocked out.

The main column finally got organized and headed south toward the broken bridge under air cover. In midafternoon the vehicles reached the blown bridge and had to stop while a bypass was built. As the vehicles began to cross the bypass they came under Chinese rifle fire. Lieutenant Campbell, wounded, was lying in the back of a truck that was under fire. Several men were hit. Campbell got out of the truck and started walking up the ditch toward the lead vehicles. After he had gone two hundred yards, he saw that someone was shooting at him. He got into a 3/4-ton truck and went on. He never learned what had become of the truck on which he was originally riding.

That truck was hung up in the stream. The whole column was stalled and under attack, and it was late afternoon before Lieutenant Hugh R. May, the motor officer, saw the last vehicle off and moved on after them. But many men had fallen by the wayside already. Lieutenant Mortrude regained consciousness and was bandaged up by an aid man. He walked along toward the reservoir and out onto the ice, half-dazed. All around he saw American dead and wounded.

The column inched on. It came under attack at another roadblock half a mile below the blown bridge. Colonel Faith got out of his jeep and walked along the column, urging the men forward, urging men to get out and make an infantry assault on the hillsides to stop the enemy harassment. Captain Erwin Bigger of Company D went up to clear out the area between the road and the reservoir. He was blinded in one eye by a mortar fragment and wounded in the leg. Using a mortar aiming stake as a crutch, he gimped along. No one noticed, for almost all of the men with him were walking wounded.

Major Robert E. Jones, the intelligence officer of the 1st Battalion, and Colonel Faith had about two hundred men in two units. They launched separate attacks against the roadblock and dispersed the Chinese. But Colonel Faith was hit by a mortar burst and mortally wounded. His men put him in the cab of a truck.

The wounding of Colonel Faith put an end to what was left of the task force's cohesion. Nearly all the officers were dead or wounded. Major Jones gathered as many men as he could and tried to hold the convoy together. But three wrecked 2½-ton trucks stood at the head of the column, full of wounded men. The men were removed, and the trucks were pushed over the cliff toward the reservoir. The wounded were now piled two deep in the other trucks. Men rode the hoods and bumpers, and half a dozen men hung to the sides of each truck. In front Major Jones led his ragged unit of perhaps a hundred and fifty men on foot. The trucks came along behind. There had been twenty-two trucks, and now there were fifteen.

A mile beyond the roadblock the column was stopped by two burned-out tanks that blocked the way. A bypass was built, and they moved on. By nine o'clock that night they had covered half of the ten miles from the last defense perimeter to Hagaru. The column came to Hudong-ni, and, as it was entering the town, it was attacked by Chinese soldiers from every direction. The driver of the lead truck was killed, the truck overturned, and once again the road was blocked. Major Jones decided it was time for the men to leave the road and strike out along the rail line. He led the way, and some of the men followed. Others stayed with the trucks and decided to make a run for it through the town. As they did so, the Chinese came at them with machine guns, grenades, and mortars, and the trucks were destroyed, spilling wounded men into the snow. Many were crushed by the trucks in which or on which they had been riding. The column was finished. The men who could walk dispersed, and those who could not were left behind.

Lieutenant Campbell led a group of men down the shoreline of the reservoir toward Hagaru. At a Korean house an ROK soldier told them where the marines were, and Lieutenant Campbell and his seventeen men went on. Only three of them still had weapons. Two miles farther they reached a marine tank post, and the tankers directed them inside the perimeter.

For several days stragglers came along into the marine line. Some of the men were captured when the column broke down in Hudong-ni, given medical treatment, and later released. Many more froze to death. Lieutenant Mortrude, wounded in the head and the knee, staggered into Hagaru from the blown bridge in the small hours of December 2. Two days later nearly all the survivors had entered the lines. The 1st Battalion of the 32nd Infantry had gone into action with 1,053 men in the ranks. Only 181 came out. The rest of Task Force MacLean had been captured or destroyed by General Almond's "Chinese laundrymen," in the worst yet debacle for the Americans in the Korean War.

9

Breakout

Tokyo was in a flap. On the night of November 28 General MacArthur called an emergency meeting at the American Embassy, where he lived. General Walker was summoned from Korea, and so was General Almond, fresh from his rousing visit to the surrounded troops of Task Force MacLean. Almond arrived at 9:30 that night. For four hours MacArthur and his principal staff assistants heard the story of the disaster they had forced, and they tried to find ways of getting out of it. At first, MacArthur tried to persuade General Almond that he had to help the Eighth Army. The way to do it, he said, was to send the U.S. Army 3rd Infantry Division west across the Taebaek Mountains to attack the Chinese forces moving down the Eighth Army's right flank, where MacArthur had left the fifty-mile gap. They would take that road that appeared on the situation map.

But in the last few days General Almond had learned that the road on the map was not duplicated by a road on the ground. There was no road through the Taebaek Mountains. The theater commander, said Almond, was preparing to put the whole 3rd Division in peril and might lose it all. If that was what MacArthur wanted, Almond would do it, but he insisted General Walker would have to agree to supply the division when it crossed the mountains. Walker could not make any such guarantee, and so one more rash move was obviated. After the long meeting, even MacArthur was convinced that there was no way he could continue the drive to the Yalu. It suddenly came home to him and his staff that the Chinese had not been bluffing and that they had moved hundreds of thousands of men into Korea under the noses of the Americans.

After the end of this meeting, Almond would say no more about "Chinese laundrymen." Walker, who had suspected earlier that disaster lay across the Chongchon, was ordered to fight a series of delaying actions, to enable the X Corps to escape from the trap on the northeast.

MacArthur still did not know the extent of the disaster and would not for several days. Typically, however, his first move was to cover his own tail. He sent a message to Washington announcing that the whole offensive had collapsed, and he did not have sufficient forces to stop the Chinese attack. "We face an entirely new war," he said. "This command is faced with conditions beyond its control and its strength."

Not so privately MacArthur was already laying the blame for his failures on Washington. Spies were telegraphing the UN strategy to the Chinese, he said. In his *Reminiscences* he quoted "an official leaflet by Lin Piao," the Chinese commander:

> I would never have made the attack and risked my men and military reputation if I had not been assured that Washington would restrain General MacArthur from taking adequate retaliatory measures against my lines of supply and communications.

There is something wrong with that quotation; it has the sound of coming from America, not China: the spies could not report that MacArthur would be restrained, because he was not, and no decision was ever made to restrain him. Further, Lin Piao was a field commander, not commander in chief of the Chinese armies. He attacked because he was ordered to attack. The decision to intervene was made at the highest political level in Peking, which meant Chairman Mao Tse-tung and the Chinese Communist political bureau.

But it was impossible for MacArthur ever to admit that he was wrong, and now the blame had to be cast on others. If only he had been able to respond with the entire power of his air forces, he said, he could have stopped the Chinese.

That contention also seems extremely doubtful, given the air force's inability to even find the 300,000 Chinese troops that had infiltrated into Korea in the past two months. Nor would massive bombing of Chinese bases and Yalu bridges have had the effect on the Chinese armies that these actions would have had on such a highly equipped army as the Soviet, or even the North

Korean. The Chinese had little mechanized equipment. Their armies traveled on their feet. By the end of November they could cross the Yalu River on the ice.

MacArthur's shocking message reached Washington very early in the morning. General Bradley was rousted out of bed, and at 6:15 he telephoned President Truman with the dreadful news. It suddenly became clear that everything MacArthur had said about his ability to carry on the war had been illusion. President Truman and the Joint Chiefs of Staff had been the victims of their own wishful thinking. The worst possible had happened: the United States was being bogged down in a land war in Asia, a situation against which all prudent political and military leaders had warned in the past.

Immediately President Truman convened a session of the National Security Council. The views of his security advisors, he found, varied widely, and there were further political complications at home and abroad. The world suddenly feared the outbreak of general war.

If MacArthur had been given his head, there was a good chance that the war would have spread. Less than twenty-four hours after learning of the disaster, MacArthur called upon the Joint Chiefs of Staff to let him personally negotiate with Chiang Kai-shek the entry of Chinese Nationalist troops into the war. Had Washington acceded, there is little doubt that China would have seen this move as a direct threat by MacArthur to carry the war to Peking and destroy the Mao Tse-tung government. A completely logical next move would have been to invoke the Sino-Soviet mutual assistance treaty, and then the fat would really have been in the fire. That is how most of the UN Allies saw the picture, and they were more than a little distressed when President Truman at a press conference allowed himself to be badgered into discussing the possible use of atomic weapons in Korea. Some elements of the military were urging that course, but the political advisors were almost entirely against it.

What emerged from those first agonized days of "the new war" was the realization that the United States had made a dreadful miscalculation. No longer was the UN talking about driving to the Yalu and resolving the political problems of Korea by military action. Their concern now was to extricate the United Nations forces from a very tight spot.

The Joint Chiefs of Staff suggested the establishment of a continuous defense line across the narrow neck of the Korean peninsula, with the X Corps linking up to the Eighth Army. MacArthur insisted that X Corps should stay where it was. The gap, he argued, was a sort of trap for the Chinese, forcing them to commit eight divisions to prevent thrusts against their supply lines.

This was a unique line of reasoning, unknown to the Chinese or to the marine and army troops of X Corps, now surrounded in the north and faced with the possibility of a disaster unparalleled in the war. It was the sort of situation the Germans had faced at Stalingrad on the orders of another egomaniacal commander.

MacArthur ordered General Almond to pull X Corps into the Hamhung–Hungnam area. This was not a retreat, according to MacArthur. "Movement in retrograde" was his nice way of putting it.

The Joint Chiefs of Staff disapproved of MacArthur's plans to hold the X Corps and the Eighth Army separate from each another, but as usual, they backed down in the face of his obduracy. They did, however, insist that the marines and the army 7th Division be extricated from the reservoir area.

No, nothing would be changed, except that MacArthur must have enormous reinforcement.

By this time the Joint Chiefs of Staff were growing more than a little uncomfortable with MacArthur's attitudes, and General Lawton J. Collins flew to Tokyo to find out what was really going on. He conferred briefly with MacArthur in Tokyo and then flew up to Korea to see General Walker.

Meanwhile on the Eighth Army front the movement in retrograde was progressing rapidly. On December 3 the Chinese again broke through the ROK II Corps lines, Sunchon fell, and Pyongyang was endangered. The next day the North Korean capital was abandoned by General Walker, who set up his new defense line at the Imjin River. MacArthur was still speaking of future surges to the north, but Walker told General Collins that he could not even defend the Seoul–Inchon area without suffering enormous losses and that he would prefer to withdraw back down to the Pusan Perimeter. He could hold there, he said, if the X Corps would reinforce him.

General Collins listened. On December 6 he flew to Hamhung to see General Almond, and there he learned about the latest developments in the war.

After the early failure to open the main supply route south of Yudam-ni, General Smith had put the 5th and 7th marines under joint operational command, to make the breakout to the south. A composite battalion was organized under Major Maurice E. Roach. Its task was to hold the high ground through which the marines would advance south out of the trap. Roach built a battalion spirit by adopting as a device a green neckerchief made from a piece of torn drop 'chute. Damnation Battalion, the men termed their unit. On the morning of November 30th the marines prepared to move out of Yudam-ni, destroying all supplies that could not be carried.

Only drivers and the seriously wounded were allowed to ride the trucks in the middle of the column. The guns of the artillery were placed at the tail end, so that if they were immobilized the column would not be stopped. The dead—eighty-five officers and men—were left behind after a field burial.

The 1st and 3rd battalions of the 5th Marines were located on high ground north of Yudam-ni, so close to the Chinese positions that the principal weapon of both sides in skirmishes was the grenade. At eight o'clock on the morning of December 1 the withdrawal began. (See Map 18.) The 3rd Battalion and then the 1st pulled out, the evacuation covered by marine and navy aircraft from Task Force 77. It was done so skillfully that the units disengaged without a casualty. After that, three marine infantry battalions moved to occupy a defense line three and a half miles long, stretching from Hill 1542 to the arm of the Chosin Reservoir. This was hard going because the Chinese were well entrenched in the area. But by late afternoon the basic positions had been taken, and the marines had the initiative. That night the 1st Battalion of the 7th Marines set out across the mountains to establish a protective barrier on the east side of the main route of supply. They reached the eastern slope of Hill 1520, and then had to stop for the men were nearly done in. It was three o'clock in the morning of December 2.

Meanwhile, the 3rd Battalion of the 5th Marines had passed through Yudam-ni, on their way to open the road south. They were led by a single tank, the only one to reach Yudam-ni before the road had been closed by the Chinese. Tank D-23 was manned by Staff Sergeant Russell A. Munsell and one crew member. After moving about a mile, they were stopped by heavy Chinese small arms fire from both sides of the road. The marines fanned out and began to clear the enemy from their flanks. They were helped by fire from the howitzers of the 11th Marines. This took until seven thirty that evening. Lieutenant Colonel Taplett gave the men a rest when they had seized the high ground on both sides of the road opposite Hill 1520. Just before midnight they renewed the attack, as the 1st Battalion of the 7th Marines were fighting on the other side of the mountain mass. The fighting here was hard and long, the Chinese resisted firmly, and the marines took casualties, including several platoon and company commanders. Company G and Company I were both reduced to platoon strength. But at daybreak on December 2 the marines counted nearly 350 dead in the Company I area alone. As day broke the marines moved down the road and wiped out a Chinese roadblock, so that the vehicle column could pass.

The 1st Battalion of the 7th Marines attacked that morning toward Hill 1653, just north of Fox Hill. They were on the way to Toktong Pass, and they would finally relieve Company F, which had been under seige on its hill for five days and five nights. The company had suffered 118 casualties, six of the

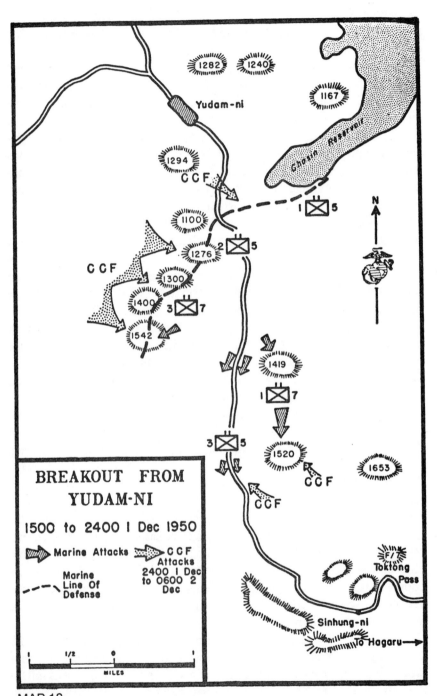

1282 1240

1167

Yudam-ni

Chosin Reservoir

1294

CCF

1|⊠|5

1100

2|⊠|5

1276

CCF

1300

1400

3|⊠|7

1542

1419

1|⊠|7

3|⊠|5

1520

1653

CCF

CCF

N

F/7
Toktong
Pass

Sinhung-ni

To Hagaru →

BREAKOUT FROM
YUDAM-NI

1500 to 2400 1 Dec 1950

Marine Attacks   CCF
                 Attacks
                 2400 1 Dec
Marine   to 0600 2
Line Of   Dec
Defense

1/2   0   1

MILES

MAP 18

seven officers were wounded, and virtually every man was hurt by frostbite, but as the battalion came up, the men of Fox Company were still holding their positions.

The Chinese counterattacked early on the morning of December 2, using their inverted V formation. Both sides took casualties, but the marines held the lines on both sides of the road and kept the escape route open.

The long, winding column of men and vehicles kept going. Colonel Taplett's battalion fought on down the road, securing one objective after another. One company would be delayed by Chinese counterattack or heavy fire from the hills, another would forge ahead on the other side of the road, the delayed company would come up, and seesawing, they moved down the road. (See Map 19.)

They fought through cold and snow. On the morning of December 3, six inches of fresh snow covered the ground. Davis's and Taplett's battalions then approached a junction at Toktong Pass, and there the 7th Marines forced the Chinese to retreat directly into the path of the 5th Marines. As day dawned the marine Corsairs caught the Chinese by surprise. The converging marine units had them in a trap; they were blasted by napalm and rockets and mortars and machine guns, and by ten thirty on the morning of December 3 one whole Chinese battalion had been slaughtered, and the marines held the ridge northeast of Toktong Pass. It had been a hard road to travel. The three companies of Colonel Taplett's battalion had been reduced from 437 men on December 1 to 194 on December 4. But they had fought their way down the road, with the 7th Marines on the north helping pave the way. They stopped at Toktong Pass to regroup, while up from Hagaru the Royal Marine Commandos set out to meet them on the road, reinforced by a platoon of tanks.

At seven o'clock in the night of December 3 the marines of Colonel Davis's battalion stopped outside Hagaru, formed up, and marched into town in column. They had been fighting for a week, without a decent night's sleep all that while, they had lived on crackers and half-frozen C-rations. They had endured conditions that not even General Smith was sure they could stand. And they had beaten the Chinese at their own game. Lieutenant Colonel Davis's 1st Battalion of the 7th Marines had plenty to be proud of, and so did Colonel Taplett's men.

At the end the going grew tough for the last part of the vehicle column. Some of the drivers of the artillery vehicles and howitzer movers of the 11th Marines panicked when the Chinese attacked the tail end of the column. But officers and noncoms pulled and pushed most of them into line. In the confusion and the fighting, however, nine howitzers were abandoned and

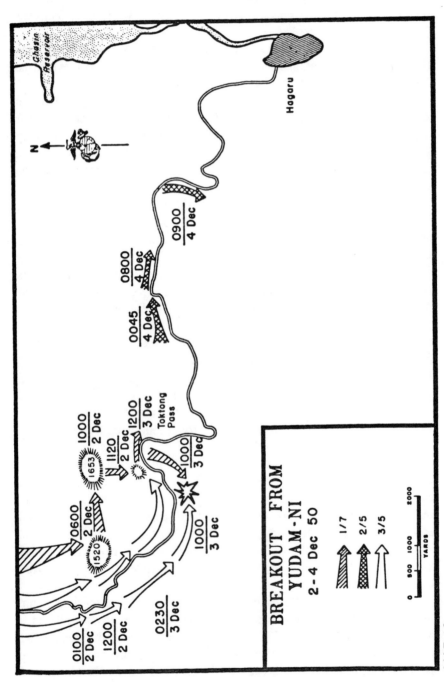

BREAKOUT FROM
YUDAM-NI
2 - 4 Dec 50

1/7
2/5
3/5

YARDS

0   500   1000   2000

MAP 19

ordered destroyed by air. At two o'clock on the afternoon of December 4 the last elements of the rearguard of marines passed into the Hagaru perimeter, and the hardest march most of those marines had ever made was history. It had taken the column three days to cover the fourteen miles. They had brought 1,500 casualties into Hagaru, 1,500 men who had been saved from what appeared earlier to be almost certain death or capture. There they joined the other marines and the survivors of the U.S. Army 7th Infantry's 32nd Infantry.

Now General Smith had to plan for the next step, the removal of casualties from Hagaru by air, and the breakout to Hamhung. Hagaru and Koto-ri were still surrounded by Chinese troops, although these had been so hard hit in the fighting that they were unable to launch a major attack in this first week of December.

On December 2 nearly 1,000 casualties were flown out to safety by C-47 aircraft. The airlift continued; by December 5, 4,300 men had been airlifted out from the half-mile-long airstrip the marines had built in the frozen ground.

The 1st Marine Division had been badly mauled by the Chinese, there was no doubt about that. The division had been equally hurt by the weather; the total casualties were more than 2,300 men, and as many of those were suffering the effects of exposure to cold as were the victims of enemy action.

But the division was still intact, still a fighting unit, and replacements began to come in to help in the fight back to the Hamhung area. The X Corps had issued orders for the retreat. (It was never called that. General Smith pointed out that there could be no retreat when there was no rear, and, from a tactical point of view, he was quite correct. From a strategic point of view, however, the retreat from North Korea was to be one of the great retreats of history.)

Over five hundred men were brought in to stiffen the battalions. If the marines were to get out without sacrificing all their equipment, they would have to fight their way, and that is what General Smith intended to do. December 6 was the date set for the attack toward Koto-ri. That was the day that General Collins returned to Tokyo from his inspection tour of Korea and sat down with MacArthur to try to plan for the future.

MacArthur complained that any restrictions placed on him could do nothing but bring disaster. He said nothing about the disaster he had brought himself. He wanted to use Chinese Nationalist troops, to bomb Manchuria and other areas of the Chinese mainland, and to use the atomic bomb. If he did not have immediate reinforcement, he wanted to pull out of Korea.

The result of the Collins visit was a growing distrust of MacArthur by the Joint Chiefs of Staff, particularly after he began making statements to the press, blaming everyone but himself for the difficulties that had arisen.

President Truman felt constrained to issue an order demanding that field commanders clear policy statements with the Department of Defense. MacArthur was not named (Truman did not want to endanger MacArthur's credibility with the U.S. public), but it was apparent that he was the only field commander in action.

What Washington was now moving toward, urged on by the British and by the other Allies, was a position that could easily have been assumed in early October: a cease-fire and the reestablishment of a line across Korea around the 38th parallel. It had taken military disaster to make official Washington realize that the Communist bloc would fight to defend what it considered to be its own perimeters and that, given U.S.–Chinese relations, China insisted on a buffer zone between its territory and the zone of American influence.

10

The Evacuation
of X Corps

Everyone in the 1st Marine Division, from General Smith on down, knew that the trip to Hamhung was going to be a hard one. The 5th Marines would take over the Hagaru defense and protect the division's rear as it marched to Koto-ri. The 7th Marines would march south at dawn on December 6. The 1st Marines at Koto-ri would continue to hold and allow the other two regiments to pass through, then become the rearguard on the road from Koto-ri to Hamhung.

The wounded who had survived from the army 7th Infantry Division had been flown south to safety. The remaining soldiers, including 385 survivors of Task Force Faith, had been provided with marine equipment and organized into a task force, called Task Force Anderson after its commander, Lieutenant Colonel Berry Anderson. The task force was attached to the 7th Marines.

Almost everyone able to walk was going to make this march on foot. The supplies and equipment that could not be carried were to be destroyed. Two days' rations and one day's firepower were to be carried. They would rely on airdrops for the future. The most serious casualties had already been evacuated by air, and those with frostbitten feet and wounds would ride the trucks. Serious casualties suffered on the road ahead would be taken out by helicopter. The less seriously hurt would be placed in sleeping bags and put aboard the trucks.

As the news correspondents who rode the evacuation planes up from Hamhung during the first week of December noted with some surprise, the Chinese were virtually inactive around Hagaru. The worst attack on the perimeter was on the night of December 5 when the area was bombed and strafed by a pair of UN B-26 bombers. The airmen said they had been ordered to make the attack, and the suspicion was that the Chinese had done the dirty work with a captured U.S. radio.

Hagaru was full of strange equipment and supplies, because in the halcyon days around Thanksgiving it had been scheduled to become a forward base. Thus, the PX department had been active, and huge stores of candy had been brought up. There was no way of sending it back, so it was given out as general issue, and the marines wandered around the perimeter munching on Baby Ruths and Tootsie Rolls. The latter were also discovered to be a fine substitute for liquid metal cement to plug up leaky vehicle radiators.

During the first five nights of December the Chinese were almost invisible. Actually, Lin Piao was shifting his strength to the center of Korea, preparing for a major offensive. For if the American high command had erred in assessing the capabilities and intentions of the Chinese, now the Chinese did the same. Buoyed by immediate success, they proposed to drive the UN forces out of Korea altogether, apparently forgetting their own army's serious limitations. The Chinese armies were moving to the center, but how? By horse-drawn wagon train, by donkey, and on the backs of men. The slow-down in attack was to be only a respite. A hundred and sixty thousand Chinese troops—six armies—were moving toward that center, along with the NK I Corps, which had already been revitalized. Their primary objective was the capture of Seoul. In Manchuria the rest of the North Korean army was being reconstituted and resupplied from Soviet sources. The Chinese and the North Koreans now believed they could take Seoul and then the rest of Korea. They believed that the Americans, the UN Allies, and the South Koreans were on the ropes.

Three Chinese armies, the 20th, 26th, and 27th, had closed around X Corps, and their mission was still to destroy the American forces. So far they had suffered many more casualties than the Americans and so there were far fewer than the 100,000 men that the size of the Chinese IX Army Group would suggest. But the marines were not yet out of the woods. The road from Hagaru to Hamhung was fifty-six miles long and it seemed likely that they would have to fight their way along every yard of it. The U.N. Navy and the Far Eastern Air Force would give them all help possible. The marine fighter bombers aboard the carriers *Bataan* and *Sicily* would provide the close air support the ground marines expected from their air wing. So would marine aircraft from the carrier *Badoeng Strait* and navy planes from the *Leyte, Valley Forge, Philippine Sea,* and the *Princeton.* The Fifth Air Force would send fighter bombers and bombers to strike the Chinese supply lines. The 11th Marines, the artillery, were to be deeply involved in the fighting retreat. Some batteries would move to the head, some would take position halfway along the road, and some would remain at Hagaru and leave with the rearguard. They began their work on the night of December 5 with a concentration of fire along the road between Hagaru and Koto-ri.

Early on the morning of December 6 General Smith made preparations to fly down to Koto-ri to begin planning for the next stage of the breakout, the drive from Koto-ri along the thirty-seven miles to Hamhung.

The 2nd Battalion of the 5th Marines paved the way by attacking East Hill, which controlled a part of that road near Hagaru. It fell more easily than anyone had expected, but Chinese resistance along the rest of the ridge line was stronger, and during the night Chinese counterattacks came one after the other, in what the official marine history describes as "the most spectacular if not the most fiercely contested battle of the entire Reservoir campaign. . . ." The western press exaggerated the Chinese method of "mass attack," but in this case their descriptions almost reflected the reality. The Chinese commanders must have felt that this ridge line represented success or failure in the containment of the marines, for they sent wave after wave of counterattackers against the line, and the marine artillery, tanks, mortars, and machine guns slaughtered them. The marines took casualties. Company D, which had suffered so in the battle for Smith's Ridge near Seoul, now suffered again. Lieutenant Karle Seydel, the only officer not wounded in the Smith's Ridge fight, was killed here. The company took sixty-three casualties in this fight for East Hill. The 1st Battalion in support took fifty-three casualties. But the marines captured some three hundred prisoners that day, and next morning someone counted eight hundred dead Chinese on the slopes of East Hill. The marines had the position and looked down the ridge line on the road. The battle had taken twenty-two hours.

Its result enabled the 7th Marines to make an easy passage out of Hagaru to the south. The 1st Battalion marched out at daybreak in a thick fog to seize the high ground southeast of Tonae-ri. (See Map 20.) They surprised two dozen Chinese on the hill and killed most of them.

The 2nd Battalion had harder going down the road, the lead tank was disabled by three rockets fired by the enemy from a captured 3.5-inch bazooka. The combination of heavy Chinese resistance and heavy fog stopped the advance until the fog lifted and the marines could call down air support. The combination of strafing and mortar fire and an infantry advance then

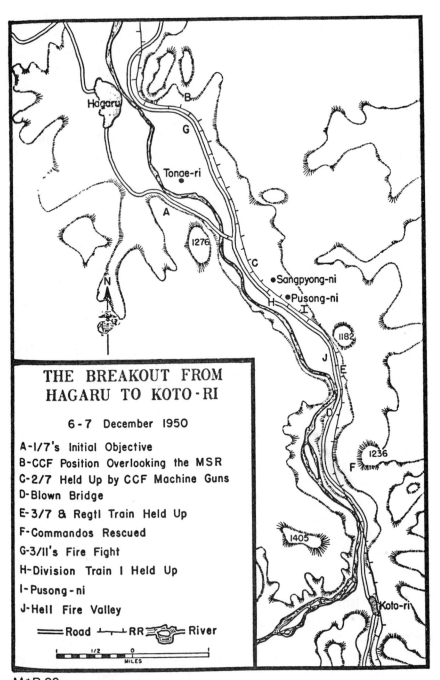

THE BREAKOUT FROM
HAGARU TO KOTO - RI

6 - 7 December 1950

A - I/7's Initial Objective
B - CCF Position Overlooking the MSR
C - 2/7 Held Up by CCF Machine Guns
D - Blown Bridge
E - 3/7 & Regtl Train Held Up
F - Commandos Rescued
G - 3/II's Fire Fight
H - Division Train I Held Up
I - Pusong - ni
J - Hell Fire Valley

Road ⊢⊢ RR River

1/2   0
MILES

MAP 20

cleared the way, and the column advanced down the road. It moved more than two miles before the next pocket of resistance appeared. That block was wiped out by three o'clock in the afternoon, and the column moved on, with the marines on the right and the marines and army troops on the left, driving down alongside the road.

By nightfall the column had moved about three miles. Colonel Litzenberg had anticipated enemy counterattacks during the night, and he was not wrong. The problem was whether to stop and establish a perimeter, or keep forging on. During the day air observers had reported strong Chinese reinforcement of the areas around the road south. The marines knew, for they had seen the long lines of Chinese moving on the skyline east of the road. The decision was made to keep moving during the night.

By ten o'clock that night, when the column had gone about five miles from the starting point of morning, it was stopped in Hell Fire Valley by a machine gun on the left side of the road. The enemy machine gun held them up until midnight, when a tank finally blew it up. Three-quarters of a mile farther down the road the Chinese had blown a bridge, and that stopped the column until the engineers repaired the bridge. The column moved on until it came to another blown bridge. This time the delay lasted an hour and a half. The column was hit by Chinese fire which did particularly severe damage to the regimental command group. Several staff officers were killed and others, including Chaplain Cornelius J. Griffin, were wounded. The chaplain's jaw was shattered by Chinese bullets as he gave consolation to a dying marine inside an ambulance. Not long afterward Lieutenant Colonel William F. Harris, commander of the 3rd Battalion of the 7th Marines, was killed. Major Warren Morris took over the battalion.

The column began arriving at Koto-ri before dawn. The 3rd Battalion came in at seven o'clock that morning, rested a while, and then moved back up the road to set up block points to help keep the road open in the face of newly arriving Chinese reinforcements.

When dawn came, air support became possible once again. The support was directed from the air by Major Harlen E. Hood, flying in a transport plane rigged up as a communications center. Quick communication helped the pilots move in swiftly when they were needed. And they were needed badly. As soon as one element of the column fought its way down the road, the Chinese closed in behind, and the next element had to fight for the road all over again.

By five o'clock on the afternoon of December 7 all the trucks, ambulances, and jeeps of the 7th Marines were safe in Koto-ri. The next element was Division Train No. 1, made up largely of vehicles and service troops. Colonel

Litzenberg had hoped that the riflemen of the 7th Marines would clear the way for the others, and they had, but the enormous number of Chinese troops assigned to the entrapment made it possible for the Chinese commanders to close in again along the road. When the division train came up, they had to fight through still another time, and that meant the artillerymen of the 11th Marines fought their way south as infantrymen.

About two miles south of Hagaru the column was stopped when several vehicles were set afire by Chinese mortar shells and blocked the road. As day broke on December 7 the Chinese attacked the column fiercely, and the guns of G and H batteries were turned on the enemy at point-blank range. There was not even time to dig in the trails of the guns. Fuses were cut for ranges of five hundred yards. And the range kept decreasing. Some Chinese got within forty yards of the guns before they were stopped, but, after two hours of continuous fire, the threat was eliminated, and an estimated 800 enemy soldiers had died in the attempt to take the guns.

Everyone fought on this trip. The convoy of the division headquarters company was made up of clerks and specialty men. They were marines—riflemen now. The trucks had light machine guns mounted on top, and all able-bodied men except the drivers walked in single file alongside the vehicles, which carried the wounded. At one thirty in the morning the column was stopped by Chinese fire. Bandsmen manned two machine guns, and a strike of night fighters was called in to help keep the Chinese at bay. Major Albert Clark and Lieutenant Truman Clark's fighter planes flew strafing runs just thirty yards from the marine line. That helped, but just before daylight a company of Chinese penetrated to within thirty yards of the convoy. The marines fought like demons. Lieutenant Charles H. Sullivan fired his carbine until he ran out of ammunition and then hurled it like a javelin at a Chinese infantryman just fifteen feet away. The bayonet impaled the Chinese.

As dawn came the day fighter bombers moved in. A four-plane division from VMF-312 unloaded 8,000 pounds of explosives and napalm on the Chinese surrounding the headquarters convoy, and the enemy broke and ran. The crisis was over for the moment.

As the column moved south, it gathered prisoners, but not very many of them reached Koto-ri. The wounded prisoners had been given food and medicine and left behind at Hagaru for the Chinese to regain. Able-bodied prisoners brought from Hagaru and prisoners taken on the road numbered about 160 by the night of December 6. When the Chinese attacked, the prisoners were left in the middle of the road as the marines scattered to the ditches. The Chinese attackers shouted at the prisoners, and the captives made a break. The Chinese fired and killed many, and the marines fired and killed more. At the end of that attack only about two dozen live prisoners remained on the road.

Farther south more prisoners were captured at Pusong-ni. A halt was called in Hell Fire Valley, and there the division train evacuated casualties by air, and more replacements came in. By midnight of December 7 the last of the marine rearguard passed into the perimeter of Koto-ri, and another stage of the breakout came to an end. The marines had suffered 616 casualties, the vast majority (506) wounded. That night 14,000 men and 1,000 vehicles clustered inside the perimeter, but not for long. The advance was to begin again at first light on December 8.

All this time the Douglas transports (DC-3 transports under various army, navy, and marine names) delivered supplies daily by airdrop. Drops could be dangerous. On a drop at Koto-ri a case of .30 caliber ammunition broke off its parachute and hurtled onto Lieutenant Colonel Allan Sutter's tent during the middle of a conference of the staff of the 2nd Battalion of the 1st Marines. The ammunition case bounced off the straw floor, just missing several people, and landed on the crate the staff was using as a map table. Some drops also fell into enemy hands; some drops broke up. Only about 25 percent of the howitzer ammunition dropped actually got to the guns, but it did the job. For small arms ammunition, food, and medical supplies, the percentage of successful drops was higher. Without the airdrops the orderly fighting retreat would have become a rout, but with them the retreat was orderly. The marines retained their confidence and fighting ability.

General Smith and his staff had reached Koto-ri on the afternoon of December 6. Immediately on arrival they began planning for the next move. Their major worry was that the Chinese were saving strength for a main assault in the mountain stretch of road—ten miles long—between Koto-ri and Chinhung-ni. Therefore, the first move would be a marine attack northward from Chinghung-ni toward Koto-ri to clear the road.

There were complications initiated by higher authority. So eager was General MacArthur to shore up the defenses of the Eighth Army that he wanted the 3rd Division pulled out of the Hamhung area and sent immediately to Wonsan. General Almond had to fly an emissary to Tokyo to explain why this must not be done: if the marines were to clear the road to Hamhung, the 3rd Division would have to take over the perimeter defenses in the south, and particularly at that moment at Chinghung-ni. This they did and MacArthur's order was rescinded just in time.

That was not the only problem. The Chinese had blown up the bridge three and a half miles south of Koto-ri where the waters of the Chosin Reservoir poured down through steel pipes to the turbines of the lower power plant. A gap of twenty-four feet had to be spanned, and there was no way of bypassing it, for the road passed along a sheer cliff line. Four sections of what was called Treadway bridging would do the job. To play it safe, the army engineers had eight sections dropped, and seven of them were recovered by the Americans, one by the Chinese. On the afternoon of December 7 the bridging was started down from Koto-ri toward the bridge site. That day the plans were made to move into steep Funchilin Pass.

On the morning of December 8 the 7th Marines moved out first, to attack objectives south and southeast of Koto-ri that controlled the winding road. The 5th Marines would follow to hit other Chinese concentrations in the same southern area, and then the 1st Marines would attack with one battalion while another protected the perimeter. The 5th and 7th marines would then move down the road toward Hamhung, and the 1st Marines would be the rearguard.

On the basis of the experience gained on the move down from Hagaru, General Smith ordered the train to get an early start and put tanks at the rear as well as the fore of the column.

It was not going to be easy. Intelligence indicated that the Chinese had moved four new divisions into the area to reinforce the six divisions already ranged around the road to Hamhung. One U.S. Marine division, reinforced by remnants of the army's 7th Division, against ten—those were the odds.

And as an addition to those odds, what value was one to assign to the snowstorm that swirled down around Koto-ri on the morning of December 8, reducing visibility to fifty feet and making air support impossible?

The key to the movement south had to be Hill 1081. (See Map 21.) Lieutenant Colonel Donald Schmuck's 1st Battalion of the 1st Marines was assigned the task of taking that height from the Chinese. These were fresh troops, having spent the past few days south of Chinhung-ni, while other marines were fighting their way out of the northern trap. They were rested and eager to do their part in this deadly game. They would come up the road behind the Chinese. They were to attack at eight o'clock in the morning. To make that schedule they started out at 2:00 A.M. from their southern bivouac to make the six-mile march through the snowy pass.

Snow and darkness plagued them from the first. Visibility was virtually zero. There was no way they could bring up vehicles, so their motorized support consisted of two ambulances and a radio jeep. They did, however, have one great advantage: they were playing the Chinese game. The falling snow covering their parkas made them virtually invisible, and the fresh snow on the ground muffled their movements. As they came up on the enemy surprise was complete, and they took their first objective with ease. At ten

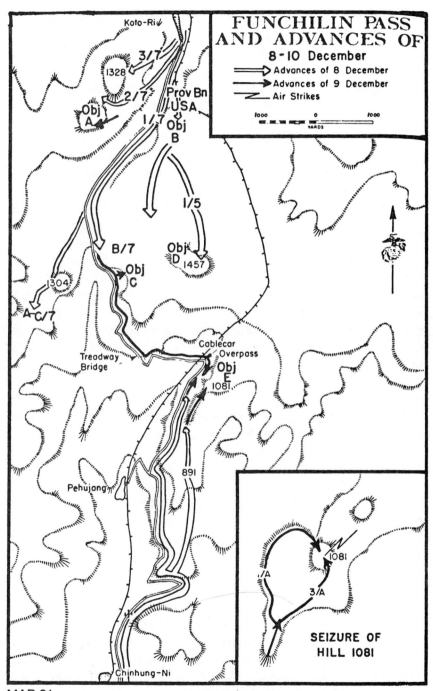

FUNCHILIN PASS
AND ADVANCES OF
8-10 December

Advances of 8 December
Advances of 9 December
Air Strikes

1000   0   1000
YARDS

Koto-Ri

3/7
1328
2/7
Obj
A
Prov Bn
USA
1/7
Obj
B

1/5

B/7
Obj
C
Obj
D 1457
1304
A-C/7

Treadway
Bridge
Cablecar
Overpass
Obj
E
1081

Pehujang
891

Chinhung-Ni

SEIZURE OF
HILL 1081

1/A
3/A
1081

MAP 21

o'clock in the morning they were ready to launch the main attack, this time supported by 81 mm mortars and 4.2-inch mortars, and five of the army's self-propelled quadruple 50 mm gun tractors and twin 40 mm vehicles. The marines moved up the wooded slope of Hill 1081 and along the ridge leading to the high point. The snow hid their movements again, and they traveled swiftly until they came to the first roadblock. The men of Company B were stopped here, until a patrol worked around the Chinese and hit them with a machine gun and mortar attack. On the western slope of Hill 1081 the surprise was complete, and the marines killed or routed every defender. They found a kettle of rice cooking in the largest bunker: it was obviously a command post.

Company A was heading for the crest of Hill 1081. Captain Robert H. Barrow led the men up along an icy ridge. When the pelting snow let up for a moment, he saw a Chinese position on a knob between his men and the top. The snow closed in again before he could direct mortar fire on the enemy. Barrow decided that surprise was his best weapon and ordered the men to keep absolute silence as they advanced. Two squads went to the left to envelop the enemy, and a platoon went to the right. Barrow led the frontal attack. After an hour the two flanking units were in place, and when they were ready, Barrow made the frontal assault. The marines whooped down like wild Indians, shouting and shrieking after their long enforced silence. They did what the Chinese had done in their first attacks on the Eighth Army front, and this time it was the Chinese who were stunned. One machine gun began firing and caused some casualties, but it was silenced by Corporal Joseph Leeds and his fire team. They killed nine Chinese in the process. Colonel Schmuck set up his command post in a comparatively luxurious log and sandbag structure. The day was about to end, and the marines had been very successful.

On the road south from Koto-ri, the column was not enjoying the same success. On the right, the progress of the 3rd Battalion of the 7th Marines was very slow. Colonel Litzenberg could not understand it until Major Morris told him that his three companies, which under optimum conditions would have numbered more than 600 men, had, after two weeks of attrition, been cut down to 130 marines. Litzenberg had to commit the reserve, the 2nd Battalion, to the right.

The slowdown had affected the whole advance. The 1st Battalion also had its troubles on Hill 1304 and lost several officers in the action, including Lieutenant Chew En Lee of Company B whose name would have given the Chinese propagandists something to think about had they known it. Because of the delays, the 5th Marines did not move out of Koto-ri until nearly noon to assault Hill 1457, and the Treadway bridge engineers did not reach their day's objective. It was not until eight o'clock on the morning of December 9 that the advance accomplished these first objectives. Company B had an easy time of it, but Company A ran into intensive small arms fire from Chinese bunkers. The hero of the assault on the crest of Hill 1081 was Staff Sergeant Ernest J. Umbaugh, who organized a squad grenade attack that wiped out the first Chinese bunker. Then, with air support from the Corsairs, the marines took Hill 1081. At this point the marines controlled the north entrance to Funchilin Pass.

At Koto-ri, the British marines took over as rearguard, while the 1st Marines led the divisional trains down the road toward Hungnam. Parts of Company B and Company C captured the site where the bridge would have to be rebuilt. The men of Company B discovered a group of about fifty Chinese soldiers in foxholes, but the Chinese offered no resistance; they were too cold. The marines simply lifted them out of their positions and put them on the road. The Chinese were used to help rebuild the destroyed bridge when they had gotten warm enough to work.

At three o'clock in the afternoon the bridge was rebuilt, and the trains began their descent into the pass. But at five o'clock one of the big construction vehicles used in the building of the Hagaru airstrip broke through plywood paneling on the bridge, and the traffic came to an abrupt stop. The future looked grim, until Technical Sergeant Wilfred H. Prosser backed the enormous machine off the wrecked bridge, and the engineers rerigged the treadways so that the outside edges made it wide enough (by two inches) for the M-26 tanks to cross, and the inside edges were made narrow enough for the jeeps (by half an inch). When the first jeep crossed, its tires scraped the metal Treadway flanges on both sides. It was now pitch dark, and the convoy edged on by flashlight and headlight, and behind the convoy came thousands of Korean refugees, who preferred to follow in the wake of the Americans rather than remain under Chinese control.

During that night's movement, there was relatively little fighting. The cold had numbed the Chinese soldiers so completely they could barely move. When prisoners were taken back to aid stations, a number were discovered to be suffering from malnutrition and from gangrene that was the result of untreated frostbite. The stories they told indicated that if the Chinese were winning a victory in the reservoir area, they were paying for it with the lives of thousands of soldiers in their IX Army Group.

At two forty-five in the morning of December 10 the leading marine elements (7th Marines) began moving into the Chinhung-ni perimeter. The column was going along steadily until a truck bogged down at a bypass across a half-frozen stream a mile beyond the Treadway bridge. Another truck stalled behind it. The column stopped while the engineers pushed the vehicles to one side and built up the road again. After three hours movement was resumed.

The Chinese launched only one attack worthy of the name. A reinforced company hit Company G of the 1st Marines early in the morning, but it did not have the staying power to stop them. The rest of the Chinese were obeying orders to move south and were slipping along the sides of the marines parallel to the road. They were marching in close order and were particularly vulnerable to air and artillery strikes. Hundreds were killed, but the rest formed up and continued on.

All day long on December 10 the marines moved south, vehicle trains interspersed with foot soldiers. In midmorning General Smith and his staff flew down from Koto-ri to Hungnam. By six o'clock in the evening most of the vehicle train was in Chinhung-ni. The rear guards came along, leapfrogging, and Koto-ri was evacuated. Marines held the high points along the road, and all seemed well. The evacuation of infantry from Chinhung-ni to Hamhung was begun by truck, since the army held the road south, and there had been no trouble.

Trouble developed on the early morning of December 11. Some of those Chinese units that had been sideslipping the road attacked at a traffic intersection in the south end of Sudong. (See Map 5.) The "safe" territory was no longer safe, and the marine vehicles of the 1st Marine regimental train were hit hard. Several truck drivers were killed by Chinese burp guns and grenades, and their vehicles were set afire. The whole train stopped, until army Lieutenant Colonel John U. D. Page and marine Private First Class Marvin L. Wasson, a jeep driver, formed a two-man task force and attacked about twenty Chinese who had halted the column at its head. Page was killed and Wasson wounded by grenades, but Wasson and army Lieutenant Colonel Waldon C. Winston got into the fight again, and Winston directed a combined force of army and marines in a successful counterattack. Wasson moved up under machine gun cover to fire three white phosphorus shells from a 75 mm recoilless rifle at a house that seemed to be the center of the enemy's activity. The house began to burn, and the Chinese ran out and were machine gunned.

Colonel Winston gradually brought order back to the column. The nine burned vehicles were pushed off, the twenty-nine casualties were taken to aid stations or laid out in vehicles, and the column began moving again. The hiatus had lasted until dawn.

At the other end of the retreating marine column another difficulty developed. The supply trains had gone on, and at the end were the tanks and the infantry of the 3rd Battalion of the 1st Marines. They were supposed to leapfrog the 1st Battalion of the 5th Marines and the composite army battalion. The last ten tanks were guarded by twenty-eight marine infantrymen. Behind them came thousands of Korean refugees, moving just as close to the marines as they could. The problem was that the Chinese soldiers had mingled with the Koreans and were waiting for a chance to hit the column.

At about one o'clock in the morning a little over a mile above the Treadway bridge, the ninth tank from the end suffered a brake freeze on the icy road and stalled. The tail end of the column came to a screeching halt. The rest of the column moved on ahead. While the marines were working on the tank's brakes, five Chinese soldiers suddenly appeared on the road, and one announced in English that they wanted to surrender. Lieutenant Ernest C. Hargett went forward to meet them, covered by a BAR manned by Corporal A. J. Amyotte. Suddenly the leading Chinese stepped aside. The other four brought out grenades and burp guns. Hargett lifted his carbine to fire and pulled the trigger, but the piece failed, as they did so often in the cold. He then rushed forward, swinging the carbine like a club, and crushed the skull of one Chinese. Another threw a grenade that wounded the lieutenant. Other Chinese from the high ground beside the road also attacked. The Chinese around Hargett never had a chance; Amyotte shot them down one by one.

But the Chinese on the high ground made it hot. Hargett's platoon fell back, and the last tank was lost along with its crew. The next to last tank's crew had closed the hatches and would not be roused by the banging on the hull with rifle butts. Lieutenant Hargett was banging away when he was stunned by an enemy explosive charge placed by the Chinese under the tank. The charge also blew Private First Class Robert D. DeMott over the drop on the side of the road. His fellows saw him go and could envisage his fall of hundreds of feet to certain death on the icy cliffs below. Hargett and the others withdrew, passing the next seven tanks, all with hatches open, the crews having abandoned and gone on after the column.

Corporal Amyotte was covering the withdrawal of the platoon with his BAR. He was down in the middle of the road in prone position, firing, when a Chinese grenade landed squarely in the middle of his back and exploded. But Amyotte was wearing a new jacket of plastic body armor, and the explosion did no more than bruise his ribs.

By this time the tank crew of the ninth tank had repaired the frozen brakes and were ready to move out. That tank and one other were brought out, the latter driven by Corporal C. P. Lett who had never operated a tank before.

At the bridge site, Captain William Gould and a demolition crew of engineers were waiting impatiently for the last vehicles and infantry to come across, so they could blow the bridge. When Hargett's platoon and those two tanks crossed over, they said that was the end of the line. Chief Warrant Officer Willie Harrison set off the charge and with a magnificent roar the Treadway bridge shattered into hundreds of pieces. The fact was that the Hargett group was not the last of the marines. The last was Private First Class DeMott. When he was blown over the cliff, he landed on a ledge overhanging the steep drop. He was only slightly wounded, and when he came to, he managed to climb back up to the road, where he found himself surrounded by Korean refugees. He heard an enormous explosion and realized that the Treadway bridge had just gone up. Fortunately he also knew that pedestrians could cross over the flumes from the reservoir at the gatehouse above the penstocks, and he and the refugees came down the mountain that way into Chinhung-ni.

At one o'clock in the afternoon of December 11, the last of the Americans left Chinhung-ni and by nine o'clock that night all but the tanks had reached the assembly areas in the Hamhung–Hungnam area. The marines and a handful of army men of the 7th Division had made the trek from Hagaru to Hamhung, sometimes moving as much as twenty hours at a stretch, carrying packs, parkas, sleeping bags, and their weapons across frozen roads and hillsides, pelted by snow and icy winds. They had mauled half a dozen Chinese divisions to the point of exhaustion.

The march of the 1st Marine Division from the Chosin Reservoir to the sea would go down in the pages of history as one of the great successful retreats.

11

The Brink of Disaster

The army historians would refer to the early part of December 1950 as "the brink of disaster." The failure of General MacArthur to anticipate the possible actions of the Chinese and his panic when the Eighth Army and X Corps suddenly suffered reverses had completely changed the American military establishment's view of the world around them. In November they thought they had the world by the tail; in December they were paranoid enough to believe that the Chinese move into Korea was the first step by the Soviet bloc in a third world war.

On December 6 General MacArthur claimed that unless he had enormous reinforcement almost immediately he would have to evacuate Korea entirely. General Collins had replied that there were no troops to send in the immediate future. Others indicated that the 82nd Airborne Division could be sent, but when Collins returned from the visit to Korea and Japan, that idea was abandoned. The military establishment had suddenly become seriously concerned about the possibility of global war and was insisting that there were much higher priorities than Korea.

While Collins was away, the atmosphere in Washington was indeed gloomy. The generals read MacArthur's reports and came to the conclusion that the UN forces ran a serious danger of being destroyed. General Bolté suggested that Korea be evacuated and that the United States put its world-wide military commands on an emergency basis. Secretary of the Army Frank Pace, Jr., suggested that the Chinese defeat of the UN forces in Korea had changed overnight the sort of world in which Americans lived. National Guard divisions were called up, and plans were made to increase the size of the American army to eighteen combat divisions (nearly a million and a half men under arms) by the summer of 1954. Several generals, including Collins, suggested that President Truman declare a state of national emergency, the next thing to a state of war. On December 15 Truman did just that.

In this atmosphere all were agreed that the general retreat had to be swift, and Pusan was seen as the next stop. The X Corps was to be brought back to Pusan and there incorporated into the Eighth Army—as many said it should have been in the beginning. General MacArthur did not like the idea; it was in a sense an admission of how far wrong he had been in the beginning, but in the face of almost general insistence, he finally approved the change. General Almond had told MacArthur he could hold at Hungnam, if that was wanted. But, suddenly, what had before seemed vital was no longer important at all. By the time the marines fought their way down to Hungnam, the rest of X Corps had assembled there as well. The next step was to move the whole corps out of the northeast as quickly and effectively as possible.

The navy was ready and had been for days. On November 15 General Smith had expressed to Rear Admiral Albert K. Morehouse and Captain Norman W. Sears his profound distrust of the MacArthur strategy of separating his forces. He had suggested that disaster might be around the corner. Those two naval officers had taken the word back to Vice Admiral C. Turner Joy, commander of naval forces in the Far East, and to Rear Admiral James H. Doyle, commander of Task Force 90, the group of fighting ships in Korean waters. Thus, when the predicted disaster fell at the end of November, the navy had contingency plans for a withdrawal of troops in a hurry.

Ships were assembled in a rush from every corner of the Far East, to withdraw 100,000 troops and (as it turned out) 100,000 Korean refugees. While the shipping was moving in the Hungnam area, the perimeter had to be protected by troops from enemy land attack, and the troops had to be supported by sea and air forces. All this was done, and on December 11 and 12, as the marines came down from Koto-ri, they began to load into transports for evacuation to the south. The Chinese were very quiet, kept quiet by an air umbrella that functioned day and night and by artillery and naval gunfire whenever targets of importance were indicated.

On December 14 the enemy gave some indication of an impending attack with heavy mortaring of the Hungnam perimeter. But the air cover and artillery of the Americans apparently discouraged the Chinese, for nothing

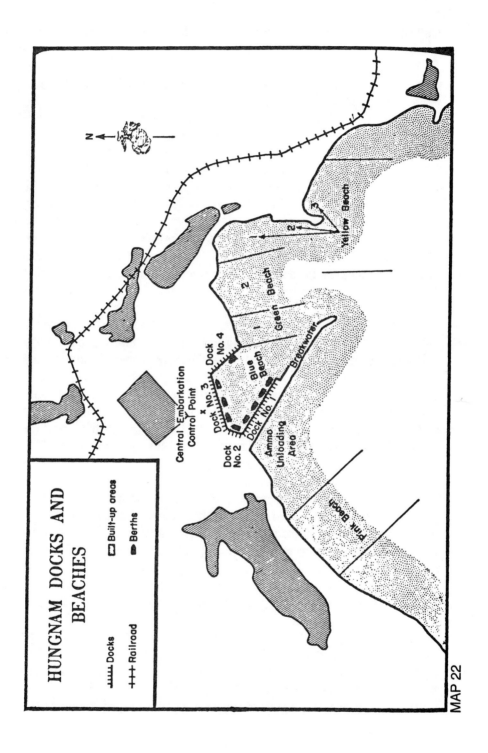

HUNGNAM DOCKS AND
BEACHES

⊔⊔⊔ Docks
+++ Railroad
▫ Built-up areas
◣ Berths

Central Embarkation
Control Point

Dock No. 2
Dock No. 3
Dock No. 4
Dock No. 1

Blue Beach

Breakwater

Ammo
Unloading
Area

Green Beach

Yellow Beach

Pink Beach

N

MAP 22

happened. On the night of December 14 the last of the marines except the amphibious force loaded aboard the transports.

On December 15 the marine convoy of 22,000 troops sailed from Hungnam. That left two army divisions, the ROK troops, and the Korean refugees inside the perimeter.

On December 16 the North Korean IV and V corps attempted a simultaneous attack on the northeast side of the perimeter but were repelled. From then on the perimeter contracted rapidly. On December 16 the U.S. 3rd Division pulled back from Hamhung to Hungnam, and the ROK Capital Divison moved down from the northeast. The perimeter was narrowed to the Hungnam area alone. (See Map 22.) The ROKs loaded for Samchok on December 17, and the next day the U.S. Army 7th Division loaded. The perimeter then shrank to a radius of five kilometers from the center of the city. On December 19 General Almond and his staff boarded the command ship *Mount McKinley,* and the defense of the perimeter became the responsibility of the navy and Rear Admiral Doyle. On December 21 the 7th Division ships left.

As the perimeter contracted, the Chinese and North Koreans surrounded it, but still they did not attack. The American artillery continued to thunder day and night, and the aircraft swarmed above the city like angry hornets, hitting troop movements on the roads and bombing any concentrations—troops, supplies, or ammunition—that they found. The evacuation was also supported by the battleship *Missouri,* with its 16-inch guns, two cruisers, seven destroyers, and three rocket craft. Finally on Christmas Eve the last of the seven embarkation beaches was cleared, and marines manned the last of the thirty-seven landing vehicles, covering the army as they went to sea.

The 3rd Division had been given the responsibility as rearguard, and the ticklish problem of getting the men off the beach without an enemy attack posed many difficulties. Seven embarkation sites were selected. H-Hour was set for eleven o'clock in the morning of Christmas Eve. Seven LSTs were beached that morning to take off the 3rd Division troops. Naval gunfire replaced land artillery support. It was not long before the force ashore was reduced to three battalions, and finally these were reduced to seven reinforced platoons manning the last strong points around the harbor. On the principle that there was always somebody who did not get the word, a final search was made for stragglers, and then the seven platoons boarded the final LST. The marines of the Amphibious Tractor Battalion were the last to leave with their thirty-seven LVTs, which evacuated army troops from Pink Beach and covered the flanks of the withdrawal.

At the very end the engineers staged a gigantic display of fireworks, blowing up all the munitions that had to be left behind, including five hundred 1,000-pound bombs and four hundred tons of dynamite that had frozen and could not be moved. The plunger was pushed, and the Hungnam waterfront erupted in a blast of flame and smoke.

Back home in America in the days of despair that followed the news that the Chinese had entered the war and destroyed General MacArthur's fine plan to clear up Korea and perhaps all the Far East, harbingers of doom had predicted a disaster that would make Dunkirk look like a Sunday school picnic. It had not come about. Marine losses from October 26 to December 15 had been 4,418 battle casualties, 3,500 of them wounded, and 7,300 nonbattle casualties, most of them from frostbite. Instead of destroying the 20,000-man marine force, as the Chinese had set out to do, they had themselves suffered perhaps 35,000 casualties. The Chinese IX Army Group had been badly hurt in the fighting and was in no position to continue their harassment against air and naval gunfire. Nor was Lin Piao basically concerned with what happened in northeast Korea now that the marines had escaped the trap. He had other moves on his mind. The Chinese plan was to build up the forces for a new offensive in central Korea. So the American "amphibious landing in reverse" was an enormous success, carrying 100,000 military personnel, nearly 100,000 Korean refugees, 17,000 vehicles, and 350,000 tons of cargo out in 109 ships. The marines were landed in south Korea and moved to Masan, where they went into reserve. On December 18 General Smith had the welcome message announcing that the 1st Marine Division had been transferred to control of the Eighth Army.

General MacArthur's panic of early December and the resulting confusion in Washington seems to have been known in detail to the Sino-Soviet leadership through the efforts of their espionage agents who were so well entrenched in the British and American establishments. MacArthur claimed that from the beginning the enemy had been reading his messages. If so, at this time, his messages and Peking's interpretation of them led to a major Chinese miscalculation. After a series of meetings in Washington and New York, the British and the Americans agreed that while there had been miscalculation, the UN must continue in Korea. There would be no evacuation as had been considered in the first flap after the Chinese attacks. If other nations appealed to the Chinese for a cease-fire, the United States and Britain would look on the idea with general approval, but not on just any conditions. No less than the status quo ante bellum would be acceptable.

The Chinese, basing their conclusions on the American panic they had already correctly perceived, believed they could do better. On December 14 the UN General Assembly in New York voted to set up the machinery to approach Peking for a cease-fire. The Chinese announced that the only basis on which they would talk about peace was if the UN forces withdrew entirely from Korea, the Americans withdrew from Taiwan, and the Western governments ended their rearmament. In other words, they demanded that the United States surrender to the Communist bloc. The Chinese obviously believed they had MacArthur on the ropes and could indeed do what on December 3 he had warned Washington could reasonably be contemplated: ". . . steady attrition leading to final destruction."

By mid-December the UN forces had established their defense line roughly along the 38th parallel. The Chinese had made no serious move to attack, although pilots reported a constant stream of traffic moving south from the Yalu. The most evident troops were North Koreans, who seemed to have regained their morale and strength. Reestablished in Pyongyang, North Korean chief Kim Il Sung began making new aggressive noises, speaking once more of the "total annihilation" of the UN and South Korean forces, as though this were the summer of 1950.

General Walker continued his frequent visits to the front line, for which he had become famous in the Eighth Army. On the morning of December 23 he set out from his headquarters in his jeep to visit the 27th British Commonwealth Brigade. An ROK truck turned across the road in front of the jeep, the general was thrown out and suffered a head injury, and he died before he could be taken to a hospital. General MacArthur made all the proper statements about Walker's ability and bravery that he had denied the general in life. He also recommended the appointment of General Matthew B. Ridgway to take over control of the Eighth Army, and that recommendation was followed by President Truman. On Christmas day General Ridgway became the new commander.

On the war front Christmas was eerily quiet. The intelligence officers of the Eighth Army kept getting information about the enemy order of battle, and every few days a new Chinese army was added to the plotting board. As the month ended the Chinese had twenty-one divisions—276,000 troops—in Korea. The North Korean army had been rebuilt to 167,000 men. And more hundreds of thousands of Chinese had been brought up to Manchuria to be ready to enter the struggle on command. The marine estimate put the number of enemy in Korea and Manchuria at 740,000.

But nothing was happening. Along the 38th parallel it was like waiting for "the other shoe" to drop. General MacArthur kept pressing for more intelligence to be secured by aggressive patroling. But the patrols too often came back empty-handed. With the arrival of General Ridgway on the scene, MacArthur abandoned his direct leadership role. He assured Ridgway that he

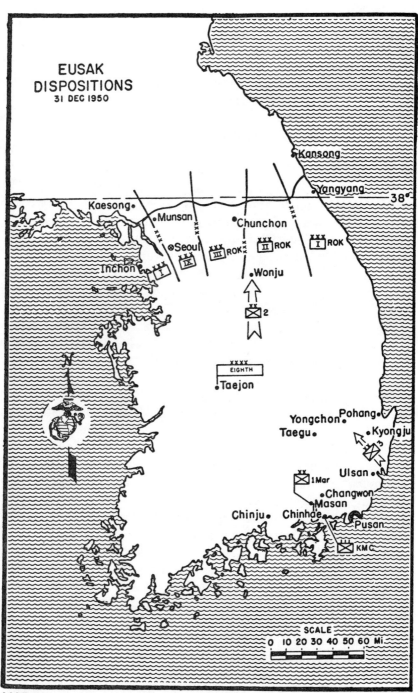

EUSAK
DISPOSITIONS
31 DEC 1950

Kansong

Yangyang

38°

Kaesong

Munsan

Chunchon

Seoul

ROK

II ROK

I ROK

Inchon

I

IX

III ROK

Wonju

2

EIGHTH

Taejon

Yongchon

Pohang

Taegu

Kyongju

3

Ulsan

1 Mar

Changwon

Masan

Chinju

Chinhae

Pusan

KMC

SCALE
0 10 20 30 40 50 60 Mi.

MAP 23

had full authority to command the Eighth Army. And from this point on MacArthur did not interfere with field operations.

Ridgway stepped into a dispirited command. Having been defeated so decisively by the Chinese, the Eighth Army's unit commanders now talked of retreat and even withdrawal. Ridgway talked of attack, but he soon learned that before he could attack he had to rebuild the morale of the army. It really was not so much a question of numbers. In January the UN forces, including South Koreans, numbered 444,000 men.

While he was working at this task, the Chinese completed their buildup, and on New Year's Eve they launched their winter offensive along a forty-four-mile front, stretching from Kaesong to Chunchon. (See Map 23.) The main drive was south toward Seoul, and General Ridgway soon predicted that the Chinese were going to attempt to flood Korea with manpower and by sheer numbers push the UN forces off the peninsula into the sea. Thus was born the new UN war strategy, which might have been taken from the book of Mao Tse-tung, to delay the enemy advance by moving back to successive positions, and meanwhile to inflict maximum punishment on the enemy armies by air and artillery firepower.

Five Chinese armies struck, the main force abetted by two flanking movements. Ten North Korean divisions also attacked down the center of the peninsula, and their efforts were assisted by the guerillas who had been left in the rear of the UN armies.

One immediate result was a new panic by the ROK forces north of Seoul. On the morning of New Year's day, General Ridgway drove north. He was establishing a tradition of his own, moving up to the front on inspection, wearing a grenade pinned to his uniform. Some said it was an affectation, Ridgway said he never knew when he might run into trouble, and the grenade was insurance. It was the sort of insurance that appealed to his troops. On this survey trip Ridgway was dismayed to see ROK soldiers streaming south by the truckload in utter confusion, many without their arms. They had abandoned their artillery and their mortars and machine guns along the road. He tried personally to halt the flight but was unsuccessful. He did, however, establish MP posts in the rear, where fleeing ROK troops were stopped, resupplied, reorganized into units, and sent off with new orders to defend certain areas. His most serious concern was for the morale of his own troops. He visited a 19th Infantry aid station where the wounded were being cleared and found that morale was dismal. General Milburn's I Corps on the western flank was hit hard, but the main enemy effort was down the middle against the U.S. 24th Division at Pochon. General Ridgway ordered the western divisions to move back to a line north of the Han River. But the enemy came on in great strength, and on January 3 General Ridgway decided to abandon Seoul. The 24th Division and the 7th Cavalry Regiment crossed the Han. General Ridgway stood on the north end of the bridge that night and watched the last of the heavy tanks and howitzers cross. Then came the refugees, thousands of them, swarming after the soldiers. Finally, at dawn on January 4 the engineers blew up the floating bridge behind them. The army moved back to establish a new defense line that extended from Pyongtaek on the west coast to Samchok on the east coast.

They expected a new Chinese and North Korean drive, but the Chinese did not choose to cross the Han. The pressure was off for the moment.

For the first time, the Joint Chiefs of Staff now made an independent decision regarding the conduct of the war. MacArthur had asked for heavy reinforcement of American troops. The Joint Chiefs refused, saying reinforcement would commit too much of America's meager military resources, and Korea was not the place the United States wanted to fight a general war, if such became inevitable. MacArthur was to fight and fight hard with the resources at hand. No more American units would be committed at this time. Meanwhile, contingency plans were made by the navy for evacuation of UN forces from Korea, if such became necessary. The mood in America and in Tokyo was more defeatist than it had been at any time since the beginning of the war. This was General Ridgway's greatest problem; almost alone he believed that the UN forces could fight the war and win it and that there was no way the Chinese could drive his army off the peninsula. But he did assign Brigadier General Garrison H. Davidson to build a defense line far to the south, covering the Pusan area. Just in case.

The next important engagement came in the Wonju area, the important road center in the middle of the peninsula. The Chinese and North Koreans pressed here against the U.S. 23rd Infantry line north of the city. One key point was Hoengsong. (See Map 24.) Elements of the ROK II Corps had fallen back, leaving a gap in the line here. It was filled by the Netherlands detachment, which had arrived on December 5 and had been engaged largely in antiguerilla activity earlier.

East of Hoengsong the Netherlands patrolled an area where the Chinese and North Koreans were reported to be active. A hundred soldiers went out on patrol and encountered about fifteen enemy soldiers busily mining the road from Chowon-ni to Hoengsong. They dispersed this group with machine gun fire but got involved in a firefight in the village and suffered eleven casualties before the day was done. The next day one company held the Chowon-ni position, and the second went on motor patrol between Hoengsong and the command post of the U.S. 38th Infantry. Word came that the enemy had broken through the right flank of the 2nd Division, and the Netherlanders were pulled back to the Wonju–Chechon area.

Wonju fell on the night of January 7. The following day General Almond ordered it retaken. Key elements in this fight would be the U.S. 23rd and 38th regiments of the 2nd Division, and the French and Netherlands battalions.

The French battalion and the two U.S. units were to hold the high ground south of Wonju, while a battalion of the 23rd Regiment was to attack and clear Wonju and the airstrip at the southern edge of the city. Those were the orders, but that day a strong enemy reinforcement made it impossible to carry them out. It was still not possible on the 9th, but on January 10 the Chinese came pouring down against the French position. The French fought off four successive waves of attack and finally the French soldiers fixed bayonets and fought their way to the top of Hill 247, the commanding position on their ridge.

On the morning of January 10 air observers reported streams of enemy troops moving south from Wonju to attack the positions of the 23rd and 38th regiments. Americans, French, and Dutch fought side by side for two days, and finally after the French attack up Hill 247, the enemy drive was blunted. An essential part of the action was the pounding of the enemy by artillery and air forces, the two elements of American might that the Chinese commanders really respected.

General Ridgway's concern for the building of morale of the Eighth Army prompted him to make a number of personnel changes, including the command of the 23rd Division, which went to Major General Clark L. Ruffner. He also made plans to employ the 1st Marine Division. On January 8 General Smith went to Taegu to confer with Ridgway on the best use of the marines. Out of this meeting came a plan to move the marines to the Pohang area, which was alive with guerilla activity, to protect the Andong–Yongdok road and the Yongdok–Pohong road.

General Ridgway wanted to go on the attack. He was having his problems within the American establishment; for example, a G-3 (operations) document from Tokyo called for phased withdrawal all the way back to the Taebaek Range and no offensive activity at all. When Ridgway received this paper, he was appalled. Headquarters was suggesting that he fall back to the old Pusan Perimeter.

Ridgway was determined to stage some sort of offensive activity in the next few days. But intelligence was his new problem. The Chinese were still employing a masterful technique of concealing their troop dispositions. This was much easier for them than it would have been for a modern army, for they had no big guns, no tanks, no half-tracks to hide. The army that moved

WONJU AND VICINITY

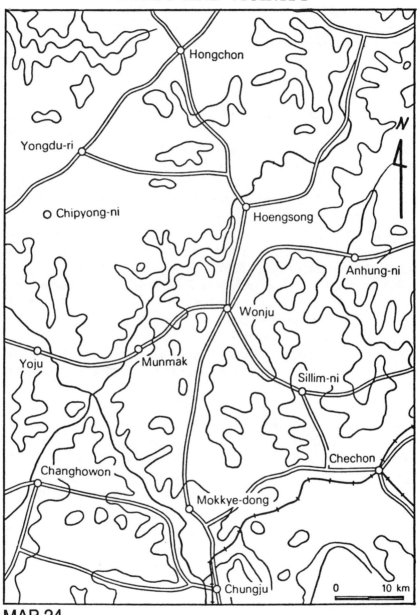

MAP 24

primarily on its legs could easily hide its tracks and melt into the forests and the valleys.

Deprived of the usual intelligence sources, Ridgway set out to find out for himself what he faced. General Partridge, the commander of the Fifth Air Force, came up with an idea. He personally brought up an old AT-6 two-seater training plane and flew Ridgway around the Korean countryside north of the American troop dispositions, sometimes twenty miles inside enemy-held territory. But they saw no more than anyone else had. There was no trace of Chinese armies, no smoke, no disturbed snow, no wheel tracks. The only way to find out what was there was to launch an advance.

On January 14, one enemy buildup was reported north of Osan and Suwon. General Ridgway ordered an immediate armor-supported attack to probe this concentration.

"Operation Wolfhound" was begun the next day—the first sign of military life in the Eighth Army since the defeat on the Chongchon River line. The 27th Infantry attacked with a battalion from the 3rd Division on the right flank. The main body moved along the main highway north toward Osan against light opposition until it was almost in the town. A brief firefight ensued, then the enemy troops retreated.

The task force converged on Suwon the next day in two columns, then withdrew back to the original American lines. Opposition was so light as to indicate only limited numbers of troops in the area.

Another probe was made on January 22 by the 8th Cavalry, with tank support from the 70th Tank Battalion, along the Suwon–Yoju road. Again the probers encountered limited resistance, which strengthened as they moved farther north.

General Ridgway had discovered what he wanted to know, and he was ready to launch his first offensive. This word was greeted with considerable relief by General Collins who came to Korea during Operation Wolfhound to ascertain the state of the Eighth Army. He left satisfied. "As of now we are going to stay and fight," he told the press. The defeatism that had permeated the American public and the military establishment was beginning to dissipate.

12

Counteroffensive

The new UN offensive was to be called Operation Thunderbolt. General Ridgway had no illusions about his situation: he would not be reinforced and would have to make do with limited support. In Washington and New York the emphasis had shifted from a military to a political solution for the Korean War. The objective now was limited to the reestablishment of the partitioned Korea of the past, despite the determined opposition of General MacArthur and President Syngman Rhee of South Korea to this policy. In view of this U.S. policy, encouraged by allies within the UN, General Ridgway planned for the carrying of the war to the enemy to discourage their militant intentions. As he had ascertained in a frank conversation with MacArthur, he was truly in charge. MacArthur had said only that he expected Ridgway to make mistakes in Korea. "We all have," he added. His attitude was so low key as to indicate that for once, at least privately, the general accepted the responsibility for his own enormous error in precipitating the Chinese entry into the war. Or, perhaps, he was only passing the buck. In any event, from this point on MacArthur's role in the Korean War was limited to politico-military discussions with Washington. He no longer tried to command the field from Tokyo.

General Ridgway had some definite ideas as to the manner of prosecuting the war against the combined Chinese and North Korean enemy. He would seek to inflict as much punishment as he could give them, and that was the purpose of this first counteroffensive.

The I Corps and IX Corps in the western sectors of Korea would carry this offensive. The marines on the east were to do something that should have been accomplished long before—eliminate the guerillas who had assembled in the mountain areas and threatened the UN force's communications lines.

"Reconnaissance in force" was the designation, and the operation was divided into five phases, lettered A through E. The two corps involved would step out at 7:30 in the morning of January 25 in the area bounded by Suwon, Ichon, Yoju, and the Han River. Only one division, plus supporting armor, would be used by each corps to attack, and one ROK division could also be used if the corps commander wanted it. The orders were to disrupt enemy communications and inflict maximum destruction on enemy communications and inflict maximum destruction on enemy personnel and supply south of the Han River.

In the I Corps area the attack was led by the U.S. 25th Division, with the now-rested Turkish brigade attached. That meant the 24th and 35th Infantry regiments and the Turks, with the 27th Infantry following in support. The first resistance came at Suwon in the middle of the afternoon, when an enemy unit of about company strength was encountered and pushed back. To the east in the IX Corps sector the 7th Cavalry took Ichon that day without meeting opposition.

UNC COUNTEROFFENSIVE (25JAN-28FEB 1951)

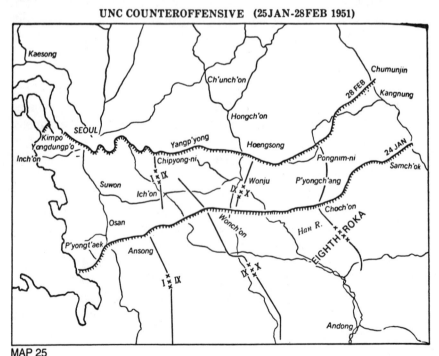

MAP 25

General of the Army Douglas MacArthur

(above) Major General John H. Church (left) with Lieutenant General Walton Walker upon the latter's arrival at Taejon airport on September 30, 1950

(below) Major General Taskin Yazici, commanding general of the Turkish Brigade

(above) Aerial view of Chosin Reservoir area

―――――

(below) Two Marine all-weather Grumman F7F fighters over the frozen mountains of North Korea

(left) Colonel Homer L. Litzenberg, who led troops in the battles at the Chosin Reservoir, in a photo taken at a later date

(right) Colonel Lewis B. (Chesty) Puller, the leader of the 1st Marines in the fight for Seoul, was promoted to brigadier general and made assistant division commander of the 1st Marine Division early in 1951.

(above) Major L. D. Van De Voort of the U.S. 1st Cavalry Division inspects the rifles of ROK soldiers attached to his unit in July 1951.

(below) Two H-5 helicopters at their base in Korea, between combat flights in February 1951

Lieutenant General Matthew B. Ridgway, commanding general of the U.S. Eighth Army, stands on a ridge overlooking the Han River and examines a horseshoe he found at the front. It was apparently dropped by a horse of a Chinese artillery unit.

(above) In May 1951, a U.S. Marine fire team takes advantage of cover as they advance against the enemy on the central Korean front.

(below) Marines disembark from an army duck after an assault crossing of Pukhan River.

Marines of the 7th Marine Regiment pour small-arms fire into North Korean positions as a prelude to a general assault.

Marines have just dropped a white phosphorus grenade on some North Korean soldiers hiding in a bunker. Front lines, December 1951.

(above) Lieutenant General Edward M. Almond, former Commanding General, X Corps, sits in his plane on July 15, 1951, as he prepares to start back to the United States and a new assignment.

(below) A U.S. Marine patrol closes in on a Korean hut in search of a Communist sniper. September 1951.

(above) Heartbreak Ridge as seen from the east on October 25, 1951.

(below) Colonel Young, one of the top officers of the 1st British Commonwealth Division in Korea, calls for a rousing cheer from members of the audience during the Danny Kaye USO show near the front lines. November 9, 1951.

(above) Somewhere along the battlefront in July 1952, Sergeant David J. Medeiros has just dropped his arm, giving the signal to fire to members of this artillery section in the 1st Marine Division.

(below) Marine M-46 tanks are moving toward the front in a night attack in January 1952.

In the X Corps sector elements of the 2nd Division, with the French and Dutch, entered Hoengsong. (See Map 25.) The corps mission was to reestablish the line from Osan to Samchok, which had been infiltrated by the Chinese during their January offensive. The ROK 5th Division was sent northeast of Hoengsong.

By January 29 it became clear that for reasons of their own, involving transport south of the Han River, the Chinese were not willing to risk a major confrontation at the moment. So the limited offensive rolled on. The UN forces had not yet encountered the enemy's main line of resistance, but this turn of events did not mean the war was winding down.

On January 28 General Almond ordered a patrol by the 23rd Infantry to the Twin Tunnels area north of the Han River, south of the town of Chipyong-ni. The orders were passed down to the 1st Battalion and thence to Company C. Lieutenant James P. Mitchell was called to battalion headquarters to get his orders at six o'clock the next morning. There he was told that his mission was to move up to the Twin Tunnels area and make contact with the enemy but not get involved in a major firefight.

The lieutenant had a hard job. The whole 2nd Division was short of jeeps and radios, a result of the losses in the fast retreat south a few weeks earlier. The 1st Battalion had to borrow three jeeps with drivers from another battalion and extra radios from the artillery. Lieutenant Mitchell had two SCR-300 radios, neither of which was operating properly. That was for communications within the patrol. To keep in touch with headquarters arrangements were made for an L-5 observation plane to circle overhead and act as radio relay. So the lieutenant needed an SCR-619 radio to get in touch with the plane. He borrowed two. But the artillery, from whom he was borrowing, complained that on a recent patrol the infantry had damaged their radios, so they insisted on sending along operators. All this horse-trading took about three hours, so it was 9 A.M. before the patrol was ready to move out.

Mitchell's patrol consisted of forty-four officers and men, most of them from his own rifle platoon of Company C, 23rd Infantry. They were riding in two weapons carriers and nine jeeps. They had one 75 mm and one 57 mm recoilless rifle, a 3.5-inch bazooka, a 60 mm mortar, two .50 caliber machine guns and three .30 caliber machine guns, mounted on the vehicles, and two light machine guns with tripod mounts. They had two Browning Automatic Rifles, and the other men carried M-1 rifles or carbines. Half the men were replacements, having joined the company only four days earlier. This patrol was their introduction to armed combat.

The patrol was to meet a patrol of the 24th Division headquarters and operate together with it. To make sure that all went well, Captain Melvin R.

Stai, the 1st Battalion assistant operations officer, decided at the last minute to come along. After the patrols met, he would come back to headquarters.

So the patrol set out from the battalion line, southeast of Munmong-ni. Lieutenant Mitchell and four men in a jeep led the patrol, out ahead about a mile. The main body was behind, led by Lieutenant William C. Penrod. The interval between vehicles was about a hundred yards.

All went as planned until the patrol reached the village of Obo-ri. There the L-5 plane, which had been circling lazily above, lost sight of the patrol because the ground was covered by the early morning haze that so often lingered in the Korean valleys. At Obo-ri, on the east bank of the Han, the patrol met the 24th Division men as scheduled, Lieutenant Harold Mueller and fourteen men. Captain Stai decided to go along on this mission, after all, and they set off for the Twin Tunnels, three miles southeast of Chipyong-ni. As they neared the little village of Sinchon, they skirted the base of Hill 453, where the road forded a shallow stream and then split, one fork going to Sinchon and the other to the Twin Tunnels. At about noon Lieutenant Mitchell stopped at the ford. Captain Stai offered to go alone into Sinchon to check it out, while the others moved to the Twin Tunnels, which were placed end to end, cutting beneath two steep ridges. When Captain Stai reached Sinchon, he left his jeep and driver on the road and walked into the cluster of houses and disappeared.

The others moved up to the railroad track and waited near a farmhouse for Stai to return. After a while they saw about twenty Chinese soldiers running from a small hill north of the railroad crossing and they opened fire on them. The Chinese replied with badly directed mortar fire. The liaison plane found the patrol at about this time and began circling again. In the plane was Major Millard O. Eugen, the battalion executive officer. He saw those troops and another group of about company size on Hill 453. He radioed a warning to Mitchell, but Mitchell never got it because of the faulty radios. The liaison plane was running low on fuel, so the pilot turned back to the American lines.

As the last vehicle crossed the ford, Mitchell saw more troops and guessed that he and his men had been caught in an ambush. The enemy on Hill 453 effectively blocked the route of retreat. Advance to the north was stopped by enemy troops on Hill 333, just north of the tunnels. The vehicles of the patrol bunched up just south of the railroad crossing.

"Let's get out of here," Mitchell shouted. He started to move his jeep to lead a breakthrough to the south.

But by this time the Chinese had started down Hill 453 to the ford. One jeep began firing its .50 caliber machine gun, but the gun was cold and the oil so sticky that it took two men to fire the gun. The rate of fire was so slow as to be ineffective.

Captain Stai's driver was waiting for the captain to reappear. He never saw him again. He did see the Chinese running down the hill and tried to speed back to join the patrol, but he was killed and the jeep overturned.

Lieutenant Mueller took his men up the hill on the east side of the road. He saw Chinese coming from the other side and hurried the men up. They began the race for the high ground. They had to abandon all the heavy weapons and much of their ammunition. They had the 3.5-inch bazooka and the tripod mounted .30 caliber machine gun and one other light machine gun.

Seven of Mitchell's men—replacements—dived into the ditch at the side of the road and refused to come out. Mitchell had to leave them there. All were killed later in the day.

It was now one in the afternoon and the fifty-one remaining men of the patrol were climbing the hill to save themselves. They were on the north side, the wet side, and they suffered for it. The snow was heavy and sticky, and soon their clothes were soaked. They lost the light machine gun and tripod when Private First Class Bobby Hensley fell over a stump and broke several ribs. Lieutenant Penrod told him to throw away the firing pin and leave the gun, and Sergeant Alfred Buchanan, who was carrying the machine gun ammunition, now abandoned it.

Lieutenant Mitchell had been injured in the back during World War II and one of his legs now gave way. He stopped. Private First Class William Stratton came up and offered to help him, but Mitchell said he had to sit for a while. Three Chinese riflemen showed up and began firing at them. Stratton and Mitchell fired back, but Stratton was no marksman with the M-1 (seven shots, all missed), and Mitchell's carbine jammed, and he had to stop and pry the offending cartridge out with his bayonet. Finally, he got the carbine operational and then killed all three Chinese soldiers with it. Mitchell and Stratton then slid down the hill into a gulley where they joined up with Private First Class Hensley, who had been left behind with his broken ribs.

Forty-seven men reached the top of the hill. One man, Sergeant John C. Gardella, lost his way, encountered a group of Chinese, hid, and lay doggo for the rest of the day and through the night.

Lieutenant Mueller led fourteen men up the hill to the top, but they found there that the Chinese occupied two other hills higher than theirs on both sides of them. The ground was frozen, and they could not dig in. Cover was poor. The Chinese began firing from north and south. Lieutenant Mueller put the remaining machine gun to guard the south approach to his hill. He had eight BARs and the 3.5-inch bazooka left to allocate.

The Chinese began moving up under a mortar barrage, but when they came in range the BARs and the machine gun stopped them. Twenty minutes passed. Lieutenant Mitchell and the two privates worked their way up the hill to join the others. The enemy machine gun on the north began firing and wounded seven men on that end of the line. One of them, eighteen-year-old Corporal LeRoy Gibbons, had already been wounded six times during this war. He got up and walked right through a string of tracer bullets to the flat of the hill where Lieutenant Mitchell was standing. His example put new life in the others, and, looking toward the machine gun, Sergeant Everett Lee said, "I'm gonna get that sonofabitch." He crawled fifteen feet north toward the gun, unlimbered his rifle and killed the two Chinese gunners. That act relieved the pressure on the north end of the line.

The machine gun was the key to the U.S. defense. Seven men were hit during the afternoon, either manning the gun or the BARs. Each time a man was hit, someone pulled him back and someone else moved up to take over the automatic weapon.

One Chinese crept up quietly until he was very close to the perimeter, stood up and began firing a burp gun. He hit five men, including Lieutenant Mueller, before he was killed.

Down south, Major Engen's plane landed and refuelled, and the major reported the ambush to headquarters of the 23rd Infantry. Colonel Paul Freeman, the commander of the regiment, ordered an air strike and a relief patrol to come out and rescue the patrol. Also he ordered an ammunition drop from a liaison plane.

At one o'clock the order for relief reached the 2nd Battalion, which was about ten miles south of the patrol. Captain Stanley C. Tyrrell got the job. It took two hours to assemble the equipment and three other officers and 142 men. Finally, 167 men started out for the relief, with 81 mm mortars, heavy machine guns, and an artillery observation party.

Back on the hill, Lieutenant Mitchell's patrol was fighting off one attack after another. A third of the men had been hit. Ammunition was getting scarce. Morale was dropping fast, although Private First Class Stratton, who had been hit in the hand and expected to be sent home on a medical survey, kept moving around, firing a BAR with his left hand and telling everyone he saw to buck up, they were going to get out of it all right. By late afternoon, however, most of the men had given up hope.

Shortly before dark Mitchell moved his men back from the crest of the hill. This way the Chinese could not see them so well. It was also true that they could not see the Chinese until they stuck their heads up over the crest, but that was fine with Mitchell, it saved ammunition.

Just before sunset came the first ray of hope—an observation plane leading eight fighters. Four were jets, and they came in first, firing machine guns and rockets at the Chinese. The Chinese hid and were quiet. The second flight of four planes dropped napalm on the enemy positions.

The air strike lasted half an hour. When it ended, a liaison plane dropped supplies to the patrol, coming down to fifteen feet overhead—so low that the men could see that the pilot had pink cheeks. Much of the material dropped outside the perimeter, but the men raced out and got what they could. There was also a message, attached to a long, yellow streamer. A soldier raced down the hill, retrieved the message, and took it to Lieutenant Mitchell.

"Friendly column approaching from the south," he read. "Will be with you shortly."

Mitchell showed the message around to the men.

But then darkness was complete, and the Chinese attack began. It started with mortar fire; several shells fell inside the American perimeter, and one man was seriously wounded. The Chinese began firing automatic weapons and rifles. The racket of the bugles began, and the Chinese infantry began approaching across the crusted snow from the south.

Four men crawled forward.

"Here they come," shouted Sergeant Donald H. Larson. Then he was hit—for the fifth time that day. Soon, all four men were hit, and they all crawled back inside the perimeter.

The column was coming up from the south, but it seemed that the Chinese were coming faster. The men of Mitchell's patrol began to lose confidence, and many of them were hurt. One man was shot in the belly but continued to load ammunition for an hour and a half before he died. Lieutenant Mueller had been shot in the leg. He was hit again, this time in the head, and afterwards he occasionally lost consciousness. Some men's clothing was freezing to the ground. Many were half-incapacitated by frostbite.

They waited for the relief, but instead came a second Chinese attack. Private Stratton, with his one-handed operation of the BAR, stood up and fired at the Chinese, moved to the edge of the perimeter and emptied the BAR at them. He was shot in the chest. Somebody pulled him back. A grenade came in and exploded between his legs. He screamed.

"For God's sake," said Mitchell, "shut up."

"My legs have been shot off."

"I know it. But shut up anyhow."

Stratton shut up. He was hit again, and he died.

Captain Tyrrell's relief column had reached the Twin Tunnels at five thirty that evening as the air strike was in progress. They had exact information as to the location of the patrol and the enemy from a liaison plane. Tyrrell's leading two jeeps reached a point about a hundred yards from the ford, and then the

Chinese opened fire with two machine guns from Hill 453. Tyrrell came up and saw that before he could mount the American hill to effect relief he would have to deal with Hill 453. He sent two platoons up the hill. They were supported by riflemen from the third platoon and by the heavy machine guns and 81 mm mortars. The barrage drove the Chinese off the hill, and the Americans moved up.

After securing Hill 453 and protecting his rear, Captain Tyrrell began to move to try to help the Mitchell patrol. But he encountered three men who had escaped downhill from the perimeter of the patrol, and they announced that Mitchell and all the others were dead. The patrol had been overrun, the three said, by "hundreds" of Chinese, and they were the only survivors. Hearing this, Tyrrell decided to wait until morning to reach the patrol, but Lieutenant Leonard Napier came up from his platoon with the information that an aid man who had made it out of the perimeter with the intention of finding medical supplies in the Mitchell patrol's jeeps reported that the patrol was still fighting, although three-quarters of the men were casualties. So Tyrell sent his men up the hill on which the Chinese were launching the attacks from the south.

Meanwhile, Mitchell's men were still fighting off Chinese assaults. Between darkness and nine o'clock the enemy made four attacks. The last was broken up by Corporal Jesus A. Sanchez, one of the men of the 21st Infantry. He loaded two BAR magazines, waited until the Chinese were almost up to him, then jumped up and emptied the first magazine into the enemy. He ejected the empty magazine, loaded again, emptied the second magazine, and then ran back and lay down. This counterblow stopped the Chinese for an hour.

The next Chinese attack came on the west. Since the machine gun was guarding the south, the Americans had only rifles and automatic carbines on the west side of the hill. They waited until the Chinese came to the rim of their perimeter and then fired at full rate. Fifteen Chinese were making the assault. Three of them managed to get inside the perimeter. Several men fired and killed the first and then the second soldier. The third Chinese soldier fired at Sergeant First Class Odvin A. Martinson, the platoon sergeant of Mueller's platoon, with a burp gun. Martinson had already been wounded five times that day. He fired back with his pistol. Neither hit the other. Private First Class Thomas J. Mortimer was lying on the ground behind the Chinese soldier. He rose up and stabbed the Chinese with his bayonet, and somebody else shot the man from the front. Sergeant Martinson picked up the body and threw it over the brink of the hill.

"I don't want them in here," he said, "dead or alive."

By ten thirty that night morale hit a new low; some wanted to surrender.

Thirty men were wounded, and some could not fight at all. Lieutenant Mueller was seeing flashes of light in one eye. Ammunition was nearly gone. Someone said they could not hold off another attack and should surrender now.

"Surrender," shouted Sergeant Martinson, "Hell no."

Two red flares went up in the west. The men on the perimeter braced themselves for another attack. But nothing happened. Half an hour went by. Still nothing.

Then they heard footsteps crunching on the frozen snow. The noises came from the south. When the footsteps came close Mitchell's men opened fire.

"Don't shoot," somebody shouted. "GIs."

"Oh yeah," shouted someone else "Who won the Rose Bowl game?"

Nobody down there could remember.

Down below somebody shouted again: "Fox Company, 23rd Infantry, by God."

Lieutenant Jones and a squad from Company F moved up the hill and entered the perimeter. The men of Mitchell's patrol who could stand up stood. The Chinese were long gone, and there was no firing. They were saved.

It took three hours to move the wounded down off the hill that night. They emptied the pockets of the dead and left the bodies. Sergeant Martinson, with his five wounds, refused a litter and hobbled down by himself. Private Hensley, with his broken ribs, helped carry another man down. They assembled at the bottom of the hill. Sergeant Gardella heard the commotion and made his way down to the bottom to join the others. They all got into the vehicles and headed back south, as the sun came up on the cold snowy mountains. Another day began in what had become a war of attrition.

13

The Battle for Chipyong-ni

During the enemy's offensive in January 1951 the troops of the North Korean II Corps had infiltrated deep behind the Eighth Army lines, and they apparently posed a serious threat to the army's communications and integrity. Before the marines arrived to flush them out several trains had been ambushed south of Wonju and north of Taegu. So the marines were given this area of 1,600 square miles to clear out, most of the terrain, as one marine wag put it "standing on end."

The 3rd Battalion of the 1st Marines was the first to get into antiguerilla action, on January 18, when they surprised and chased a number of troops east of Andong. They were North Koreans of the 10th Infantry Division. That division had been reorganized after the UN capture of Seoul and sent back down south under Major General Lee Ban Nam to infiltrate into the Andong–Taegu area and harry the UN lines of communication. Now the element of surprise was lost, and the manhunt was on. It was centered in the Pohang–Andong area. (See Map 26.) The area was so large that the marines carried out rice paddy patrols each day, in squad strength or less. On a given day the 5th Marines alone had twenty-nine such patrols out. All roads usable by vehicles were patrolled daily by motorized patrols, including at least one tank. Marine aircraft based at Pusan gave some help, though most of their effort was in support of the Eighth Army troops in the north. The little

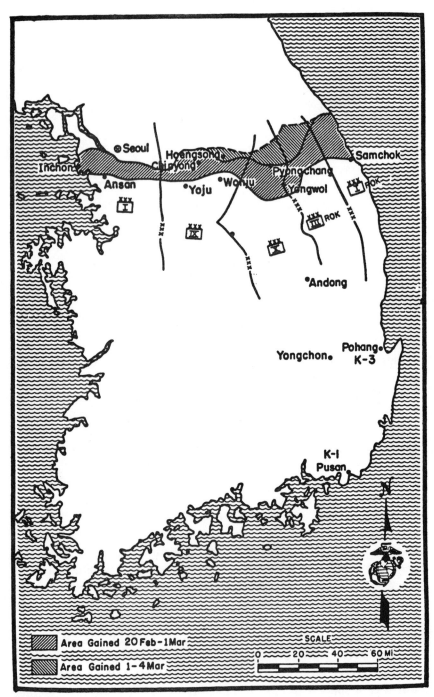

Seoul
Inchon
Ansan
Hoengsong
Chipyong
Yoju
Wonju
Pyongchang
Samchok
Yongwol
ROK
ROK
ROK
Andong
Yongchon
Pohang
K-3
K-1
Pusan

☒ Area Gained 20 Feb-1 Mar
☒ Area Gained 1-4 Mar

SCALE
0   20   40   60 MI

MAP 26

observation planes of VMO-6 were the best helpers. The problem with the guerillas was finding them, and the observation planes often did just that.

When the marines reached the Pohang–Andong zone in the fourth week of January, the North Koreans were already rueing their decision to set up guerilla activities on such a scale. General Lee was instructed to withdraw, if possible, to join the II Corps north of Pyongchang. Beginning January 22 the marines caught small groups of guerillas in the hills. On January 26 the 1st Battalion of the 7th Marines flushed a force of about four hundred North Koreans in the Chiso-dong area. Usually their efforts were much less dramatic, although very thorough. For example, Company C had reports of a strong guerilla force near Chachong-dong, and Lieutenant Richard J. Schening took a scouting force out to trap the enemy troops who were reported to be getting ready to make a raid for food. The marines moved silently in before dawn, concealing themselves under porches, beneath bramble bushes, in heavy bushes, and in trees. Some were even dressed in the white robes of Koreans apparently out in the woods to gather firewood. But . . . they found no guerillas.

The marine pressure kept the guerillas constantly off balance, their morale declined rapidly, and they began to slip away. By February 5 it was apparent to General Smith that the marines were wasting their time, and he so reported to General Ridgway. The marines had searched high and low but had killed only 120 of the enemy and captured 184. This was obviously no manner in which to employ the toughest fighting force in Korea, so on February 11 General Smith flew to Taegu to discuss the matter with General Ridgway. They agreed that the marines would have to be otherwise employed, but they did not that day decide just where the marines should go. The matter was settled for them at midnight, when the Chinese launched their second offensive of the year, this time on the central front.

After the harrowing experience of Lieutenant Mitchell's patrol up to the Twin Tunnels, the 23rd Infantry was ordered by 2nd Division to move up to the town of Chipyong-ni. On February 3 this was done, and the troops moved into this half-mile-long town that lay along the single-track railroad. Most of the buildings were the usual Korean huts of mud and straw on a stone foundation. There were, however, a few modern buildings, the railroad station and some business houses in the center of town, built of brick or frame. About half the town was already rubble as a consequence of previous military action.

Chipyong-ni was in the valley, circled by eight hills that rose about 800 feet above the rice paddies. Colonel Freeman would have had to establish a perimeter four miles around to cover them all, so he chose a compromise and

THE BATTLE OF CHIPYONG-NI (3—16 FEB 1951)

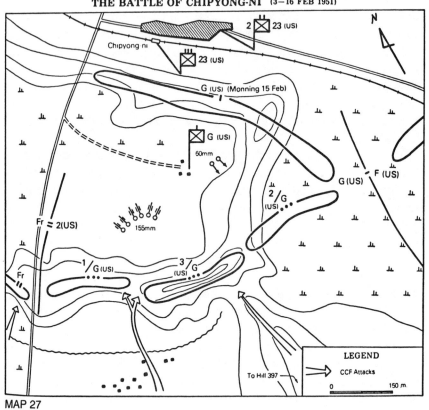

MAP 27

established a mile perimeter on lower ground on small hills and running through the rice paddies on the northwest. (See Map 27.)

General Ridgway was planning to increase his offensive efforts. The effect of the January offensive appeared to have been salutary in inflicting losses on the enemy and dissuading them from pushing farther south. Ridgway hoped to send his troops up as far as the Han River line where they would dig in and hold. He also planned an attack on the central front, between Yangpyong and Hoengsong.

During the ten days after Colonel Freeman's regiment reached Chipyong-ni, augmenting forces continued to arrive. The 37th Field Artillery Battalion came in on February 5. A battery of antiaircraft artillery added ten flakwagons to the defenses. Batttery B of the 503rd Field Artillery Battalion brought up six 155 mm howitzers.

Colonel Freeman's men set up their area defenses, digging in the machine gun sites, registering mortars, sowing mines, and running patrols around the high ground outside their positions. The artillery registered on all the obvious avenues of enemy approach; the heavy mortars were distributed among the platoons. The communications men set up telephone lines connecting all the units. In other words, the defenses were established carefully and efficiently.

To the south of the 3rd Battalion was the French battalion under Lieutenant Colonel Ralph Monclar, actually a lieutenant general in the French army who had asked to be reduced in rank so that he could lead the French contingent in Korea. They had taken over the Twin Tunnels area, Hill 543, Hill 279, and Hill 459 near the village of Kudun. They had a tight hold astride the road to Chipyong-ni. (See Map 28.)

The French were attacked by the Chinese on February 1. Early in the morning a large force surrounded the French positions, and the fighting began with the usual preparation by Chinese mortars. The infantry then tried to envelop the French positions, but the French infantrymen held and counterattacked just at first light, driving the Chinese out. The Chinese were more persistent than usual this day and came in from three sides. Lieutenant Nicolai of the 3rd Company was killed in this fighting. So fierce was it that at one point a 57 mm recoilless rifle manned by the 2nd Company knocked out twenty-three Chinese soldiers with five shells fired at point-blank range. Machine gunners saved the headquarters company command post, but Captain LeMaitre, the commander, was killed. Major Barthelmy and Captain Serre of the 3rd Company were wounded, and the company was completely surrounded. The men were saved by an air strike and an airdrop of ammunition. After that, the company fought off the Chinese, who retreated after they had suffered several hundred casualties. The French were hit hard too; they

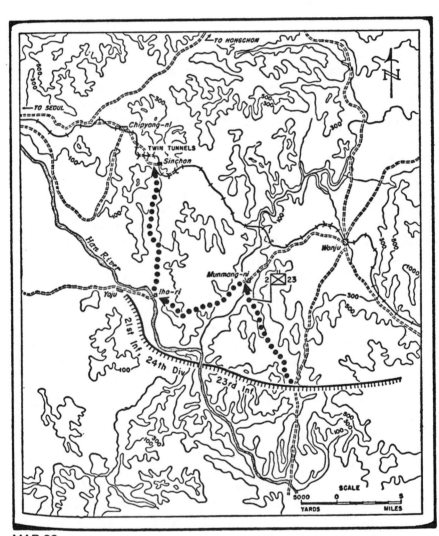

TO HONGCHON

TO SEOUL

Chipyong-ni

TWIN TUNNELS

Sinchon

Han River

Munmang-ni

Wonju

Yoju

Iho-ri

21st Inf

24th Div

23rd Inf

2 ☒ 23

SCALE

5000   YARDS   0   MILES   5

MAP 28

lost twenty-seven men killed and a hundred missing in this engagement. After it, they moved up to Chipyong-ni with the 23rd Infantry, and Colonel Monclar placed his three rifle companies on the west side of Chipyong-ni.

Meanwhile, on February 5 General Ridgway began his general offensive, with X Corps leading the attack in the center of the line. The plan was to make a double envelopment of the town of Hongchon with the ROK I Corps and the ROK III Corps.

The ROK 5th Division was to attack on the right, northeast of Hoengsong to the Hongchon–Pungam line. The ROK 8th Division would attack on the left to the Yongdu-ri–Hongchon line. The U.S. 7th Division would attack up the Pyongchang–Hoengsong road, and the U.S. 2nd Division would remain in reserve along the Chipyong-ni–Wonju line. The 187th Airborne Regimental Combat team would supply tanks.

The attack was begun by the South Koreans at eight o'clock in the morning of February 5. Almost immediately it ran into trouble. The Chinese and North Koreans put up stout resistance, and the weather turned worse, cutting back air operations. General Ridgway ordered the ROK 3rd Division into the area northwest of Hoengsong to bolster the effort, but on the night of February 11 the Chinese counterattacked, using the Chinese 66th Army, the Chinese 40th Army, and the North Korean V Corps. They hit the ROK 3rd, 5th and 8th divisions and shattered them. The ROK troops, who had an inordinate fear of the fighting qualities of the Chinese, fled before them, and the total dissolution of the ROK 8th division on the 2nd Division's flank left the flank wide open. Soon Wonju and Chipyong-ni were threatened. Radio Pyongyang and Radio Peking now boasted that this was the offensive that would drive the UN forces into the sea. In the first hours the enemy drove the UN forces back between five and twenty miles along the broad front, and Chipyong-ni, which was well behind the lines when the offensive began, by February 13 had become a bulge on the left of the X Corps line.

Patrols returned that day to report heavy Chinese movement on three sides of the town, north, east, and west. The artillery began firing against the enemy troops in range, and air strikes involving forty flights of planes were directed against those farther off. But the Chinese were coming in force.

Colonel Freeman wanted to withdraw from this salient, but General Ridgway insisted that Chipyong-ni was to be held. Colonel Freeman cheerfully acceded.

"We'll stay here and fight it out," he told his unit commanders on the afternoon of February 13.

The early part of the evening found the Chipyong-ni area quiet enough. At Battery B, Lieutenant Robert L. Peters was writing a letter home. The battery executive officer, Lieutenant Randolph McKinney, debated with himself whether to wear his clothes to bed or to strip down to his skivvies. He compromised by leaving his clothes on but taking off his shoes.

Before Lieutenant Peters finished his letter he heard a burst of gunfire that seemed a long way off. He stepped outside the dugout and saw six torches on the hillside. The machine gunners began to fire at figures moving along the rice paddies. Peters stepped back inside.

"Get up, McKinney," he shouted. "This is it."

On the east end of Company G Private First Class Donald Nelson and Private Jack Ward were sitting in their foxhole in the 2nd Platoon area, arguing about which one ought to stay awake during the first part of the night. Suddenly they heard digging sounds. Then two squads of Chinese attacked the center of the line and the 3rd Platoon with grenades. Corporal Eugene L. Otteson began firing his machine gun. The men on watch in the foxholes woke up their companions. "There's some firing going on," said Private First Class Herbert Ziebell to Private First Class Roy Benoit. "Get up and get ready."

Ziebell looked out over the countryside, but there was nothing to shoot at. He sat and waited.

When Lieutenant Paul McGee heard Corporal Otteson's machine gun, he telephoned Lieutenant Thomas Heath, the company commander. He also telephoned his squad leaders and informed them that they were under attack. But to conserve ammunition, he said, they were to fire only when they could actually see the enemy.

In a few moments the area was all quiet again. The attack had been the usual Chinese probe to locate the enemy positions.

The perimeter was quiet for an hour. Then the Chinese moved up again in force. The 3rd Platoon became aware of the Chinese movement about 11 P.M. when a grenade came bouncing into the foxhole of Corporal James C. Mougeat and wounded him.

"Lieutenant McGee, I'm hit," shouted Mougeat, as he crawled out of the hole and started west along the hilltop toward the company command post.

The Chinese threw more grenades at Mougeat, and one knocked the M-1 out of his hand and tore off the stock. Two other Americans shot the Chinese down as Mougeat recovered his rifle and ran on to the command post. There he decided to go back to his post. "I'm not hit bad," he said.

Lieutenant McGee saw several men below the platoon. One of them called his name.

"Who's that?" McGee demanded.

"It's a Chink," said the BAR man beside him.

McGee rolled a grenade down the hill. It exploded near the Chinese and wounded him. The enemy soldier rolled down the hill farther. McGee borrowed the BAR and put a burst into the Chinese. After that the soldier lay still. The others disappeared.

When the firing began, Lieutenant John Travis of Battery B and his machine gun sergeant, Corporal William H. Pope, grabbed several boxes of ammunition and moved up to the road cut where the battery's machine guns were centered. Ahead of them they could see many figures moving across the snow-covered rice paddies. Someone put up flares and the light silhouetted the Chinese soldiers against the snow and the dark hills.

Then into the machine gun position came a mortar shell, which killed the two men closest to Lieutenant Travis and wounded him and Pope. Travis hurried to the fire direction center tent and yelled out for six men to man the machine guns and another six to come and carry the wounded.

Captain John Elledge gathered up ten men and started out. Five of the men dropped out and went back to their holes. Elledge and Private First Class Leslie Alston got to the cut and found one gun jammed. They went back for another gun, carrying a wounded man with them. Then they made several trips, carrying ammunition up and wounded men back. The two machine guns fired steadily. The main attack, however, seemed to be centered on the French battalion just to the right of the machine gun position.

The Chinese swarmed up the French hill with the usual cacaphony of whistles shrieking and bugles bellowing. The French responded in kind, cranking up a hand siren they had acquired somewhere. It produced an alarming sound. The Chinese were startled, and more so when the French came at them. When the French soldiers were thirty feet from the Chinese line they began hurling grenades, and the Chinese line broke. The area quieted down.

Back in the American sector the artillery kept up a harassing fire all night, firing illuminating rounds every five minutes opposite the perimeter. During the night the Chinese launched four separate attacks at Company G, most of them against the 3rd Platoon. At light on February 14 there were still Chinese soldiers right on the line of the 3rd and 1st platoons. Three Chinese reached the line, one was killed, and the two others were captured. At the juncture of the 1st and 3rd platoons a dozen Chinese withdrew, leaving another dozen bodies on the south slope of the hill. The 3rd Platoon sergeant, Bill Kluttz, saw a number of Chinese in the creek bed just ahead of his position. He began firing at them. Lieutenant McGee told him to fire the bazooka into the creek bed, and he did. The rocket hit a tree and burst over the creek bed, and about forty Chinese came running out across the rice paddies in front of the 1st

Platoon. The Americans fired on them as they ran. In a few minutes the area was quiet again.

During the day the men of the 23rd Infantry and the artillerymen prepared for another attack. Lieutenant McGee took out a patrol that morning to cross the rice paddies. They found a dozen Chinese in the paddies and in a culvert, seven of them wounded. They counted eighteen dead bodies. Near Mawsan they saw a small haystack. McGee walked up to it. A Chinese soldier popped up in the haystack and tried to shoot him. Sergeant Kluttz shot the Chinese. Another Chinese, badly wounded, tried to fire on them with a Soviet-made burp gun. He was too weak to operate it. Corporal Boleslaw Sander shot him down.

Captain Elledge and several other artillerymen checked the area around the battery position. Eight hundred yards from the road cut Elledge saw a house that he decided should be destroyed before the Chinese attacked that night. The howitzers took the house under fire with white phosphorus shells. After the third round the house began to blaze and fifteen enemy soldiers came running out. The two machine guns and the French battalion riflemen killed eight of them, and the others escaped.

As the day wore on the artillerymen dug the foxholes and trenches around the guns deeper. They relaid the howitzers in pairs. Lieutenant Heath went to Battery B to work out mutual defense plans with Captain Elledge and Lieutenant Rochnowski. They agreed that the enemy was most likely to attack on the center of the Company G front, the high part of the perimeter where Lieutenant McGee's 3rd Platoon was located. So they reinforced the area with two more BAR teams. Rochnowski agreed to send artillery men up to fight with the infantry if that became necessary.

During the day the 23rd Infantry received twenty-four airdrops of ammunition. The air force also made a number of air strikes, all around the perimeter, for the Chinese now surrounded on all sides. Enemy activity was hardly seen, although a number of mortar rounds fell inside the perimeter during the day.

Except for that, all was quiet. The men of Company G were served hot meals, and it was so quiet that some men began making bets that the Chinese had withdrawn. But as darkness fell those bets were off. First came flares in the southern sky and then the squawk of the Chinese bugles. Half an hour later came the probe, directed this time against the machine gun in the center of Lieutenant McGee's platoon. The gunner was wounded immediately. The Chinese wormed forward, covered by a machine gun of their own. Two squads penetrated the front of the 1st Platoon and occupied several foxholes. They planted pole charges in two of the 1st Platoon foxholes, and thus killed four men. They set up a machine gun on the left side of the 1st Platoon sector and began firing on McGee's 3rd Platoon. The leader of the 1st Platoon sat in a hut when the fighting started and did not come out. McGee called the company command post and asked if the 1st Platoon was still in position. Lieutenant Heath called the leader of the 1st Platoon, and he called his sergeant on the hill. Sergeant Schmitt was on the right end of the position and did not know that the left-hand side had been taken by the Chinese. He said the line was solid. McGee didn't believe it. He shouted at the 1st Platoon areas on the left side next to his own:

"Anyone from the 1st Platoon?"

There was no answer.

Now the enemy began trying to overrun the 3rd Platoon. They took one foxhole. McGee saw four Chinese with shovels on their backs crawling on hands and knees about fifteen feet behind the hole where a squad leader was crouched.

McGee shouted:

"There are four of them at the rear of your hole. Toss a grenade up and over."

A burst from a machine gun—enemy—prevented the squad leader from standing up to toss the grenade. McGee and Private Cletis Inmon, firing a BAR and a rifle, killed the four Chinese.

At ten o'clock McGee saw a group of Chinese coming up out of the creek bed toward the squad leader's hole.

"Fifteen or twenty of them coming up on your right front," he shouted at the squad leader. The Chinese machine gun kept the squad leader down. The Chinese began throwing grenades toward his hole. There were three men in there. The squad leader and one man, a sergeant, jumped out and ran to McGee's hole. The sergeant was hit on the way. The Chinese threw a satchel charge into the hole the two men just left and killed the man who had stayed in there.

With the two new men piled on top of him, McGee could not see or move.

"Get the hell out of here and back to your squad," he shouted.

The two men did not move.

McGee repeated the order. The sergeant jumped out of the hole and was immediately shot in the shoulder. McGee called for a litter team and the two men were evacuated under fire.

By this time Chinese soldiers were crawling up the slope toward McGee's hole. One Chinese threw three grenades at him before McGee killed him with the BAR. But the BAR was jamming on every tenth round. McGee used his pocket knife to extract the cases, until he dropped the knife and could not find it in the dark. He abandoned the BAR and picked up his carbine. The cold oil stopped the bolt from slamming home. McGee grabbed the operating handle and slammed the bolt in, fired four rounds and killed the Chinese who was raising up on his knees to attack the hole. Men in other holes killed three other Chinese right on the Company G line.

It was now nearly eleven o'clock at night. McGee sent a runner to the company command post to tell Lieutenant Heath that his platoon needed men, ammunition, and medics. Heath called Rochnowski, and the artillerymen sent fifteen soldiers up to help. But on the way up the hill two men were hit by a mortar round, and the rest turned around and went back. Heath stopped them at the bottom of the hill and led them up himself. By the time they got up there the line was alive with firing. The Chinese held much of the Company G line. Once again the artillerymen broke and ran down the hill. Heath ran after them and began shouting:

"Goddam it, get back up on the hill. You'll die down here anyhow."

By this time it was nearly one o'clock in the morning, and the hill was alive with fighting men. Captain Elledge heard the racket and went out into the gun park and called for men to come up and help the infantry. He went forward himself. He ran into a group of Chinese and began firing his carbine on automatic. He killed one Chinese with a bullet through the chest, the next with one through the head. A third Chinese threw a small "ink bottle" grenade, which exploded and numbed Elledge's arm. When the arm went numb, Captain Elledge figured he was badly hit, and he slid down the hill and went back to the battery mess tent.

Lieutenant Heath's main line of resistance was breaking up. The Chinese had directed the brunt of their attack against his company positions.

Down below at the Company G kitchen tent the men were paying for their failure to dig foxholes that afternoon. There was one hole—the garbage pit. Eight men jumped into it all at once. They stayed there.

The Chinese captured the saddle that was the boundary between the 3rd and 1st platoons. The 1st Platoon leader's failure to discover for himself the condition of his defenses had given the Chinese plenty of time to organize up there. They put a machine gun into operation and began firing toward the howitzers. Up on the hill, however, the weapons were rifles, grenades, and satchel charges. The Chinese fought for every foxhole. They took heavy casualties, but they also took a lot of foxholes.

At about one o'clock in the morning Lieutenant Heath tried to organize the artillerymen into a counterattack force to retake the saddle. Three attempts failed, but Heath did not give up.

"We're going up that goddam hill or bust," he shouted, and he organized the artillerymen for another assault.

On the hill Lieutenant McGee's runner, Private Inmon, was hit in the eye. There was no way he could be gotten to an aid station just then, but an aid man came over and bandaged his head. Inmon loaded clips then for Lieutenant McGee to fire.

Corporal Ottesen continued to man his machine gun, until two Chinese came up to his hole and tossed in grenades. The gun stopped firing. Ottesen disappeared.

Sergeant Kluttz reported to McGee that Chinese were coming through between Ottesen's squad and Corporal Raymond Bennett's squad. McGee shifted men around to stop that and called to Lieutenant Heath for help. Heath called Colonel Edwards, who sent a squad up from Company F.

Bennett's squad tried to recapture the Ottesen position and got involved in a firefight. Bennett was hit first in the hand, next in the shoulder, and then in the head. McGee lost contact.

It was two o'clock in the morning when Sergeant Kenneth Kelly came up with the squad from Company F. The Company F men were unlucky—instead of taking back the Ottesen position, they were all killed or wounded within the first ten minutes.

Sergeant Kluttz went back to tell McGee the news. Worse, the 2nd Platoon fell back, taking with them a machine gun that had been supporting McGee. The 3rd Platoon was now in bad shape, and McGee began to lose heart. Down below, Lieutenant Carl Haberman was reorganizing the artillerymen for another move. They were clustered in a squad tent when he came in.

"Hell," he said, "a squad tent won't stop bullets."

His logic seemed appealing at that moment, and the men went with him, but when they saw the hill and heard the firing, none would climb.

On the hill McGee finally gave up when Sergeant Kluttz's machine gun jammed. The two of them called to the other men to retreat, threw all their grenades, and walked down the hill. Three other men followed, all that were left of the 3rd Platoon of Company G.

Lieutenant Heath had the task of reporting to Colonel Edwards that company G had been driven from its position with heavy losses. The colonel's battalion reserve was now reduced to the support platoon of Company F, minus the squad that had been lost in attacking McGee's hill. Colonel Edwards appealed to Colonel Freeman, the regimental commander, for more men. Colonel Freeman's reserve had been reduced by Chinese attacks on the 3rd Battalion, and all he could give Edwards was a platoon of Rangers and a tank.

Colonel Edwards organized the two platoons under Lieutenant Robert Curtis. They reached the Company G area at about eleven thirty in the morning. The Ranger company commander (a captain) did not want to take orders from Lieutenant Curtis so more time was lost while Colonel Edwards put Captain John H. Ramsburg in charge of the composite group, which then went forward. Soon Company G and the new men were intermingled at the bottom of the hill, and they began firing up to discourage the Chinese from coming down.

The Ranger officer continued to interfere, and after several Rangers were wounded Ramsburg sent him back with the casualties to get rid of him. The counterattack was a mess; friendly machine guns and mortars opened fire on the Rangers and wounded many of them. Other guns wounded Curtis's men. Somehow a few of them made it to the top of the hill. Captain Ramsburg was wounded by a grenade fragment. Heath came up and took over the attack for Ramsburg. Then Heath was shot in the chest, and someone dragged him down the hill. The Ranger platoon leader was killed. One by one the soldiers who had reached the top came down. The counterattack had failed. The Chinese still held Company G's defensive line, but the artillery was still in position. Curtis went back to the command post, only to learn that the whole command organization was about to fall apart. Captain Elledge got an abandoned half-track working again, and he took that machine with its quadruple .50 caliber machine guns and swept the length of the hill that was now held by the enemy. An enemy squad captured a 75 mm recoilless rifle and pointed it at Elledge. He could see the light through the tube as they prepared to slam home the charge. He opened fire and killed the Chinese squad just in time.

By dawn the artillerymen had become the front line of the area. They continued to stay on and fire their howitzers. Captain Elledge moved around, pounding the enemy-held hill with his four .50 caliber machine guns, and the three tanks available also kept firing at the hill. The Chinese stayed up there. The artillerymen manned the howitzers and fired white phosphorus shells at the hillside, stopping at least one putative attack in this fashion. As day grew bright, the artillery was still in position. The Ranger company and Company B made an attack and were supported by several air strikes. Colonel Edwards came up to direct the assault himself. Artillery and tanks were employed, and, finally, the Chinese withdrew from the area. The enemy assault on Chipyong-ni had failed. Hundreds of Chinese bodies lay on the hills and in the paddies. General Ridgway's forces had held and won a victory.

14

Northward

The Chinese had been held off, but they still surrounded Chipyong-ni. What was needed now was a rescue by a strong force. It was on its way.

While the men of Company G and the artillery fought for that vital position at Chipyong-ni, the French and other elements of the 2nd Division did the same. At three o'clock in the morning of February 15, there was scarcely enough ammunition left inside the lines of the 23rd Infantry to stage a turkey shoot, but, as in the motion pictures, the cavalry was coming. This time it was the U.S. 5th Cavalry, and their mounts were tanks. Colonel Marcel G. Crombez, commander of the regiment, had been ordered by General Moore to attack up the road fifteen miles from Yoju to Chipyong-ni, to relieve the Americans and the French trapped there. (See Map 29.)

They had moved at five o'clock in the afternoon of February 14, five platoons of tanks, three battalions of cavalrymen, and two battalions of field artillery, including a number of self-propelled howitzers. They moved in the dark, in column over the rutty road, which was covered with snow and ice. All but the artillery crossed the Han River that night. At dawn the 1st Battalion moved forward on the right-hand side of the road, and the Chinese began to fight back. Colonel Crombez sent the 2nd Battalion up the left side of the road, and a full-scale regimental attack began, supported by artillery and air strikes. But the advance was much too slow: there were too many Chinese

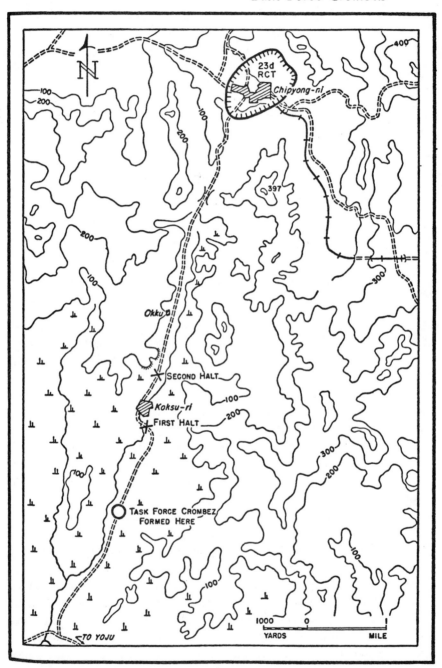

MAP 29

against them. Colonel Crombez decided to establish an armored task force to penetrate the enemy territory, the infantry coming up behind.

Twenty-three tanks from the 6th and 70th tank battalions were assigned to this task, along with Company L of the 5th Cavalry and a handful of combat engineers. The 6th Tank Battalion had M-46 tanks with 90 mm guns. The 70th Tank Battalion rode M-4A3 tanks, with 76 mm guns. There were other important differences: the M-46s could turn completely around in place, an important factor on a narrow road. They also had heavier armor.

The infantrymen would guard the tanks against Chinese with satchel charges and grenades, and the engineers would look for antitank mines. When not engaged in operations, they would ride the tanks.

As the tanks prepared to move out, Colonel Crombez went up in a helicopter and looked over the terrain ahead. He saw a typical Korean farm road, narrow, flanked by mountains on the left and rice paddies on the right, with a deep cut a mile south of Chipyong-ni where steep cliffs lined both sides of the road. That, he could see, was going to be a bad point.

The M-46 tanks took the lead. There would be no supply train behind, for that would only slow the force. The tanks would burst through the Chinese lines, the infantry would come and mop up, and the supply trains would come along when the road was safe. Colonel Crombez rode in one tank. Lieutenant Colonel Edward J. Treacy, Jr., commander of the 3rd Battalion, rode atop another, and Captain John C. Barrett, commander of Company L, rode on a third. A hundred and sixty infantrymen were also atop the tanks, and when the tanks stopped they would jump down to protect the engineers who might be moving mines. When the tanks moved, the tankers were supposed to signal the infantry. A truck came up behind to pick up wounded infantrymen, and any infantrymen who were left behind were instructed to try to make their way back to the lines, or to wait for the return of the tanks, promised for later in the day.

The column moved out at three o'clock that afternoon, with planes strafing and bombing the road ahead. About two miles along the road the column came under Chinese fire and stopped. The infantrymen jumped down and began firing back. Suddenly, without warning, the tank column moved forward, and about thirty infantrymen were left behind. They began making their way back to the UN lines.

The column moved through the village of Koksu-ri and stopped again. Once more the infantrymen dropped off the tanks, and again the tanks started up without warning. Many more men were left behind this time, including Colonel Treacy, who was later captured by the Chinese.

Captain Barrett nearly missed the column, too. He was unable to catch his own tank but did manage to crawl aboard the fifth in line and so went on. By this time, through repeated error, the original contingent of a hundred and sixty infantrymen was reduced to about seventy.

The tanks fired at the Chinese along the road, and the Chinese tried to destroy the tanks with bazookas and satchel charges. The infantrymen shot the Chinese down as they came, some of them to within fifty feet of the roadside. Captain Barrett personally shot down three Chinese who were carrying a bangalore torpedo up to try to get themselves a tank.

The big trouble came when the tank column reached the cut in the road south of Chipyong-ni. There the road passed between two embankments for about the distance of a city block. Both banks were lined by Chinese.

The tanks moved on through. The lead tank, commanded by Lieutenant Lawrence DeSchweintz, was hit by a rocket, and DeSchweintz was wounded, but the tank went on.

The four engineers were riding on the next tank in line, and one of them was shot off the deck as they passed through the defile. The tank kept on going.

Captain Johnnie Hiers, commander of the tank company, was riding in the fourth tank. It was hit by a bazooka rocket, which killed the men in the fighting compartment, including Captain Hiers. The driver gunned the engine, drove on through the cut and turned off the road, even though his tank was burning. That heroic act let the rest of the column move on through.

The last truck was disabled. Some of the wounded managed to climb aboard tanks, but many were not able to and were killed or captured. But the column moved on, the tanks firing at the enemy along the sides of the road as they went through this dangerous territory.

As the column moved up toward Chipyong-ni, four tanks from the 23rd Infantry area came down, driving Chinese before them. When the Chinese soldiers saw tanks on both sides of them, they began to run. Hundreds of the enemy abandoned their positions south of Chipyong-ni, and as they moved across the paddy fields they were taken under fire by the tanks.

The defenders of Chipyong-ni continued to hold, and at noon the relief column came up, preceded by napalm-throwing aircraft that forced more of the enemy to flee. At four in the afternoon the defenders could see the tanks, and at 5:15 twenty tanks rolled inside the perimeter.

Of the one hundred and sixty infantrymen who had started out only twenty-three remained. Thirteen of them were wounded.

Colonel Crombez then had to decide whether to remain in Chipyong-ni for the night or to return, and because the weather was turning worse he decided to stay. Next morning they started back and discovered that there was not a single Chinese soldier left in the area. Everyone had moved out overnight.

February 16 was spent flushing out pockets of enemy and counting corpses. General Ridgway arrived at Chipyong-ni, and in some awe he viewed two thousand Chinese bodies stacked around the French battalion position alone. Only then was the difficulty of the fight and the extent of the defensive victory appreciated on high. Colonel Freeman had been wounded in the fighting and was replaced in command by Lieutenant Colonel John H. Chiles. The 23rd Infantry and the French were relieved by the IX Corps. The war went on.

In the third week of February, General Ridgway decided that the success of his program to build morale and fighting power of the Eighth Army was such that he could venture a more powerful attack: to cross the Han River east of Seoul. Once again, however, he made it clear to all concerned that his was a limited objective, aimed at cutting the enemy supply lines and wiping out forces massed on the west. There was no talk about driving to Pyongyang or to the Yalu, for as the Chinese armies attacking Chipyong-ni were decimated, other Chinese forces had moved south, bypassing Wonju and attacking down to the Chechon area. There they had been stopped, but north of Wonju the dissolution of the two ROK divisions had given the Chinese control of Hoengsong, and General Ridgway wanted it back. To get it back, he would use the 1st Marine Division.

Colonel Lewis B. (Chesty) Puller, the leader of the 1st Marines in the fight for Seoul and the defensive action at Chosin, had been promoted to Brigadier General and made assistant division commander of the 1st Marine Division a few weeks earlier. General Puller flew to Chungju on February 13 to look over the area. The next day the marines began moving north.

The Chinese drive south in the central area had brought them to the outskirts of Wonju, but on February 18 Ridgway's probing patrols learned that the enemy was withdrawing along a broad front. Ridgway set February 21 as D-Day for his new offensive operation. The marines would now become part of IX Corps, under Major General Bryant E. Moore. Their efforts would be integrated with those of the army's 24th Infantry Division, the 1st Cavalry Division, the ROK 6th Division, and the 27th British Commonwealth Brigade. The marines would attack northeast from a point north of Wonju and cut off those enemy forces that had penetrated south and east of Hoengsong. The 1st Marine Regiment and the 5th Marines would move into action immediately.

The enemy, according to intelligence estimates, consisted of elements of three Chinese armies, the 66th, 39th, and 40th field armies. The terrain was Korea at its roughest: rocky hills and deep valleys, swiftly running streams, and bad roads.

On February 20 General MacArthur flew to Korea to confer with General

Ridgway—really to show himself and announce to the press that he was still running the show.

"I have just ordered a resumption of the offensive," said MacArthur, revealing plans made by General Ridgway two days earlier. And having told the world the secret General Ridgway was trying to keep to preserve the element of surprise, MacArthur mounted his command plane and flew back to Tokyo, leaving the responsibility for defeat with Ridgway but preparing to take the responsibility for victory for himself.

The offensive began at ten o'clock in the morning of February 21. General Ridgway had made some careful preparations, and one of his last messages was to warn the commanders that they must not bypass any "hostile force of sufficient strength to jeopardize the safety of your forces." There would be no repetition of the MacArthur error of September. No major enemy forces would be left to fight in the UN rear if Ridgway could help it.

February weather meant thaws, and thaws meant mud; it was so great a problem that the marines wondered if they would be able to move north along the roads fast enough to meet their timetable. General Puller telephoned General Smith to ask what to do if all his elements did not arrive in time to attack simultaneously. General Smith told him to attack with the elements that did arrive. As H-Hour approached, the trucks of the 5th Marines pulled up to the line of departure, and the marines of the 1st Battalion scrambled out of their trucks on the double and advanced without any time for reassembly and nose counting.

The MacArthur announcement of the previous day had guaranteed that the kickoff of the offensive would have that growing element of warfare: plenty of press coverage. Correspondents swarmed around the senior command posts. Generals were on hand in coveys. MacArthur came again, this time to visit the 187th Airborne Division. General Ridgway and General Moore were watching the marines take off, standing on an embankment above the paddy fields. Ridgway saw a marine, loaded down with a communications radio, stumbling along with one combat bootlace untied, flapping along the snow. The general slid down the bank on his bottom, landed at the marine's feet, and tied the man's shoe in a trice.

What a show! How the correspondents lapped that up—and how the foes of the war and the foes of grandstanding curled their lips at Ridgway's theatrical gesture. At least, there was one element to Ridgway's theatricality that made it far more forgivable than MacArthur's: the former's gestures were made to appeal to the troops, while the latter's were made to impress the world.

Slipping and sliding, the marines advanced. On the shady sides of the steep hills they clawed their way up crusty snow. On the sunny sides they slipped on the slush, and quite by accident they developed the technique of purposeful sliding: the first marine of the 5th Marines slipped and fell and slid a hundred feet down the bank. The next man plopped himself down and slid all the way, and so did those coming after.

The marines were quite unbothered by the enemy during these antics. It was not until late afternoon that they began to encounter serious resistance. The 5th Marines then engaged in two firefights before digging in for the night. They were both at long distance, and only three marines were wounded. Far worse than the depredations of the enemy were the activities of nature on this first day. The men had clambered through snow, ice, slush, and mud. At noon it began to rain, and the rain did not stop. It rained through the night, and the men rested in foxholes half-filled with water, with their parkas soggy and their weapons dripping, wet to the bone.

On the left flank the 1st Cavalry Division faced the same wet misery. The Han River began to rise in the flooding rain, and the ford west of Koksu-ri, which the cavalry had counted on, would no longer allow the passage of jeeps. A pontoon bridge built at Yoju broke loose. The rain did not stop until just before dawn on February 23.

On that day the real enemy resistance began. The 1st and 2nd battalions of the 1st Marines encountered dug-in Chinese resistance on two hills, but they fought through. The 5th marines had it much easier. "All we did was walk, walk, walk," said Captain Franklin B. Mayer, commander of Company E. Their fighting would come on the next day.

On the left, the 1st Marines sent an artillery barrage into Hoengsong, then an air strike, and then a tank and infantry patrol. When the patrol came in, it was met by strong machine gun fire from the hills to the west, and the antennae were shot off two tanks by sharpshooters. The tanks were still able to knock out the enemy positions—their fire was directed by runners. Captain Robert Wray, leading the patrol, was eager to go on, but an aerial observer reported to battalion that the Chinese were massed on high ground beyond, waiting to ambush the patrol. So Lieutenant Colonel Donald Schmuck ordered the patrol back, and it came back through Massacre Valley, named for the fate of an army convoy ambushed during the Chinese winter offensive.

Either the Chinese had laid mines along the road during the winter, or they had done it since. The patrol made it through safely, but later in the day when the road had thawed in the sun, a jeep was blown up by a land mine.

On the afternoon of February 24 Chinese artillery began firing from the hills north of Hoengsong. Nevertheless, by the end of the day all the major objectives of the 1st Marine Division had been achieved. One reason for this was the effective air support given the ground forces by the 1st Marine air wing.

When the marines became a part of the Eighth Army, the marine air wing then became a part of the U.S. Fifth Air Force. The marines were frankly concerned about being controlled by air force General Partridge and army General Ridgway. General Smith had tried without notable success to secure a statement from the army and the air force that the marine air wing would be used in support of marine operations. That's how they had been trained, that's how they had performed brilliantly in Korea up until this point. No such statement was forthcoming by the moment of attack. The air force policy was to combine operations and use the nearest available craft to make any given air strike. On February 23 the marines grumbled when an air strike requested by the 5th Marines did not materialize. But later that day two air force strikes did come in right on schedule.

The trouble, the ground marines complained, was that the marine air wings were just too good. The U.S. Army and the British Commonwealth commanders had all requested marine air when it came to close support, because they saw how effective it was. Thus, in this offensive the marines carried more than their share of the load, most of it in support of U.S. Army units. They flew 101 of the 800 sorties carried out by the Fifth Air Force that day. VMF-312 sent up part of a sixteen-plane strike behind the Chinese lines. That afternoon two four-plane flights supported the army's 2nd and 7th divisions. On February 24 Major Daniel H. Davis, executive officer of VMF-12, flew off with four planes in support of the British Commonwealth Brigade. The ground artillery marked the Chinese positions with white phosphorus shells, and Davis's planes came in low with napalm, rockets, and fire from 20 mm cannons. The Chinese fought back with machine guns and antiaircraft guns. Major Davis's plane was hit on his eighth strafing run and lost a wing. It crashed, and the major was killed.

That day—February 24—General Moore, the commander of IX Corps, died of a heart attack. General Ridgway took the unusual move of appointing General Smith—a marine—to command a corps of troops that were primarily army. General Puller took over the 1st Marine Division.

This new offensive bogged down in the mud. On February 25 General Ridgway announced his dissatisfaction with progress. Logistics was the big problem for the UN forces. The next phase of battle would have to be fought on soggy ground north of Hoengsong between two streams virtually at the flood point. The 1st and 7th marines would carry the action in this area. To cross the Som River, Lieutenant Virgil Banning's 3rd Battalion of the 1st Marines would have to do some engineering, because the regimental engineer company was busy with road repairs. The Som was two hundred feet wide at this point in the season and chest deep.

From somewhere in his duffel, Major Edwin H. Simmons of the battalion weapons company produced a manual titled "How to Build a Swiss Bent Bridge," and Technical Sergeant Carmelo J. Randazzo's Antitank Assault Platoon was given the job of building such a bridge. The marines cut down trees for timbers and acquired telephone wire for lashing. They built trusses and hooked them up to spars and stringers and carried them all out into the chilly water and put them together. By the night of February 28 they had assembled two spans: one, 120 feet long, reached a sandbar in the middle of the river, and the other, 60 feet long, reached the other side. On the morning of March 1 the troops walked across the bridge, and no one got his feet wet. Under cover of an artillery barrage they moved forward three-quarters of a mile.

Before noon the marines encountered real hostility. The Chinese had booby-trapped the terrain ahead and were dug in under log-covered bunkers. The artillery and air strikes did not dislodge these troops, who had taken great pains to prepare a defense. The going was so slow that in midafternoon the marines called a halt. Next morning, with heavier air strikes and more artillery support, they attacked west of the river. The Chinese had mostly moved out, and west of the river the resistance was very light. The same was true east of the river. Lieutenant Colonel Allen Sutter's 2nd Battalion of the 1st Marines linked up with the 3rd Battalion in the afternoon after taking its assigned objective, Hill 208. Sutter had expected a hard fight, but only three men were wounded.

On the morning of March 3 the marines approached their final objectives of this operation—five hills that were dead ahead. They moved up. The worst resistance was in the area of the 7th Marines. Fighting for two hills, called Hill 333 and Hill 536, they took 118 casualties (104 wounded), at the end of the day and the Chinese still held the hill tops. On March 4 they attacked again, but as had happened in the past, the heavy fighting on the day before seemed to have sapped the Chinese resistance, and the enemy had moved out during the night. As of the night of March 4 the operation was officially over. The Eighth Army had not accomplished all that General Ridgway set out to do. Mud and rain were as much responsible for the slow going as was the enemy, but, for the first time since the UN forces began fighting in Korea, they had a solid line, with no gaps, no appreciable guerilla resistance behind them, and no soft spots. (See Map 30.) The marines had accomplished their objective: keeping the Chinese off balance as they tried to prepare for another major offensive.

UN OFFENSIVE (1 MAR–21 APR 1951)

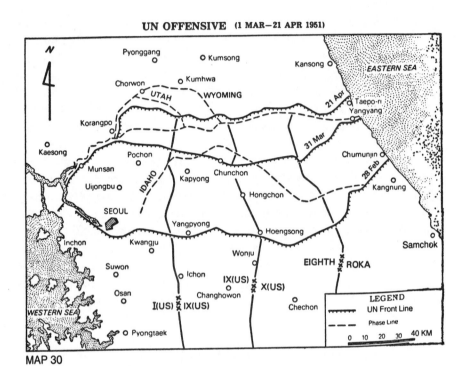

MAP 30

The next move by General Ridgway was called Operation Ripper. By the time it was ready to move in March, Major General William H. Hoge had arrived from the United States to take command of the IX Corps, and General Smith reverted to command of the 1st Marine Division, and General Puller to his post as assistant division commander. The purpose of the new operation was to move the UN line north, recapture Seoul, and then reach the 38th parallel once more. The war was entering a new phase.

15

The Recapture of Seoul

The strange nature of the Korean War is nowhere better illustrated than in an exasperating footnote to that first new UN offensive around Chipyong-ni. For shorthand and security purposes the military always gave colorful names to its various military operations, and this one had been termed "Operation Killer" by the staff planners. When that title reached Washington it caused an enormous flap. The Republicans in congress picked it up and charged that the whole effort of the Democrats was to kill Chinese. The State Department said the name increased the difficulty of arriving at a diplomatic arrangement with the Chinese to end the war. The Joint Chiefs of Staff protested to Ridgway that the name was a public relations gaffe and suggested that General Ridgway be more careful of his operational titles in the future. So, the politicization of military operations—something hitherto strange to the American services—proceeded apace.

This whole matter was all a part of growing politicization of the war and a growing critical media attitude toward the war and the American military. The major problem developing was the failure to convince a broad section of the American people that the killing was worth the effort, and Ridgway's plan—to inflict maximum damage to the enemy with minimum cost in lives and material—did not have "sex appeal." Many Americans did not believe Korea was worth the effort. Others shared General MacArthur's view that if

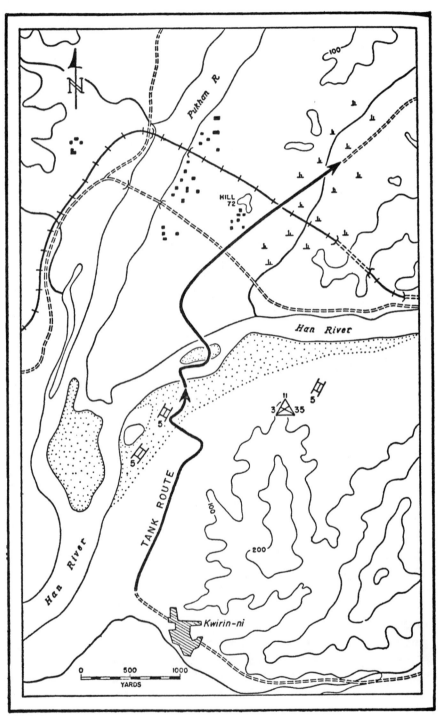

MAP 31

you were going to fight a war, you ought to fight it all the way and win. From General Ridgway there were no brave words about driving on to victory, or clearing the Korean peninsula of the enemy. There was just slogging effort, to capture territory if necessary, but, above all, to make the Chinese offensives so expensive that the Chinese would have to begin thinking about their own withdrawal from the political trap that Korea had become.

Thus, the March offensive planned by General Ridgway did not promise anything, certainly not the capture of the South Korean capital. And it was called "Operation Ripper," which really could not affend anyone in Washington. The *goals* of the offensive were much more extensive than Ridgway's promises. The offensive was intended to secure and straighten out the Hong-chon–Kangnung line, to capture Seoul, and then to secure once more the line along the 38th parallel, all the while punishing the Chinese so severely that they would have difficulty mounting the offensive they were obviously planning for spring when the ground unfroze. The IX Corps and the X Corps would advance in the center, with the ROK I Corps and III Corps covering the eastern side of the line and the U.S. I Corps on the west around Inchon.

The UN offensive began on the morning of March 7. In the center of the line were the marines, with the 1st Cavalry Division on the left and the 2nd Infantry Division on the right. The ultimate objectives were the important communications centers of Hongchon and Chunchon. On the west was the 25th Division with the 89th Tank Battalion, which would cross the Han River and establish a bridgehead on the north bank of the Pukhan River, which flows into the Han. (See Map 31.)

Five miles beyond the point of departure of the marines lay Oum mountain, a bare peak that jutted up to 2,900 feet, amid a surrounding fortress of wooded hills. The roads in the area were virtually nonexistent, the maps called them "secondary," in Korea that usually meant a cart track.

The marines faced three divisions of the Chinese 66th Field Army, the Chinese 196th, 197th, and 198th divisions. In all, the enemy had around 24,000 men there in defensive positions.

The assault on the first day was carried by the 1st Marines on the right and the 7th Marines on the left. It was a cold morning, but clear, although a light snow was falling. The marines were ready for anything, but the resistance they encountered was slight. They reached their objectives in midafternoon and counted noses. In both regiments, only seven men had been wounded. One reason for the light casualties was the air support offered by Marine Air Group 33, whose planes blanketed the sky all day long. On the second day the resistance stiffened somewhat, but the combination of air power and the efforts of the artillery men of the 11th Marines made it possible for the infantry to take their objectives before dark. The hardest fighting of the day was that of Company A of the 7th Marines, which was held up for hours by a handful of enemy entrenched in log bunkers on a hill east of Oum-san. They were equipped with mortars and used them effectively, causing several casualties before the marines brought up tanks, and the 90 mm guns knocked the timber bunkers apart.

It was apparent that the Chinese were following Maoist strategy—when the enemy attacks, withdraw. The marines had pushed out in front in their area, so they stopped on the night of March 9 to wait for the rest of the force to move up on west and east.

On the west, the 35th Infantry of the 25th Division was moving ahead to cross the Han, supported by tanks of the 89th Medium Tank Battalion. On the morning of March 7 the tankers of Company A crawled out of their sleeping bags at three thirty and went to breakfast. The company was bivouacked in the battered village of Kwirin-ni, about two and a half miles south of the Han River. The company consisted of fifteen tanks and one tank recovery vehicle. The eight lead tanks pulled trailers, which carried nests of twelve-man assault boats for the infantry to use to cross the river. According to the Eighth Army plan, the tanks were not to cross, since the engineers estimated that the depth of the Han that day would be about nine feet. They would stay on the south bank in support of the infantry. At least those were the orders from higher up. The tanks would await the construction of a 50-ton-capacity floating bridge, which was supposed to be built across the Han on the afternoon of the first day.

Lieutenant Colonel Welborn G. Dolvin, commander of the 89th, wanted to get his tanks across as soon as possible to support the infantry, and when he had the plan on March 4 he told Captain Herbert A. Brannon, commander of Company A, to look for opportunities. That day Brannon went to the engineers and secured photos, but they proved to be of little use in determining a specific crossing area. The Chinese had kept up such an effective fire that observation planes had not been able to fly low or stay over the area for long. Brannon *thought* the aerial photos indicated a shallows at the crossing, but he was not certain. He went down to the south bank of the Han and walked along until he found a spot that might do. He was going to give it a try, at the point where the Pukhan joins the Han. A thousand yards upstream from the confluence is a small, flat island, which divides the Han into two channels, one 250 feet wide and the other 200 feet wide. Brannon would send one tank across here, towing a cable attached to the winch of the tank recovery vehicle. If the tank got stuck and bogged down in midriver, the recovery vehicle would tow it back. If it made the trip across, then the other tanks would follow.

On March 6 Captain Brannon brought his platoon leaders down to the river bank and showed them what he intended to do.

The tank column began to move at 4:30. The snow had stopped falling, which helped visibility, but it was still dark, and the drivers of the tanks could scarcely see the outlines of the road. They moved slowly, careful not to race engines, until they reached the riverbank. Here the engineers uncoupled the trailers, each carrying five assault boats. The tanks moved out to selected positions on the riverbank, prepared to open fire in support of the infantry. The area at the bank was quiet, except for an occasional shellburst across the river. At 5:55 the UN guns began to fire, 105 mm and 155 mm howitzers of the U.S. artillery and the guns of the British 45th Field Artillery Regiment. The tanks also began to fire across the river, although it was so dark the tankers could only hazily see the outlines of the hills where the Chinese were entrenched.

On schedule, at 6:15, the infantrymen of the 35th Infantry pushed the boats into the water and started the crossing, several hundred yards below the sandbar and island. The crossing went well, only a few boats were holed by enemy machine gun fire and a few men wounded. But on the far side, the troops were pinned down by enemy machine gun fire from the high ground and enemy artillery fire from the hills beyond. The enemy artillery also began shelling the south bank, which interfered with the engineers trying to build the bridge.

While they waited, Captain Brannon conferred with Lieutenant Colonel James H. Lee, commander of the 3rd Battalion of the 35th Infantry, whose troops had just crossed the river. Lee was skeptical of the tankers chances of making the crossing, but he agreed that Brannon could try if he wished. So Brannon called on Lieutenant Thomas Allie who had volunteered to make the effort.

The cable was attached to the tank and the recovery vehicle winch, and the tank started across, Lieutenant Allie standing in the open hatch and giving directions to the driver below. Midway across they discovered the depth was only three feet, which was easy enough for the Sherman tank. But the cable got hung up on the bottom and broke, tearing the coupling out of Allie's tank. It did not make much difference, the tank went across to the sand island.

On the island Lieutenant Allie saw that there were footings for an old bridge at the east end, and he decided to try that route. The water on the other side suddenly deepened, and for a moment it closed over the hatches of the drivers, wetting down Sergeant Guillory Johnson, but Johnson speeded up to keep the water from closing in behind the tank and drowning the engine, and in a moment they had reached the first footing for the old earthen bridge and were out of danger. The same wetting occurred two more times, but in less than two minutes overall the tank was across the river. Allie then called back for his second tank, and five minutes later he was joined by Sergeant First Class Starling W. Harmon. Then the third tank started across, but its escape hatch had jarred loose during the early morning barrage against the enemy, and it flooded out in midstream. The two other tanks of the platoon made it across safely, and Lieutenant Allie was ready for action with 80 percent of his force intact.

Even before they arrived, Allie was moving. The infantry had stalled about a thousand yards north of the Han, when they ran up against two fortified positions, one on a hill and the other on the railroad embankment. The tanks moved up, firing on the hill position. When fire stopped coming from there, they turned to the embankment, where half a dozen burned out freight cars stood. The Chinese had placed their machine guns to fire underneath the freight cars on the area below. It did not take the two tanks long to destroy the machine gun positions, and the infantry moved up six hundred yards, to be stopped by three more machine guns that began firing from concealed positions. Lieutenant Allie spotted one and turned his 76 mm gun on it. Two rounds sent parts of bodies and pieces of shattered metal up into the air. The other two tanks came up, and Master Sergeant Curtis D. Harrell located another machine gun, which he destroyed. The four tanks then used their machine guns for half an hour to cover the infantry as they advanced another seven hundred and fifty yards to the north side of the rail line.

Meanwhile, Captain Brannon had been sending other tanks across by platoon, and by ten o'clock all were across except the one flooded vehicle. Supported by the tanks, Lieutenant Commander Lee's 3rd Battalion reached its objective at noon. The flooded tank was hauled ashore by the recovery vehicle, repaired, and crossed over again early in the afternoon.

The U.S. X Corps, in the center of the peninsula, had the hardest going, largely because in the mountainous terrain it had to move through every enemy position was a "strong point" and demanded far more than the usual effort. The 23rd Infantry started the assault. Soon it became apparent that the front had to be kept very narrow, and massive artillery assaults had to accompany the infantry movement. In spite of the thawing that came in the second week of March, turning the roads into mud lanes and the paddies into quagmires, the troops moved. On March 13 the 38th Infantry relieved the 23rd in the line. The line moved steadily north, ragged, then straightening out, from west to east. On the east the ROK III Corps and I Corps had secured the eastern end at Kangnung.

The marines in the center of the UN line began advancing again east of

Hongchon after the two ends had caught up. Their objectives were along a narrow front, north of Oum-san. On March 11 the 3rd Battalion of the 1st Marines was engaged in heavy fighting for the prominence known as Hill 549. (See Map 32.) The Chinese here were dug in behind log-faced bunkers and were well armed. They let the marines come up close before opening fire and in the first burst killed one marine and wounded nine others. It took hard work at grenade range to quiet the enemy down, and then the artillery finished the job. Except for this place, the resistance was light as the marines moved up toward line Albany. They reached that line and held all points by March 14. The 38th Infantry had its own objectives, Reno line and Idaho line. Reno was achieved by March 14. All the way across, the enemy was definitely on the retreat by March 14. On that day a patrol from the ROK 1st Division crossed the Han River on the west side, and at 5:30 in the morning of the next day the Eighth Army forces marched on toward Seoul without meeting resistance. At 11:30 that morning the ROK troops reached the capitol building, and for the second time the enemy flags were hauled down. This time, South Koreans hauled up the ROK colors. Seoul was a sad and battered city. Once it had been a metropolis of a million people, now scarcely two hundred thousand remained, and they were suffering all the exigencies of war, from shock to malnutrition. Its buildings were mostly destroyed. The shopping district had been reduced to rubble by artillery fire. The streetcars were hunks of twisted steel, the tracks were bent, broken, or missing entirely. Power and water lines were smashed. But Seoul was back in South Korean hands, and the symbolism was meaningful. The war had come full circle. The UN forces were virtually astride the 38th parallel once more. Now what was to be done?

In Washington and New York the Americans and their Allies were attempting to find a political solution to the war. In January the Chinese had rejected attempts of the American bloc to achieve a cease-fire, an action which had at least made it impossible for the Soviet supporters and sycophants to achieve much success in trying to brand the UN forces as "aggressors." But solution to the war on the political level seemed as far away as ever, largely because the Chinese still believed they could amass enough force during their spring offensive to actually drive the UN forces out of Korea. Peking obviously had not had enough time to absorb the lessons of January and February. The "neutral" bloc, backed by Britain's Attlee government, favored the seating of Communist China in the UN, which was one of the Peking demands if the war was to end. Taking a great gamble (that the Chinese would not accept), the Americans voted in the UN for a motion that would bring a cease-fire, a conference of the United States, Britain, the USSR, and China to settle "Far Eastern problems," including the status of Formosa

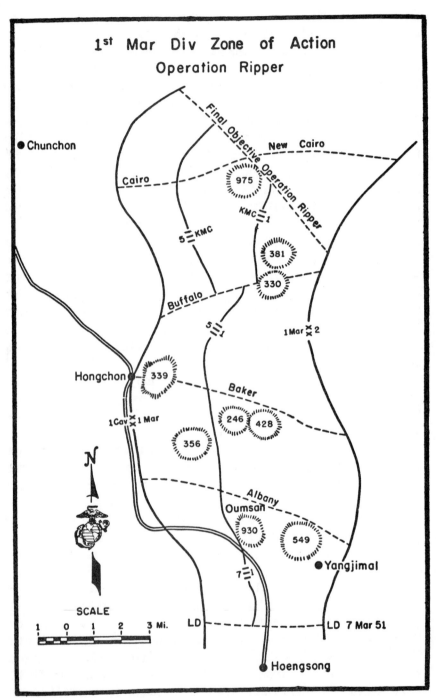

MAP 32

and China's UN seat. Never had the Chinese been closer to retrieving Formosa and settling the Korean War than at that moment.

At this juncture, Peking again miscalculated. Thinking they had the UN on the run, they insisted on prior admission to the UN and the prior U.S. withdrawal of protection from Formosa.

No United States politician dared make such concessions in the political atmosphere of 1951. Given the misunderstanding of Pacific affairs engendered by both parties, such a move would have been suicidal.

The war would continue. As for the 38th parallel, the same debate raged again in Washington and Tokyo. The State Department wanted the line stabilized there. The Joint Chiefs said it was impossible to tie the hands of the military thus. Everyone knew what MacArthur wanted, his view had never changed.

The matter ceased to be academic with the recapture of Seoul. What was needed was a clear statement of war aims. One was beginning to emerge in the Department of State. It called for a basic line of demarcation between the Koreas at the 38th parallel. The UN forces might move beyond that line in the fighting, but the idea of driving the Communists out of North Korea, destroying the North Korean regime, and unifying Korea under the Rhee government by force had been given up by the U.S. government, if not by MacArthur. The hawks in the State Department had been overcome.

In the field, General Ridgway opted to continue his advance north of the 38th parallel, but not with any idea of driving to the Yalu. He wanted to be certain he had done enough damage to seriously impede the Chinese spring offensive. So another limited military operation was to be launched immediately. Called Operation Rugged, its purpose was to establish "the Kansas line," which would generally be on the 38th parallel, except on the west, where it would follow the Imjin River to the sea and would include the Hwachon Reservoir, which was important for military and civilian reasons.

By the beginning of the last week in March, the UN forces were massed behind their line and ready to move. The marines had reached line Cairo. (See Map 32.) The Eighth Army had moved up about thirty-five miles in the past three weeks.

Military operations continued in Korea, even as in Washington a new chain of events had been precipitated by General MacArthur.

On March 15, while the administration in Washington was struggling with the question of the 38th parallel, General MacArthur told Hugh Baillie, president of the United Press Associations, that if the U.S. government in Washington forced the Eighth Army to stop at the 38th parallel it would prevent him from accomplishing his mission—which he saw as the reunifica-

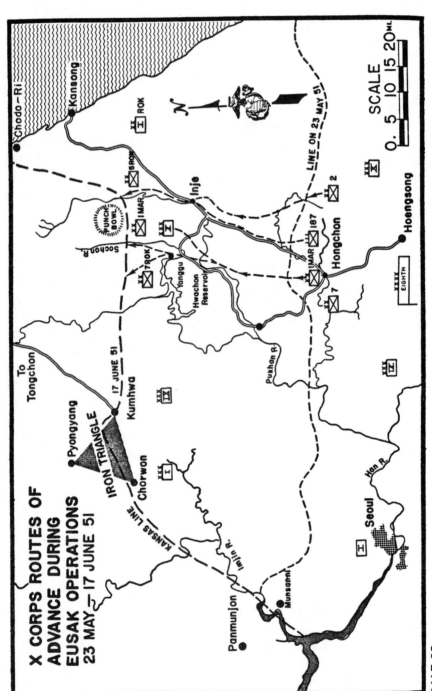

X CORPS ROUTES OF
ADVANCE DURING
EUSAK OPERATIONS
23 MAY — 17 JUNE 51

MAP 33

tion of Korea under the Rhee government. For months President Truman had been struggling with the problem of U.S. war aims in Korea. One thing of which Truman was certain was that at this moment, March 15, 1951, the aim was certainly not what MacArthur said it was. But there was no question—no question at all—but that General MacArthur was doing all he could to change American policy to bring about a resumption of full-scale war, if possible, a war that would wipe out Communist China. President Truman knew this was so. The source of his knowledge was a series of messages intercepted by American espionage agencies from Spanish and Portuguese diplomats in Tokyo, with whom MacArthur had been having most undiplomatic conversations. From President Truman's point of view, the general had crossed the line between loyal disagreement and political treachery. He was determined that MacArthur had to go, but he could not use those espionage intercepts to fire the general without creating a real mare's nest on the international scene.

When the UN force reached the 38th parallel again, the way was paved for a new U.S. diplomatic demarche. The State Department wanted to reopen the question of peace talks, without making any promises, and Truman agreed. MacArthur was informed of this impending development. He chose this time to make his own personal call on the Chinese to "talk peace," in the full knowledge that they could no longer win the war. Such a statement was calculated to infuriate the Chinese, and it did.

It also angered official Washington. MacArthur's continued criticism of official Washington policy during the next two weeks brought tempers around the White House to the boiling point.

The plan for Operation Rugged was issued on March 29. It called for the attachment of the 7th Marines to the U.S. Army 1st Cavalry Division for attack north of Chunchon. The 1st Marine Division, now augmented by the ROK 1st Marine Regiment to replace its own 7th Marines, would continue in the line, although it had expected to be relieved. It would support the 1st Cavalry and 7th Marines in the drive north.

The plan was regarded as set until April 6 when General Ridgway altered it to take cognizance of a strong enemy buildup in the Iron Triangle, a broad plain in the mountains bounded by Kumhwa, Chorwon and Pyongyang. (See Map 33.) The 1st Marine Division was moved up to relieve the 1st Cavalry Division and prepared to attack.

That day in Washington President Truman met with his closest advisors, Secretary Acheson, Secretary Marshall, General Bradley, and Averell Harriman, to decide what was to be done about MacArthur. On April 5 Representative Joseph Martin of Massachusetts, a bitter enemy of the administration, had read a letter on the floor of the House of Representatives in which

MacArthur had put forth his old views about the necessity of winning the war against communism in Asia.

Truman's advisors agreed that the general was beyond the pale. The only differences among them concerned what to do to stop MacArthur from subverting official government policy. When the Joint Chiefs of Staff informally indicated that they agreed to MacArthur's dismissal, and so told Secretary Marshall, the President decided to act. Army Secretary Frank Pace, Jr., was in Tokyo at the moment on a trip, and he was supposed to deliver the message quietly. Before he could do so, however, the press got onto the story, and the White House panicked and put out the announcement from Washington on the night of April 10 that General MacArthur had been relieved of command.

The war virtually came to a halt for the next few days.

General Ridgway was ordered to Tokyo to take command of the American forces in the Far East. Lieutenant General James A. Van Fleet was ordered to Korea to take Ridgway's old Eighth Army job. MacArthur returned to America to unleash a bath of emotionalism that for several days paralyzed the entire nation and made the Korean War a source of political upheaval for two months.

Meanwhile, the Chinese were preparing in earnest for their spring offensive. The thaws that had turned the icy land of Korea into a quagmire were nearly over.

At seven o'clock in the morning of April 21 the 1st Marine Division resumed its advance up the center of Korea, with the 7th Marines on the left and the 5th Marines in the center, the Korean marines on the right, and the 1st Marines in reserve. It was very quiet, eerily quiet, as they moved forward four miles that day. Other IX Corps troops had the same experience. The only ominous sign was a pall of smoke, green wood smoke, that hung over the line of advance. The enemy was burning the forests again, using the smoke screen to mask its troop movements. The marines up and down the line could sense that something was about to happen.

16

The Chinese Spring
Offensive, 1951

The Chinese preparations for their spring offensive were not confined to ground operations. For the first time an effort was being made to oppose, and perhaps to dominate, the United Nations forces in the air. It had begun in February, after the failure of the Chinese January offensive, which some officers laid to the failure of the Peking government to produce adequate air support for the ground troops. The Chinese had been able to put only about six hundred aircraft into the air over Korea in January, and General Liu Ya-lou, commander of the air force, intended to double that number by summer, when the drive was supposed to end with the push of the UN forces into the sea.

With the retreat of the Eighth Army south of Seoul, the U.S. Fifth Air Force had moved most operations back to Japan, which meant the Chinese were able to dominate the air corridors in northwest Korea and along the Yalu. During February and March the Chinese had also repaired and rebuilt ten important airfields and brought in many planes, including new MIG fighters. The territory between the Chongchon and Yalu rivers had become known as MIG Alley.

In the winter the Americans began bringing into Korean air action the F-84E fighters and F-86 Sabrejets, which were more of a match for the Soviet-built MIGs than the F-80 had been. The new Sabrejets, however, were run out of Kimpo airfield in January by the advance of the enemy, and it was not until the second week of February that Kimpo and Suwon were back in UN hands. The odds were more even, but the air war was a real war. On March 1, for the first time, a B-29 raid against the Yalu River bridges ran into real trouble, in spite of an escort of F-80s. A strong head wind had sapped the F-80s' fuel, so that the fighters had only a few minutes over the target, and the MIGs came up to haunt the B-29s. They damaged ten of the big bombers that day, three of them so badly that they had to be scrapped after their return to UN territory.

Obviously, MIG Alley was a formidable air corridor in the spring of 1951.

The air forces of the UN were continuing to hit the Yalu River bridges on the Korean side, and with good effect, but the going was difficult because the F-86s sent along to protect the bombers still could not fly successful MIG sweeps from so far south. Consequently, the B-29s *always* now had a rough time, as they did on April 12. The mission: hit the Yalu bridges again. That day twelve B-29s loaded with 2,000-pound bombs were sent from Okinawa against the bridges near Sinuiju, within sight of the MIG bases up there. They were escorted by F-84s and F-86s, but it was understood that by the time they got to MIG alley, the fighter cover would be nearly exhausted. They would have to go in to bomb alone.

The planes took off at dawn from Okinawa. It was a clear day, and two hours and forty minutes out they climbed to their assigned altitude and there met the fighter cover. At noon they approached the target. When they were five miles away from the bridges, the tail gunner of one B-29 suddenly shouted "MIGs."

Everybody looked, and there they were, about thirty enemy jet fighters, coming in on the formation at six o'clock. They broke off at four o'clock and tried to shoot up the tail gunners, then swung in for amidships shots. They were so close that the American gunners could see the muzzle blasts from the 23 mm cannon. They came in daringly, and one of them was shot down by Gunner Billie Beach, riding in "No Sweat," one of the veteran B-29s of the 19th Bombardment Group.

Three minutes later another MIG came in on the "No Sweat." Gunner Beach shot this one down, too, when it had reached a point only four hundred yards away.

In the course of this action the "No Sweat" had been hit bad, but she was still lucky. Two of the four planes in the "No Sweat"'s bombing formation had been shot down, and the third had turned back for Okinawa before bombing. The "No Sweat" was all alone in skies that were definitely unfriendly. The number two and number four engines were out, and the props feathered. The right aileron was gone. The interphone was out.

The commander of the aircraft considered bailing out at this point and rang the warning bell. But they were over enemy territory, and the antiaircraft fire was coming up in nasty black puffs far too close to the nacelle and wings. The aircraft commander decided against bailing out just then; he would make his bomb run. And he did, the plane limping in over the bridges.

After the bombs were dropped, every thought was for survival, and the next hour, moving slowly back through enemy territory was a long one. The number two fuel tank started to burn. The bomber lost altitude and barely cleared a peak or two but finally managed to reach one of the advance fighter bases along the Han River, to try a landing. The runway was too short, but there was no option. The "No Sweat" sideslipped in, hit hard on her landing gear, which collapsed, and slid along on belly and nosewheel. She collapsed with her nose across the road along the strip, and that was the end of her. But she had done her job.

In April a new job was given the B-29s: the destruction of General Liu's new airstrips up and down North Korea. Between April 23 and April 27 the major bombing and strafing effort, was devoted to the plastering of those Chinese airstrips. The UN forces intended to deny General Liu the air control he wanted to accompany the Chinese spring offensive.

Air forces and ground forces were not under much illusion about the state of the war, even though General Ridgway's early spring operations had been quite successful, particularly in restoring morale among the soldiers and in America.

In the winter of 1951 the Republic of Korea forces began to improve their performance at the regimental and divisional levels. Too often in the past a decision to place a South Korean unit in a strategic defensive position had led to disaster. But in the course of Operation Ripper the ROK 1st Division performed well as usual, and so did some other units. A battalion of the ROK 2nd Regiment virtually annihilated one Chinese battalion without losing a man. The ROK troops in this operation also captured four artillery pieces and seven mortars. At the command level, however, the situation was still dismal. One of General Ridgway's last acts before turning over command of the Eighth Army to General Van Fleet was to send an emissary to Seoul to inform President Syngman Rhee that a major overhaul of his high command, from defense minister down to the corps level, was very much needed. Until the South Koreans developed a proper military organization, he warned, there would be no further development of South Korean military forces by the American advisory groups.

As matters stood that April, it seemed that the United Nations and the Chinese and North Koreans were headed for stalemate. The forces committed were now nearly equal. The United States had sent 227,000 servicemen to

Korea. The British and other United Nations contingents numbered 21,000. The ROK forces numbered 250,000. So altogether the UN had nearly half a million men in the field. The Chinese had sent sixteen armies into Korea, or about 400,000 men. The North Koreans had reorganized and put 120,000 men in the field. The superiority in numbers that the enemy held over the UN was very slight, and that was at least matched by the UN superiority in weaponry and air power. The weakest segment of the UN force, by far, was the ROK Army. Altogether, the match was quite close. Some in Washington believed that stalemate was near, but General Ridgway warned that the loose positions of the Chinese above the 38th parallel could mean speedy withdrawal, but could also mean preparation for a new offensive.

That, of course, was what was coming, as the men in the UN line knew. Prisoners captured in March said that the fifth Chinese offensive was scheduled to begin on April 22 and the main line of attack would be down the center in the Pakyong–Chunchon region, against the IX Corps.

Once the UN command problems were sorted out after the sacking of General MacArthur, the UN forces, as noted, began to move again on April 21, but, on the left of the 1st Marine Division, the ROK 6th Division failed to maintain contact, and at the end of that day a gap of a mile and a half existed between the ROK forces and the marines.

The Chinese were prepared to launch their attack in the Iron Triangle. The marines had expected it for several days. In patrol encounters they had found leaflets that pointed to an enemy advance and crude propaganda signs with messages like: "Your Folks Like See You At Home."

That night the Chinese attacked the ROK forces, and the marines, poised to resume their drive the next morning, were warned that the Chinese advance was about to begin. They had two hours to prepare for the blow, and that was not enough time. Within minutes after the Chinese attack on the ROK 6th Division began, that unit started to collapse, and before midnight it was routed. The marines moved the 1st Battalion of the 1st Marines to the left of Chunchon to hold. The 1st Battalion of the 5th Marines was in Hwachon.

The division MPs were ordered to stop all ROK stragglers and put them under guard. Even so, the marine trucks rolling north had enormous difficulty getting through the thousands of ROK troops straggling along the roads.

The first marine units to be hit were the Korean marine battalions on Hill 509. By midnight they were virtually encircled. At Hwachon the Chinese made a determined attack on Hill 313, at the end of a long ridge that overlooked the town. Captain James T. Cronin's Company B began a footrace with the Chinese, the prize being the control of the hill. As the marines neared the summit the slope was so steep they had to crawl on hands and knees. Chinese machine gunners on the other side were raking the summit. The Americans could not get up, but they would not let the Chinese up either. The result was a stalemate with heavy casualties on both sides. Seven marines were killed and seventeen wounded. When Company F sent up reinforcements at dawn, they discovered that the enemy side of the hill had been abandoned. The Korean marines had also staged a counterattack and broken through the enemy surrounding them, so the area around Hwachon was stable on the beginning of April 23.

The major Chinese attack had been directed on the west, which was held by the 7th Marines. Major Webb Sawyer's 1st Battalion had the job of stopping the enemy from widening the salient gained by the collapse of the ROK 6th Division. About two enemy battalions were thrust against the 7th Marines here, and Captain Eugene H. Haffey's Company C took the brunt of the assault. The line bent, but, to the glory of the marines, it did not break. The deciding factor was the marine artillery, which responded nobly. After three hours of bitter fighting, the 1st Battalion of the 1st Marines arrived on the left flank of the 7th Marines and closed up. On the far side of the gap left by the fleeing South Koreans the U.S. 24th Infantry bent its line back and closed with the marines, and in the rear the British 27th Commonwealth Brigade was moving forward to meet the Chinese head-on and stop the penetration.

As daylight arrived, so did the marine air support. The Chinese behind Hill 313 and Hill 509 were worked over thoroughly, but on the edge of the Iron Triangle the U.S. 24th and 25th divisions were giving ground. The enemy seemed to be driving toward Seoul. General Ridgway had made the decision that Seoul was not to be given up again, because the significance of the capital was too great. The enemy was slowed while crossing the Imjin River that night.

On the morning of April 23 the marines were in good shape, but they faced the threat of the enemy on their left flank after the ROK collapse, and there was no alternative but to draw back to a line that faced west as much as north. The line's key was a horseshoe-shaped ridge held by B and C companies of the 1st Marines. In effect, the 1st Battalion of the regiment was facing three ways to block Chinese attack. The 3rd Battalion had moved to the village of Todun-ni on the west bank of the Pukhan River. (See Map 34.) Their key positions were Hill 902, a 3,000-foot prominence that dominated the area and the three ridge lines that led down. All these heights were manned by the battalion. The 1st Marines had built a new line of defense against an enemy they knew to be determined.

The expected attack began at eight o'clock on the night of April 23 west of Horseshoe Ridge with the bugle calls and the arching green flares of the

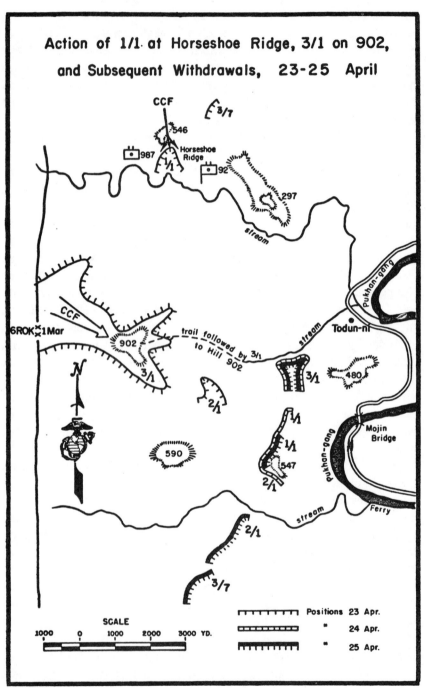

Action of 1/1 at Horseshoe Ridge, 3/1 on 902,
and Subsequent Withdrawals, 23-25 April

CCF

3/7

546

987   1/1   Horseshoe
               Ridge

92

297

stream

CCF

6ROK   1Mar   902   trail followed by 3/1   stream   Todun-ni
                       to Hill 902

3/1

2/1   1/1   480

Pukhan-gang

1/1

590   547

2/1   Mojin
       Bridge

Pukhan-gang

stream   Ferry

2/1

3/7

SCALE

1000   0   1000   2000   3000 YD.

Positions 23 Apr.
           24 Apr.
           25 Apr.

MAP 34

Chinese. There was no probing, the Chinese came on by the wave, chanting as they came "Awake, Marine. . . ."

It was the usual attack with burp gun and grenade, and the grenades were flying like snowflakes. In that first rush the enemy knocked out both the outpost machine guns of Company C and wounded ten men. Through the hole in the line they prepared to advance farther, and they were so numerous that the rest of the company had to give ground. Company C did so stubbornly and set up its position again about fifty yards behind the old line.

For four hours the Chinese attacked Horseshoe Ridge, but the marines held. The two companies in the line were reinforced from time to time by squads from the other companies. Men carrying back the wounded returned to the line carrying ammunition. Most notable was Corporal Leo Marquez, who led the carriers, bringing grenades and rifle ammunition forward all night long. He was hit in the cartridge belt, helmet, and the heel of one shoe, but he was not wounded. And the line held.

Meanwhile, the Chinese were harassing the 3rd Battalion of the 1st Marines on Hill 902 with mortar fire, and at midnight they attacked. Company G at the top of the ridge was nearly thrown off by the first wave but recovered, and the line stood. One reason for their success was the excellent artillery coverage by the 11th Marines and the U.S. Army's 987th Armored Field Artillery Battalion, which sent up three teams of observers and registered their defensive firing with pinpoint accuracy on the Chinese attackers. The two forward battalions, the 1st Battalion of the 1st Marines and the 3rd Battalion of the 7th Marines, had a wide gap between them but the enemy could not take advantage of it, because each time troops moved into the gap, the artillery and the American tanks mowed them down. At daybreak the gap was further covered by the airmen. The intelligence officers were busy, and they discovered that the two battalions that night had faced off the 359th and 360th regiments of the Chinese 120th Division of the 40th Field Army.

On the morning of April 24 the 1st Marine Division faced the problem of orderly withdrawal. There was no reasonable alternative, given the collapse of the ROK forces on their left. Besides, General Van Fleet was continuing General Ridgway's policy of attrition. It was important to destroy the enemy's material strength. It was not nearly so important to hold any position. The withdrawal was on, and the most seriously wounded were taken out by helicopter. Then the men of the 1st Battalion of the 1st Marines fought their way down the hill, carrying the other wounded, while the 2nd Platoon of Company C held as the rearguard.

The 3rd Battalion of the 7th Marines fought its way down from Horseshoe Ridge. The Chinese followed closely and threatened the army artillery, but the artillerymen picked up rifles and fought as infantry and drove them off, saving their guns. The airmen of the 1st Marine Aircraft Wing hovered above the ridges like cats, pouncing on the enemy as the Chinese tried to drive forward to break the retreating line. In the former ROK 6th Division sector, the 27th British Commonwealth Brigade came forward and held, stopping the enemy breakthrough that threatened to cut off the marines. But the British 29th Brigade was in more serious difficulty.

The 29th Brigade, operating under the control of the U.S. I Corps, was holding the line of the Imjin River 56 kilometers north of Seoul, from Choksong on the west to the junction of the Imjin and Hantan rivers on the right, when the Chinese started their offensive. They were flanked on the left by the ROK 1st Division and on the right by the U.S. 3rd Division. This was hill country, the highest peak being Kamak-san, a point of about 2,000 feet. The Imjin is shallow here, fordable almost everywhere, so it was not much of a barrier to the Chinese or the UN forces. The 29th Brigade was positioned south of the river and was making daily patrols across to the north side.

On April 22 the early morning patrol encountered strong enemy forces and was withdrawn. At ten o'clock in the morning a patrol of the Northumberland Fusiliers made contact with the enemy and later in the day so did the Belgian battalion on the right flank. Information from prisoners and air observation indicated that the enemy was moving in great force into the Iron Triangle area. By dusk, the Chinese had reached the river in front of the main position of the 29th Brigade.

Lieutenant G. Temple sent an ambushing patrol onto the south bank that night, and they observed the Chinese crossing. First came a half dozen Chinese, and then another half dozen, and in a few minutes the river was full of enemy troops. Temple's men held their fire until the Chinese were thirty feet away, then he gave the order to shoot. The Chinese fell like ninepins; Bren Gunner Private L. Allen counted ten dead Chinese before his position.

Lieutenant Temple's men beat off four separate Chinese attempts to cross the river here, then moved south to the lines of Company C.

The southern bank of the river was commanded by an eminence called Castle Hill. Company A was settled here, and it received a major attack at midnight. Company D was astride the road on the east, Company B was sitting on a hill in front of Kamak-san. The X Company held the right center, and two companies of the Belgian battalion held the far right. Before dawn the Chinese had infiltrated around the right to the south, and in the early morning hours the 29th Brigade had to move out. Company A was badly hit. Its commander, Major P. A. Angier, was killed, and by midmorning only one officer of the company was left on his feet.

Castle Hill fell. Then Lieutenant Philip Curtis counterattacked with men from Company A to try to take out a Chinese machine gun emplaced on the top of the hill. Covered by artillery fire, he led twenty men up the hill, across open ground. Before they had moved twenty yards three men fell dead. Four more were wounded in the next minute. Curtis was hit twice but continued to lead the advance. The men were stopped, but Curtis went on. Once he fell but got up. Staggering from multiple wounds, he made his way alone to the top of the hill and hurled two grenades into the Chinese machine gun position. The gunners fired into Curtis's body, and then the grenades blew them up. Curtis was awarded the Victoria Cross, posthumously.

The British position was battered and partly overrun. They faced at least three battalions of the Chinese 187th and 188th divisions, and by midday they were surrounded, holding a front seven miles long with only five companies. It was impossible to prevent penetration by Chinese elements. On the morning of April 23 the units closed into smaller defensive perimeters. On the left the Gloucester Battalion held one hill. On the far right the Belgians managed to withdraw to a point behind the main force, with the assistance of some American tanks.

By the evening of the 23rd, however, the 29th Brigade faced at least an entire Chinese division. Brigadier T. Brodie, commander of the brigade, might have retreated yet, through the thin line to the south. But he chose to hold and blunt the Chinese attack here, with his four infantry battalions.

On April 24 the surviving men of the Gloucestershire Battalion withdrew from Choksong to a hill to the south. The battalion was quickly surrounded. During the afternoon the other units of the 29th Brigade tried to extricate them by counterattack and failed. A detachment of Filipino tanks came up, but they also failed to break through the Chinese line. That night British Centurion tanks tried again and failed.

American planes came over to drop supplies to the beleaguered battalion, but the drops fell into the hands of the enemy. An American helicopter tried to land on a flat spot to evacuate the wounded, but the Chinese fire was so severe it had to withdraw. Still the battalion held its hill and thus held up the advance of thousands of Chinese.

Lieutenant Colonel J. P. Carne kept his men fighting until he could see that there was no more hope of stopping the enemy. He then told them to separate into small groups, infiltrate through the enemy lines and escape to the line of the brigade. In the end only forty men made it.

Piled around what was to be known as Gloucester Hill were the bodies of five hundred Chinese soldiers, and the brigadier estimated that at least a thousand more had been wounded and evacuated.

On the night of April 24 came orders from corps headquarters for the brigade to withdraw. The troops moved out next morning and arrived at noon at Uijongbu, about twenty-five kilometers north of Seoul. From there they moved further south for reorganization and went into reserve. The 29th Brigade had lost 25 percent of its men, with the Gloucestershires practically wiped out. Still they had frustrated the Chinese effort to break the UN front, and for three days they had stopped the drive along the road toward Seoul. Total brigade casualties came to a thousand, but Chinese casualties were ten times as high. The fifth Chinese advance had been halted here in the battle of the Imjin River, primarily through the efforts of a small heroic band of Britons.

17

The Second Chinese
Spring Offensive

The Chinese spring offensive failed. In the east the Chinese made gains in the Yanggu–Inje area against the ROK forces, but by April 29 they were halted all along the line.

General Van Fleet organized the UN forces along the No Name line, which ran from a point above Seoul to Sabangu in the center, and then roughly along a line slightly north of the 38th parallel. Van Fleet also strengthened the western side of the line by adding more American units. The 1st Marine Division was returned to the X Corps command and held the center of the line along with the U.S. 2nd Division.

During the first week of May the UN forces moved forward about ten miles above the No Name line. Uijongbu, which had been abandoned at the height of the Chinese offensive, was recaptured, and the Kimpo peninsula was cleared of enemy troops. Chunchon was recaptured, and the Seoul–Kapyong road was taken back.

The Chinese were not finished for the spring, however. They planned to renew the offensive, and they had a thousand planes and fifty new air bases in preparation. When intelligence indicated that the Chinese air power was really becoming a threat, the U.S. Fifth Air Force stepped up its operations and in the second week of May struck hard with B-29s and fighter bombers at these bases. For example, on May 9, 312 UN planes hit Sinuiju air base, and knocked out fifteen enemy jets on the ground and a hundred buildings that housed repair shops and stored parts.

On the ground General Van Fleet spent the first ten days of May strengthening the UN position all long the line. At first he expected the enemy assault to fall on the western side of the line, but that changed when the Chinese moved five armies eastward to the center of the peninsula, in the Chunchon–Inje area. The attack seemed to be headed for the X Corps line, and captured prisoners, who knew a remarkable lot about the Chinese plans, indicated that the U.S. 2nd Infantry Division would feel the brunt of it.

Major General Clark L. Ruffner, the commander of the 2nd Division, got ready for a fight. His division occupied the center of the No Name line, along the crest of hilly country between the Hongchon and Soyang rivers. The division's front line covered a distance of about sixteen air miles, but at least twice that much lineage if measured up and down the hills and ravines. On the right was a tank-infantry task force. On the left was the 38th Infantry Regiment. Colonel John C. Coughlin, commander of the 38th, stationed his 1st and 3rd battalions in the line, with the 2nd Battalion in reserve. Each of the line battalions centered its defense around a high point; the 1st Battalion around Hill 1051 and the 3rd around Hill 800.

The latter hill was typical of the X Corps positions, located on a dirt track ten miles from the main route of supply. At the base of the hill the road ended, and the way up was by shank's mare, 1,600 feet of hike to the top of Hill 800. All the equipment of war was to be carried up over a footpath.

When Lieutenant Colonel Wallace M. Hanes was told that he was to defend Hill 800, he took the job seriously. He told his officers that they were to clear fields of fire and construct bunkers. He meant bunkers, not glorified foxholes, and that became eminently clear on the second day of the assignment. He put the men to work hauling up logs and sandbags. Someone said something about needing 5,000 sandbags. More like 20,000, said the colonel. Hanes was not kidding: he wanted bunkers that could withstand artillery fire, because during a Chinese offensive he might have to bring the artillery fire right in on top of the men.

Seven hundred Korean civilians were employed to help build these defenses on Hill 800. They carried up 237,000 sandbags, 385 rolls of barbed wire, 6,000 pickets for the wire, and other supplies. Thirty-two oxen were used to drag up the hill a section of 4.2-inch mortars and all the ammunition the colonel thought they would need. Grenades were brought up by the case.

Hill 800 was joined to Hill 916 by a bald ridge. It was here, the colonel believed, that the enemy would attack, and so two barbed wire aprons were laid along the ridge, one near Hill 913, and the other surrounding three sides of

Hill 800 and facing Hill 916. Inside the barbed wire the engineers built trip wires and laid flares, booby traps, and mines. The most important weapons were thirty-nine fougasses, made of fifty-five gallon drums filled with gasoline and napalm, triggered into flame by explosives with detonators. These fougasses would spread a flame ten yards wide and forty yards long. The colonel also demanded that his men bury their telephone lines and dig communications trenches. In the end, twenty-three bunkers of logs and sand were built on the little hill.

Some of the men could not understand all the fuss. They christened the colonel's hill Bunker Hill (not to be confused with the marines' Bunker Hill of a later date). Some, told to bury the communications lines, goofed off on the job. They could not understand the need for so much trouble. Even General Van Fleet, when he visited the area, said he had never seen such a fortification in all the corps defenses. Each bunker was equipped with at least twenty grenades and a stack of ammunition. The colonel, it seemed, was preparing for a siege.

While this fortification was going on the 2nd Infantry Division established an advance patrol base about five miles in front of the main line of resistance and sent patrols up as far as the Soyang River. By May 10 the patrols reported that the enemy was building for a new offensive, moving troops along the roads and dispatching more aggressive patrols to probe UN positions. There was another telltale clue, the number of refugee civilians from the north increased suddenly.

On May 16 the Chinese struck. The day was dark with a heavy overcast that prevented the fighter planes and observation planes from flying over the area. That afternoon the Chinese sent their probing patrols south, and that night they attacked in strength and took Hill 1051 from the 1st Battalion. The area around Hill 800 was quiet. The next day, May 17, the men strung more wire around the hill and made more fougasses, which they placed along the probable enemy lines of approach. Late in the afternoon a patrol moved over to Hill 916. It ran into heavy enemy fire and came back. Some enemy troops pursued the patrol until they were driven off by supporting fire from Hill 800. The men of Company K, the defenders of Hill 916, had to assume that the enemy lurked in force behind it.

As dusk came, Captain George R. Brownell moved up to the farthest forward observation post on the tip of the hill and took over a bunker there with his runner and two intelligence observers from the battalion headquarters. Night came silently. It was too quiet. Then at 9:30 came the sound of whistles and the blare of a Chinese bugle. Silence again. A few trip flares exploded but not many. Then the Chinese attacked. They had slipped around the side of the hill, avoiding the first line of barbed wire and cutting it as they came up from the side. They now faced the second line of barbed wire and had to attack this frontally. Immediately the flares began to go up, and the Americans responded with grenades and rifle fire.

Captain Brownell wanted artillery fire immediately and tried to get it. Unfortunately his artillery observer was in another bunker, and the telephone line failed, either because the Chinese cut it or because it was hit by a mortar round. Then the telephone line to the 1st Platoon failed. The Americans were paying the price of their failure to bury the wires deep.

In that area were a number of men of Company M who had been sent in to help, under the command of a lieutenant just up from the replacement depot. When the firing became heavy, the lieutenant decided he had had enough of the war for that day and headed down the hill. About twenty of his men followed him, leaving an enormous hole in the center of the hill's defenses, which the Chinese almost immediately found. They began to occupy the bunkers and crawl toward the top.

A shell landed in Captain Brownell's bunker, knocking out the radio set with which he was in touch with battalion headquarters. With all its bunkers, the hill was now vulnerable because of the failure of communications.

Captain Brownell started back down the hill to round up his second platoon and bring those men to counterattack and retake the positions abandoned by the lieutenant and the men of Company M. Back at battalion headquarters Lieutenant Colonel Hanes ordered artillery fire onto the hill to drive the Chinese off. Two men manning a recoilless rifle in one bunker had a good view of the action and a telephone, and they kept giving the colonel instructions about the placement of the artillery fire.

Lieutenant Blair Price lined up about thirty-five men to make a counterattack and moved up. And at the bottom of the hill the lieutenant from Company M found Colonel Hanes waiting for him when he came down, and Hanes sent the lieutenant and the men right back up the hill to fight again.

Captain Brownell, Lieutenant Price, and Lieutenant Herbert E. Clark, leader of the second platoon, launched their counterattack and ran smack into a pair of machine guns, one Chinese and the other a Company K gun that the Chinese had captured. The enemy in the bunkers were throwing American white phosphorus grenades and so were the Americans, so it was hard to tell friend from foe, or position from position.

Captain Brownell's men moved up slowly and finally reached the apex of the hill where they killed three Chinese. By one thirty in the morning they had spread out to occupy the rest of Hill 800. They reoccupied all the bunkers except the one farthest north, and that one was already held by privates first class George Hipp, Clarence Rick, and Rodney R. Rowe, who had waited out the surge of Chinese all around them. They had a worse time from their friends than from the enemy, because the men of Company K, assuming that the three were all dead, kept firing at their bunker all night long. Not until daylight were they able to identify themselves.

By daylight communications were reestablished on Hill 800, and all was secure.

On the left flank of Company K's front, the Chinese attacked in force. They overran the right flank of Company I and the left flank of Company K, but the reserve platoon of Company I sealed up the gap and restored the line.

When morning came on May 18 the men on Hill 800 went out to scout and found eight bodies of Chinese soldiers, most of them along the barbed wire in front of the American position. They also found many unexploded grenades on the side of the hill. The Chinese had thrown them without pulling the pins.

That day Company K rebuilt its defenses. This time the telephone wires were dug in deep, under eight inches of dirt. This time the forward observer of the 38th Regiment's artillery registered the artillery in a semicircle around Company K for future reference.

Colonel Hanes examined his defenses and found a gap between Company K and Company I. He had been told that the gap was slight, but he discovered that his troops had not after all recovered all the bunkers that the Chinese had captured and that it was estimated that several hundred Chinese soldiers were occupying them.

He would have to dislodge the Chinese before dark or have plenty of trouble in the night. So he organized a counterattack force and prepared by ordering the firing of a thousand rounds of 4.2-inch mortar ammunition into the bunkers he had planned so carefully.

As the counterattack began and the mortar fire picked up, the Chinese panicked and abandoned the bunkers, and, as they started down the hillside, the artillery opened up on them, using the coordinates secured earlier. Also a pair of half-tracks in the Company I sector poured the enfilading fire of their quadruple .50 caliber machine guns into the Chinese as they tried to scramble through the barbed wire entanglements. The mortar men fired so rapidly that they bent the base plates of some mortars and burned out some tubes. The infantry moved up and attacked the Chinese as they scurried away. The casualties among the enemy were very high, the position was completely closed, and the 3rd Battalion did not lose a man in the counterattack.

By the end of the day Company K had rebuilt its defenses, and they were stronger than ever. As dusk fell, the Chinese massed behind Hill 916 and prepared to attack.

East of the 3rd Battalion of the 38th Infantry, the Chinese had been more successful the night before. They had driven out two ROK divisions and parts of the U.S. 2nd Infantry from the No Name line. Because the ROK troops had failed again, X Corps was forced to turn on its right flank to prevent envelopment.

Back on Hill 800 all was well. As night came, Colonel Hanes called for artillery fire behind Hill 916, and this fire disrupted the Chinese as they were assembling for their night attack. When the Chinese formed up again, and the bugles began to blow, Hanes called for more artillery fire and got it. This happened still another time, and then the Chinese got their attack under way. When it came, Hanes did what he had said he might do: he called for fire on top of the American bunkers. The shells came in, exploded just above the American bunkers by proximity fuses. In eight minutes the artillery put two thousand shells into the air to explode over the American positions on Hill 800. Hanes called Captain Brownell for a reaction:

"The position is completely covered with fire," said Brownell. "Nothing above ground could live in this."

The men of Company K sat in their bunkers as hell raged around them and waited out the night. The observers shifted the fire around to meet enemy concentrations. The 38th Field Artillery Battalion fired ten thousand rounds between ten o'clock that night and four o'clock the next morning. When daylight came, the Chinese had completely disappeared, and Company K was in full possession of the hill. All around them the UN forces had fallen back, and in the morning the 3rd Battalion of the 38th Infantry showed as a big bulge in the center of the UN line. That would never do. The UN strategy was not to seek territory, but to punish the enemy. It would be far less costly to bring the battalion back than to bring the army up. So the battalion was withdrawn, and the men of Company K, having taken everything the enemy could hand out, had to abandon their positions and retreat to solidify the UN line once again.

Elsewhere, the Chinese attack was temporarily more successful. The ROK 5th and 7th divisions in the Hangye and Inje areas fell back. The Chinese virtually surrounded the U.S. 2nd Division, but the 9th Infantry drove north, and the 23rd and 38th Infantry regiments pushed south, and the threat was wiped out. The Eighth Army straightened out its lines. The 1st Marines fought a brief engagement with the Chinese on May 20 and defeated them soundly. The Chinese had suffered badly for their attempts. Casualties of the X Corps were around a thousand, those of the Chinese around 70,000.

The enemy retreated as fast as possible, but the retreat was more like a rout. As the weather cleared, the UN air forces were out in strength, bombing and strafing the roads. The Chinese forces were even trying to move in the daylight hours. By May 31 Chinese casualties were estimated to be 105,000, including 17,000 dead and 10,000 prisoners of war.

But in the line, some, like the men of the 38th Infantry, were wondering what had happened to the war, and what the brass was trying to do.

18

Punchbowl

With the failure of the Chinese spring offensives, General Van Fleet decided to undertake another limited drive north, to punish the Chinese even more severely. The 1st Marine Division would be sent to capture Yanggu on the eastern end of the Hwachon Reservoir. The 187th Airborne Division would move against Inje, to retake that ground sacrificed by the ROK default of a few weeks earlier. They were to move in connection with the U.S. 2nd Division. The final objective of the 187th was the town of Kansong on the west coast, and, if all went well and they moved rapidly enough, the UN force might surround and cut off an enormous number of Chinese—all the Chinese south of the Inje–Kansong road. (See Map 35.)

The marines moved out at 8 A.M. on May 23. The next day the 5th Marines hit a strong pocket of enemy resistance on three hills north of Hanggye, but with tank and air support they took the positions before midnight.

General Almond, commander of the X Corps, was eager to try to close his trap, so he ordered the 187th Airborne to move out on the road to Inje. Two battalions attacked on May 23 and gained four miles. That was not enough for Almond. On the morning of May 24 he ordered a mobile task force to move up to the Soyang River and seize the bridge site—that day. Colonel William Gerhardt, executive officer of the 187th Airborne, decided that he would personally lead the task force. It would consist of an infantry battalion, a

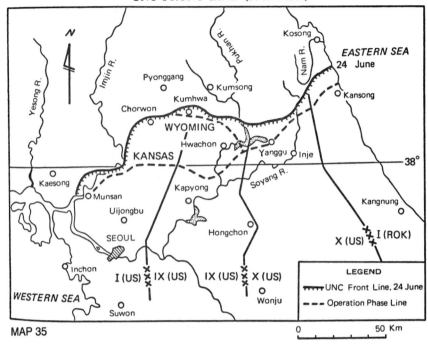

MAP 35

0   50 Km

company of engineers, a squad from the reconnaissance platoon, and a battery of artillery. The 2nd Division would supply two companies of tanks and four half-tracks mounted with quadruple .50 caliber machine guns. In his usual precipitate fashion, General Almond insisted that all this be done and the task force be moving two hours and twenty minutes after he had the idea. There was no way that could be done. Most of the 72nd Tank Battalion was located on the wrong side of a difficult mountain pass twenty miles south of Hangye. It would take them at least three hours to reach that town. The single company readily available was Company B, already in support of the 187th Airborne at Hangye.

Lieutenant Colonel Elbridge Brubaker, commander of the tank battalion, and Major James H. Spann, his operations officer, flew up to Hangye by liaison plane and learned what was required. They instructed Captain William Ross that his Company B would send a platoon to make the point of the task force along with a platoon of engineers and the squad from the 187th's Intelligence and Reconnaissance Platoon. Task Force Gerhardt they called it.

Captain Ross chose his 3rd Platoon for the task. Shortly after noon Colonel Gerhardt told him to send the point platoon three miles forward to Puchaetul, which was to be the point of departure. (See Map 36.)

But who was to command the point?

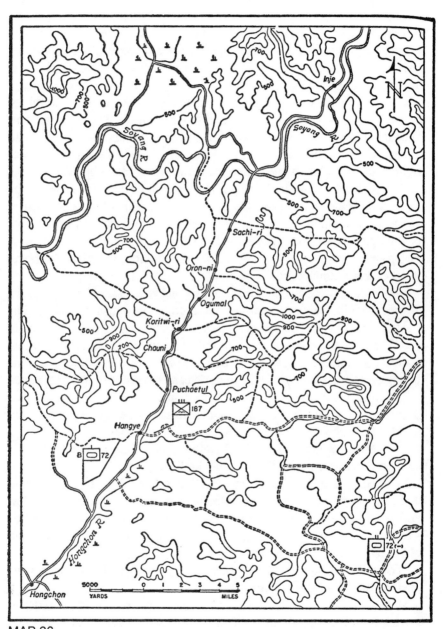

MAP 36

Colonel Brubaker had planned to send his executive officer to do the job, but the exec was two hours away with the battalion. Brubaker happened to encounter the assistant executive officer, Major Charles Newman, who was inspecting the wreckage of tanks destroyed in the Chinese spring offensive. Newman was chosen to organize the point. Brubaker rode up to Puchaetul in Newman's jeep, and they met Colonel Gerhardt there. The operation was already in motion. The eleven I and R men in three jeeps and the engineers in two 2½-ton trucks were on the road with the engineers, looking for mines. Gerhardt had borrowed a company of tanks from the 3rd Division. This company would move out with the main force. Gerhardt informed Newman that he had arranged for air support. All they had to do to put it in motion was to fire white phosphorus shells, and the planes would soon be over.

Shortly after 1 P.M. Major Newman's M-4 medium tanks moved out, led by the platoon leader, Lieutenant Douglas L. Gardiner. Each tank was armed with a 76 mm cannon, a .30 caliber machine gun in the bow, and a .50 caliber machine gun at the turret. They carried seventy-one rounds of ammunition for the big gun, forty-nine boxes of .30 caliber ammunition, and thirty-one boxes of .50 caliber ammunition.

Two miles out of Puchaetul the tanks met the I and R men and the engineers. Major Newman reformed the column. Two tanks led, followed by a jeep. Two more tanks followed the jeep, and they were followed by another jeep. Then came the two trucks and the last jeep. The column moved out again and advanced a mile to the outpost at Koritwi-ri, where it stopped while the engineers moved forward with mine detectors to probe the road for mines.

As the column waited, a helicopter landed on the road, and out of it stepped General Almond. He demanded an explanation, and, when he got it, he did not like it. He shook his swagger stick at Major Newman.

"You get those tanks on the road and keep going until you hit a mine. I want you to keep going at twenty miles an hour."

Newman ordered the column to move forward in fifth gear, which meant about twenty-two miles an hour. Almond got into his helicopter and flew back to the 187th Airborne command post, where he began to raise hell because the main body of the task force had not yet moved out. Major Spann told him the tanks were waiting for the infantry.

"You tell Brubaker," said the general, "to get that tank column moving whether the tanks have infantry support or not."

Meanwhile, Colonel Gerhardt had formed up his task force and was moving onto the road north, the tanks intermingled with trucks and other vehicles. It was quite a job to get them out of the mass and alone onto the road north. But he got the 1st Platoon moving.

The Newman column had come across several enemy positions, firing on them with the cannon and machine guns, and had killed a pair of Chinese infantrymen alongside the road with a bazooka rocket before the enemy could fire. This encounter had taken place near a destroyed bridge across a stream where a number of Chinese were holed up. The column had received some rifle and machine gun fire here and had killed the enemy machine gunner and routed ten men, five of whom they shot down. The others escaped.

The point force moved on, firing at anything that seemed suspect. They saw a Chinese in a cave and fired into it. Here they killed seven enemy soldiers. A mile farther along the road they routed another band of Chinese.

South of Oron-ni the column had to pass through a narrow defile, and Major Newman expected trouble here. Lieutenant Gardiner's lead tank approached the pass gingerly. He saw two houses there that commanded the road and so informed Major Newman. Newman told him to set fire to the houses, and he began shooting. The houses burned, but no one came out. The column then sped on through the pass. As the last two tanks passed through, two machine guns on a fifty-foot hill east of the road opened fire on the rear of the column. The I and R jeeps were all equipped with machine guns, and the gunner of the last jeep returned the fire, and so did the gunmen of several of the tanks. A liaison plane came over and dropped a green smoke bomb to attract attention and then dropped a grenade container. One of the I and R men retrieved the container. It held a message: over the hill the pilot had spotted a large number of troops east of the road. Did they want an air strike? If so, the tanks could fire several rounds of white phosphorus, which would bring the aircraft in a hurry.

Major Newman was in too big a hurry to wait for an air strike. They destroyed the two machine guns and moved on into Oron-ni, where they encountered more Chinese among the shabby white houses. A brief firefight brought forth four Chinese prisoners, who were put in one of the trucks at the rear. Major Newman sent a message back to Colonel Gerhardt: they were hurrying on, and he hoped more tanks would be on the road coming to join them. The 1st Platoon was already moving out, ahead of the Gerhardt column.

Newman's column sped on through Oron-ni. They passed more Chinese on a ridge west of the road and fired their machine guns without even slowing. When the lead two tanks crossed a culvert, a group of Chinese ran from the east side of the road into it. Major Newman sent the I and R men to take care of them and prevent them from firing on the tanks. Thirty-seven Chinese came out and surrendered. They, too, were sent back to the trucks. But the I and R men on foot had encountered a much larger force at the end of the draw, and the sound of firing continued. The last two tanks opened fire on the draw, and the enemy firing stopped.

This firefight had consumed about twenty minutes, and, after it, the Americans piled into the vehicles and sped on up the road. The column moved forward to Sachi-ri, where they encountered about two hundred Chinese who opened fire from both sides of the road. Some of them were dug in on hills beyond the village. The tanks stopped and fired, while the I and R men moved forward on foot. Another thirty Chinese surrendered.

Newman now had too many prisoners. He detailed four of the engineers as guards and left them there, with all the Chinese prisoners, to await the coming of the Gerhardt column. He also radioed back to Gerhardt to hurry those other tanks forward because matters were becoming complicated.

Just beyond Sachi-ri, the tank column encountered a group of about a hundred enemy soldiers, marching with several pack animals. The tanks opened fire and dispersed this column, killing perhaps half the Chinese. A few miles farther on they came upon another group and repeated the performance.

A plane came over and dropped another message. Four thousand enemy troops were moving a mile north of the column, and two flights of American planes were on their way to make a napalm strike on them. The tankers were warned to wait until the air strike was finished.

Lieutenant Gardiner, who had retrieved the message, took it to Major Newman.

"What are we going to do now?" he asked.

"We're going to attack the Chinks," said Newman. "If we turn back we'll run into General Almond."

So they did. As they moved up, along came the jets, so low that the tankers could feel the heat from their engines as they passed overhead to bomb and strafe the Chinese. The enemy column was only five hundred yards away by that time. The tanks moved in and attacked as the enemy column was still trying to recover from the air strike. It was completely disrupted: the Chinese scattered and fled into the hills. The tanks were now within sight of the Soyang River, and the tankers could see large groups of Chinese moving along the river banks. The tankers were busy firing most of the afternoon. The other two platoons of tanks soon came up, and, finally, the Gerhardt column arrived at about 6:30 that evening. That night the task force camped on the bank of the Soyang River. But the trap did not close; the Chinese managed to get the majority of their troops out of the area before they could be surrounded. General Almond's big gesture was widely applauded, then and later, as an example of creative leadership by high authority, but just what it accomplished was not quite certain. Certainly, many Chinese had been killed and captured, but the Chinese still had about 700,000 men in Korea or ready to be committed to Korea. It was going to take a lot more than tank exploits and "creative leadership" to bring the war to an end.

The Chinese had begun playing an entirely new game, using the North Koreans, to protect their own movements. The marines discovered this change at about the time of General Almond's exploit.

On the left of the 187th Airborne area the marines moved up along the south shore of the Hwachon Reservoir and routed and captured large units of troops. Most of them were North Koreans, and the marines learned that the Chinese had assigned the NK 12th Division the task of fighting delaying actions so that the bulk of the Chinese army could move north.

During the last five days of May the marines advanced steadily on the road to Yanggu. On May 31 the 7th Marines fought their way up parallel ridges in the steep pass that led to the town and, aided by tanks, took Yanggu.

On June 1 they continued to slog along toward the line called Kansas. The going was hard against heavy enemy resistance. On June 2 they fought along an extended ridge that ran northeast from Yanggu and gave access to the southern rim of the Punchbowl—so called because it was an area of flat terrain surrounded by hills. The North Koreans were manning log bunkers on the hills around the Punchbowl, and they made life hard for the marines, even when air strikes came in to help. Hill 610 gave a great deal of trouble. It was captured on June 2. The North Koreans counterattacked that same night. The marines fought off the counterattack, got a few hours of sleep, and the next day had to repeat the performance on Hill 680—and then later on Hill 692.

A single apparently small incident can affect the course of an entire military operation, and what happened to the marines on June 2 is a good example:

On that morning the 1st Marines relieved the 7th Marines in the forward line. At 8 A.M., Lieutenant Colonel Homer Hire, commander of the 3rd Battalion of the 1st Marines, went forward to make a reconnaissance. His group was hit by a mortar barrage, one officer was killed and two forward observers, four company commanders, the battalion operations officer, and thirty-two enlisted men were wounded. The battalion was stunned, and its attack had to be postponed for an entire day so that it could be reorganized. One handful of well-placed mortar shells had stopped the marines cold.

The drive was toward the Punchbowl, and that meant the mountain range north of Yanggu. In this area the North Koreans had been assigned to hold until death. For five days the South Korean marines carried the action, but the North Koreans fought as fiercely as they ever had. On June 10 the South Korean marines did something quite unusual for them—they staged a night attack. It caught the North Koreans completely by surprise, and the result was the capture of Taeam-san, the central mountain defense position.

On the left flank the 1st Marines prepared to attack the ridges north of the

Hwachon Reservoir. The going here was equally hard. It was June 14 before the 1st Marines reached a point three thousand yards north of the Kansas line. They called it the Brown line, in honor of Colonel Wilburt S. Brown, who had recently taken command of the 1st Marines. On June 18 the enemy staged a counterattack to retrieve the high ground. The 3rd Battalion of the 7th Marines made five separate defenses against superior Chinese forces. Through many acts of individual bravery, the marines held, and, as night ended, they were still on the high ground.

Next morning, when the marines looked for the enemy, they were gone. By the morning of June 20, the new line was secure. The marines had been fighting steadily for two months and had reached the Punchbowl. They now held the southern rim.

In June the U.S. 3rd Division advanced to hold line Wyoming from Chorwon to Kumhwa, on the southern axis of the Iron Triangle, the area between Pyonggang, Chorwon, and Kumhwa that had for over a year served as the major mobilization area for North Korean and Chinese troops. On June 11 Chorwon was captured, and the 25th Division took Kumhwa. Only Pyonggang remained to be cleared up. On June 13 elements of the 3rd Division, called Task Force Hawkins, entered Pyonggang, and the Iron Triangle was in American hands. This advance, however, had taken the

THE IRON TRIANGLE AREA

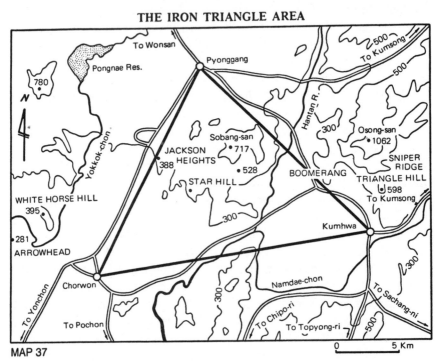

MAP 37

American troops too far from their stabilized line, and they moved back that same day after clearing out the enemy troops. The Chinese and North Koreans moved back in.

On June 30 the Eighth Army ordered the U.S. I Corps to launch another limited offensive toward Pyonggang, because the Chinese had begun a new buildup in the Iron Triangle. (See Map 37.) Task Force Hawkins was reconstituted; it now consisted of the 64th Tank Battalion, the 3rd Battalion of the 65th Infantry, and a company of engineers. Its assignment was to conduct a "reconnaissance" and inflict maximum punishment on the enemy forces building in the area. This action was to work in conjunction with an attack by the 7th Regiment on Sobang-san, Turyu-bong, and Palli-bong, three prominent and troublesome hill positions. The ROK 9th Division was also involved in the action.

At 4 A.M. on July 1 the 7th Regiment started off in the center. The troops advanced easily until 5:30 that evening when they began receiving heavy enemy fire. They stopped short of Turyu-bong to set up their perimeter. (See Map 38.)

On the west side Task Force Hawkins made good progress, cleared the area, and retreated that same day. The other elements fought for two more days, exhausted the enemy in the center of the Iron Triangle, and withdrew.

ATTACK ON SOBANG-SAN AND PYONGGANG (1–4 July 1951)

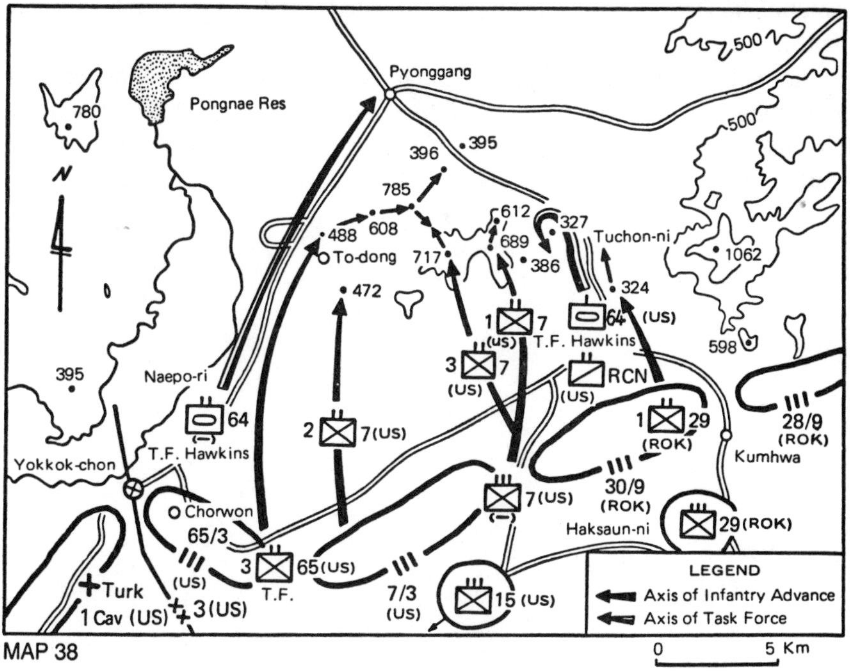

MAP 38

The Van Fleet strategy was still to exhaust the enemy, so the line remained more or less static.

On the east-central front the IX Corps was within ten miles of Kumsong. The ROK I Corps had advanced well above Kansong.

By taking this territory they had eliminated the enemy's major staging ground for attacks in the south. Here they stopped, because General Van Fleet's limit of advance had been reached. To go farther would demand a change in strategy. The Eighth Army went on the defensive again. They had suffered many casualties: the 1st Marines alone had more than 60 killed and a thousand wounded during the struggle. The Korean War had by this time taken an enormous toll. Later observers put the total figure of military casualties at this point at 1,250,000 killed, wounded, or captured; a million of these were from North Korea and China. That was minor compared to the cost to the civilian population of Korea. Two million civilians had died, and three million more had been made homeless. The line the UN now held generally embraced all the old territory of the Republic of Korea, and then some. This line, plus an extension on the west, would end up generally being the final line of demarcation of the two Koreas, although no one knew it at the moment. In essence, everything that occurred in Korea after the summer of 1951 was a waste of time and lives. The issue had been decided: the North Korean military adventure had failed, the UN attempt to impose a military solution had failed, and the Chinese attempt to force the UN out of Korea had failed.

As the UN forces consolidated the line, a major political development was occurring in New York. The Soviet Union, seeing the failure that had befallen first the North Koreans and then the Chinese, proposed truce talks. The war entered an entirely new phase. Now it was the turn of the politicians to fail.

19

The Static War

The relief of General MacArthur in the spring of 1951 had established the principle of political settlement, rather than military victory, as the cornerstone of American policy in the Korean War. When General Ridgway took over as commander of the forces in the Far East, it was with the understanding that no large-scale ground operations would be conducted without the prior approval of Washington. In fact, advances were confined to the general area of the Kansas–Wyoming line.

While truce talks began on July 7 at Kaesong, the war went on. The Eighth Army established patrol bases forward of their Main Line of Resistance, the Kansas–Wyoming line. (See Map 35.) It was not a very happy situation; the enemy could bypass the bases at any time, and thrust against the UN positions on the line, and they did so from time to time.

On June 26 the 3rd Battalion of the 1st Marines established a patrol base on Hill 761 but it was bombarded so severely by enemy mortars that it was moved back to the main line the following day. Thereafter, the movement of troops was more or less confined to straightening out the line and securing advantageous positions against the enemy, or to punitive action designed to destroy enemy troops and installations. This latter was undertaken to remind the recalcitrant Chinese and North Koreans at the peace table that the UN still held the balance of power in the field, and that, although the Communist forces could inflict heavy casualties on the UN forces, the cost in lives to the Communists was much greater.

The marines in the Punchbowl sector, who had been in action steadily for two months, were relieved by the U.S. 2nd Infantry on July 15 and went into reserve.

The truce talks continued in August, and the troops held their lines, with occasional forays. At this stage the Van Fleet strategy was to keep the enemy off balance, to capture prisoners to find out what the enemy was doing, and to prevent the Chinese from secretly preparing a major offensive. One such operation was that against Million Dollar Hill, on August 2.

The hill had been occupied earlier by the 24th Division and then abandoned. It stood out in sharp contrast to the surrounding green hills because in the fighting so much ammunition had been expended on it that the vegetation was completely blasted off the thousand-yard-long ridge. Thus, its name, Million Dollar Hill, referred to the money expended on ammunition.

From Million Dollar Hill the Chinese had a fine view of the whole 24th Division line. Therefore, Eighth Army directed that it be captured again and held. The attack began on the morning of August 2 and lasted two days. After the hill was taken, Company K of the 24th Infantry's 3rd Battalion was assigned to hold it. On the evening of August 3 the 2nd Platoon led the way up the hill in the dusk. The march took an hour, and at the end of it the infantrymen's fatigues were wet with sweat. Lieutenant Wilbur C. Schaeffner and his thirty-one men moved out from the crest to take up positions on the east end of the ridge line, which was broken into five mounds grading down in size from west to east.

During the night Lieutenant Robert H. Hight brought up the rest of the company and posted the men on the two larger mounds, at the west end of the ridge.

On the east the men of the 2nd Platoon had to prepare their own defenses. The attack troops had not dug in here. The sides of the ridge were so steep that the only reasonable approach for the enemy was over the eastern tip. Lieutenant Schaeffner placed a machine gun on top to cover the saddle that led to the tip of the ridge. Two BAR men covered the machine gun. When the Chinese saw what the Americans were doing, they began mortaring the ridge. A Chinese soldier moved up to throw a grenade at the machine gun, and the BAR men shot him, and he rolled down the ridge line. This fight drew the attention of a Chinese machine gun about sixty yards away at the eastern tip of the ridge. For the rest of the night the machine guns traded fire, and the mortar rounds flew. When light came on August 4, Lieutenant Hight made the men dig in deep, since the Chinese were so close at hand. He then planned artillery registrations around the whole company area. He could call on two batteries of 105 mm howitzers, two batteries of 155 mm, and two companies of 4.2-inch mortars for help. The men put out trip flares and boobytraps. During the daylight hours Korean laborers came up, bringing ammunition and food. As the day wore on, the men finished preparing, and Hight established a flying squad—eight men who could be rushed to any point in the perimeter that needed help. As the afternoon ended, the sky clouded up. The men napped. Shortly before dark one squad leader registered the company 60 mm mortars on the eastern tip of the ridge, three hundred yards out.

As night came, the company settled down. On the south side of the ridge three searchlights on the main defensive line were arranged to give night illumination to the ridge. One was pointed at the hill, and two were aimed up at the cloud cover, reflecting back like moonlight.

As the last glow of daylight faded, the searchlights came on. It began to rain as Lieutenant Hight set out for a check of the position. It was 9 P.M. He walked along the slippery clay just below the rim of the ridge. As he returned to his dugout, two trip flares went up in the valley below. The Chinese had begun probing his defenses.

A group of Chinese started up the steep side of the ridge in the center of the company perimeter. Then another group came to the eastern end in Lieutenant Schaeffner's sector, hurling grenades. One grenade cut the wire on the telephone but most exploded harmlessly along the slope. The BAR men who protected the machine gun crawled up the ridge line and peered over. Every time they saw a Chinese move down below they dropped grenades. The machine gunner and the riflemen concentrated their fire on the eastern tip of the ridge, to keep the Chinese heads down. After about twenty minutes, the Chinese moved back. The rapid action was replaced by a desultory spattering of rifle fire.

At about ten o'clock the thunder began to roll across the hill, and the rain increased, whipped along by a brisk wind. Under this cover, an enemy soldier sneaked up on machine gunner Corporal Gilbert L. Constant and Private First Class Robert J. Thomas who was loading for him.

In the hard rain they did not see the Chinese coming. But Private First Class Walter Jeter, Jr., did, and he shouted, "Look out on your left!"

Just then the Chinese let go a red flare from a flare gun to mark the position of the machine gun. It hit the ground directly in front of the machine gun and blinded Constant. Thomas, a black man who was considered one of the crack marksmen in the outfit, picked up the machine gun and unhooked the elevating and traversing mechanism so the gun swung free on the pintle. He fired a long burst, killed the soldier who had fired the flare, and worked the gun around. But another Chinese had come up on the left, and the grenade he threw into the machine gun pit wounded Thomas and Constant. The squad leader, Sergeant First Class Raymond M. Deckard, shouted at the men to come out, and he sent Corporal John W. Diamond to take over the gun. On the way Diamond was wounded in the face and arm, and Deckard took over the machine gun himself.

Trouble then appeared in batches. Both members of one BAR team covering the machine gun were wounded. The other BAR jammed. The machine gun feed mechanism went bad, and the rate of fire slowed. Suddenly, Deckard was missing five men and a BAR, and his machine gun was on the blink. He called for the reserve squad to come up and plug the line.

The rain was now coming down in sheets, blinding the men. Lieutenant Hight, who had served in World War II in the South Pacific, where it came down in torrents, thought this rain beat any he had ever seen before.

The Chinese now laid down a barrage from five machine guns on the ridges across the way and on the eastern tip of Schaeffner's ridge. Several squads of Chinese infantrymen were also adding rifle fire from positions near the 2nd Platoon. Grenade and mortar explosions accompanied all this.

Lieutenant Schaeffner's platoon was in the middle of it. He called by telephone for the flying squad and reported on Deckard's machine gun. Hight sent the men straightaway. He also called for mortar fire on the tip of the ridge and sent the 3rd Squad's machine gun up to the 2nd squad. All this reinforcement solved Schaeffner's problem, but he was using ammunition very fast. Lieutenant Hight called the battalion commander, Major Ernest H. Davis, to ask for more ammunition. Davis said he would get it up as soon as possible, but, until he did, they must stretch their ammunition and hold their position.

Fortunately, the heavy enemy assault ended at about 1 A.M. The enemy must also have been bothered by the rain, because there were no more infantry rushes. The ammunition problem was growing serious, however. Korean porters sent up the hill with ammunition were fired on and turned back. This was reported to Hight, and he told his officers they would have to get through the night without more ammunition.

"What are we going to do when this is gone?" one asked.

"Well, by God," said Hight, "we'll just wrestle them."

All he could do was get help from outside, and he ordered artillery fire and mortar fire around his line. It lasted for an hour and a half. At 4:30 in the morning the enemy fire slackened off, and soon the rain slowed and light began to show on the horizon. Chinese appeared now to try to recover arms and equipment, and the Americans fired on them. When day broke they counted thirty-nine bodies in front of their perimeter. Company K had five

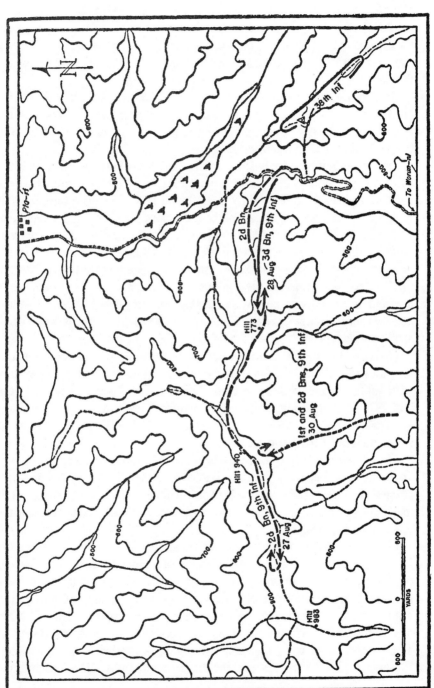

MAP 39

men wounded, but they had held their hill. Once again, however, higher headquarters decided the price was too high and the difficulty too great, so, in the afternoon Lieutenant Hight received orders to abandon the hill. The men rigged up demolition charges and booby traps and marched down to join the regiment.

The cease-fire negotiations continued at Kaesong. The Chinese and the North Koreans were milking them for their full propaganda value, but the Americans were not yielding. Peace seemed a long way away, and even further to the men on the firing line.

One important range of hills west of the Punchbowl was held by part of the ROK 5th Division. One night in August a surprise Chinese attack drove the ROK troops off the hills—Hill 983, 940, and Hill 773. (See Map 39.) This would never do, said Eighth Army headquarters. The hills must be retaken.

The South Koreans tried and tried again. They failed, for the enemy was there in force, and, as the fighting lulled, the Chinese built and rebuilt the bunkers until from the air the maze of trenches appeared to have been plowed in. The trenches connected the bunkers, and the bunkers were built of heavy logs and sandbags, capable of withstanding heavy artillery fire. Some of these bunkers could shelter sixty men. They were protected by mortars and small artillery pieces. The Chinese camouflage, as always, was superb.

On August 17 the ROK troops launched another attack, and on August 25 they took the hills and the four razorback ridges that converge on the western extremity to form Hill 983, the highest of them. To the east, separated from Hill 983 by a sharp draw, was a section of ridge 1,100 yards long, which came to a peak at Hill 940. Another 1,000 yards to the east is Peak 773. The ROK troops suffered a thousand casualties here.

The Chinese and North Koreans had been rebuilding their forces furiously, apparently still believing that they could drive the UN troops out of Korea altogether. A new effort was begun to dominate the airways, and Soviet pilots in MIGs joined the Communist air forces in the skies. They did not achieve the dominance they sought.

On the ground the Chinese had moved about half a million men into the Korean line. On August 22, on the flimsiest of pretexts, both the Chinese and the North Korean Communist delegations walked out of the truce talks. General Ridgway and General Van Fleet suspected what was coming, and all military elements of the UN were alerted. The force now included 229,000 men of the Eighth Army. It could scarcely be called a U.S. Army any more. Troops had come from Canada, Colombia, Australia, Belgium, France, Ethiopia, Great Britain, Greece, the Netherlands, India, New Zealand, the

Philippines, Norway, Sweden, Thailand, Turkey, and South Africa. The ROK Army now numbered 357,000 men.

Against them were the sixty divisions (more than 500,000 men) of General Peng Teh-huai's Chinese army, plus the North Korean army of about 150,000.

On the night of August 27, the Chinese attacked, this time beginning at that ridge line held by the ROK 5th Division, because it was just west of the Punchbowl and in the center of the UN line. They broke through, and the whole line was in danger.

General Van Fleet called on the American forces nearby to stop the enemy.

On August 27 the U.S. 9th Infantry entered the fighting. Its 2nd Battalion moved up to Hill 940. The battalion then tried to seize Hill 983 and failed. It withdrew that night to Worun-ni. The next day the 3rd Battalion attacked but did not even reach Hill 773. It also fell back to Worun-ni.

On August 30 the 9th Infantry was ready to go again. This time it would be a frontal assault straight north against Hill 940.

The 1st and 2nd battalions started up the hill. They made it to within a few hundred yards of the top, but then heavy enemy fire brought the advance to a sudden stop. Both battalions took heavy casualties. Half the men of Company A were down, including the company commander, wounded, a platoon leader killed, and another wounded. Lieutenant John H. Dunn took over the company.

By dusk it was apparent that the two battalions were not going to reach the top before dark. The regimental command post ordered them to withdraw. An artillery officer, Lieutenant Edwin C. Morrow, who was serving as a forward artillery observer, was the only officer left on his feet. He was sitting behind a knob when a sergeant crawled up and told him that Lieutenant Dunn was dead, only twenty-two men of the whole company were left. Suddenly, artilleryman Morrow joined the infantry. He tried to organize a retreat. He arranged for the artillery battalions below (seven of them) to fire smoke as the infantrymen came down the hill, carrying the wounded. There was no question of bringing down the dead or the heavy equipment; there were not enough men on their feet.

The withdrawal took most of the night. At four o'clock on August 31 the 1st Battalion reassembled in the area below the ridge line. They moved then to an assembly area near Worun-ni. Two hours later they were expected to be reorganized for another attack.

It was foggy and cold for August. The bad luck of the last day had doused morale in the battalion. It helped a little to get hot coffee, dry socks, and plenty of ammunition. Most important of all was mail. Also replacements joined up to fill the holes in the ranks.

There was all too little time. Before noon the men were loaded on trucks again, heading north to attack Hill 773. After two miles they got down, formed into company columns, and began to march, with Company C in the lead. As they marched along the road, they passed dead North Korean soldiers in their distinctive greenish uniforms.

They approached the eastern tip of the ridge line, where the land drops down to the pass between Worun-ni and the Pia-ri valley. Company C turned left toward the ridge and climbed the first knoll, which was held by the 38th Infantry. This knoll had a good view of Hill 773, so Lieutenant Colonel Gaylord M. Bishop, commander of the battalion, set up his command post here. Bishop and Lieutenant Charles W. Mallard, his intelligence officer, were already on the scene, looking over the terrain ahead. They watched the men of Company C turn off the road and start up the ridge to attack. It was not long before the infantrymen moved into the fog, very late in rising this day, and soon they moved into the low cloud cover that hung over the top of Hill 773 and were gone from view.

As the company advanced, it slowed, and the scouts set the pace. The infantrymen were grateful for the occasional halts.

From his hilltop Colonel Bishop heard the sound of a machine gun firing, but he could see nothing. Corporal John Truax, the radio operator with the company, kept him informed. Company C had run into a machine gun emplaced in a bunker two hundred yards in front of the column on the ridge. The first bursts wounded a number of men, including Lieutenant Orlando Campisi, the company commander. The Americans returned the fire, but their efforts had no effect on the gun.

Corporal Truax informed the colonel that all the officers were now wounded. The attack had been stopped cold by one machine gun.

Colonel Bishop ordered Company B, back at the base of the ridge behind Company C, to move on through and resume the attack. He also sent his intelligence officer, Lieutenant Mallard, forward to take over Company C and get it moving again.

Mallard was to provide supporting fire for Company B, and that was all they were likely to get. The fog and cloud cover precluded the use of air strikes and artillery.

The Commander of Company B, Captain Edward G. Kryzyzowski, told Lieutenant Joseph W. Burkett to take his 1st Platoon into the lead. Companies A and C would provide fire cover.

Burkett looked up the ridge. The fog and clouds had closed in, and now were so thick he could not see far ahead; in fact, he could not even see the route that Company C had followed. He went scouting ahead, leaving his platoon sergeant, Sergeant First Class Floyd Larney, to brief the squad leaders.

In the few moments when the fog drifted off to reveal the land, Burkett got glimpses of what lay ahead, and he planned his attack. By walkie-talkie radio he informed the support companies of his needs, and they shifted machine guns and BAR men to cover him. He went back to the platoon and moved them up the ridge line. As they reached the first knoll, where Company C had run into trouble, he had the covering fire of four machine guns. If the enemy machine gun was still there, it was silent. Even the rifle fire was very slight. Lieutenant Burkett was grateful for that—he was concerned about maintaining control of his platoon since three-quarters of his twenty-two men were raw replacements, who had come up from a depot in the last forty-eight hours. They were very nervous and did not know what was expected of them. They tended to lag behind the men ahead, or to bunch up, equally dangerous procedures on a ridge line.

At the base of that first knoll, only about thirty feet high, Lieutenant Burkett half expected to run into a shower of grenades. No such thing happened; they were protected by the knoll. As they began to move up, however, the enemy riflemen fired. Burkett took three men and went carefully up the hill. Asking his three men to cover him, he crawled ahead, reached the brim of the knoll, raised up on his knees and, pulling the pin from a grenade, leaned back, and lobbed the grenade over the top of the knoll where it exploded on the other side. As he did so, his helmet fell off and went clattering down the knoll side. The three men came up to Burkett, and the four of them went over the top. They found several empty foxholes on the reverse slope.

The platoon came up, and Burkett resumed the advance. Fifty yards ahead was another little knoll. As Burkett moved the men toward it, he noticed something was missing: the machine guns behind had quit firing. He called for his runner, who carried the radio, but the radio had gone dead. They could not raise the other platoons or companies.

After the American machine guns stopped firing, the Chinese counterfire picked up. Burkett tried to move ahead, and now the inexperience of his recruits told. They were strung out, so that only about ten of them were within hailing distance. Twenty yards from the crest of this knoll the men came under grenade fire. Burkett saw the grenades come rolling down the face of the hill. The men dropped, and the grenades exploded harmlessly. More grenades came, this time hurled high, toward the rear elements of the platoon. These were more effective, because the recruits had not learned to see a grenade coming, and scramble aside and down to get out of the way. Several men were wounded as they lay dumbly and watched the grenades come at them. Burkett spotted the source: a well-camouflaged bunker on top of the knoll. He saw the men hurling; they were North Korean soldiers.

Burkett did not know it, but the reason the American machine guns had stopped firing was that the fog had rolled in between the guns and the platoon, and the gunners could not see ahead. Captain Kryzyzowski sent three BAR teams up. The first BAR man to arrive was Private First Class Domingo Trujillo. He came up to Lieutenant Burkett and told him why he was there. What should he do? Burkett pointed at the bunker, and Trujillo, standing erect, fired a burst into the bunker and then lowered his gun. A North Korean rose up with a burp gun. Behind Trujillo was Private First Class Robert L. Spain with another BAR, and he pulled the trigger, but the gun misfired and the burp gun did not. Trujillo was killed instantly by a burst of lead in the chest.

Men began throwing grenades toward the bunker. They were bad pitchers, none of them came even close. Burkett crawled forward, under covering fire. Avoiding the fire of the machine gun, Burkett crawled from the north to the south side of the ridge line, and then west toward the top of the knoll. When he estimated that he was even with the bunker on the north side, he crawled back to the ridge line. He could see the top of the ridge and knew where the bunker was. He lifted a grenade, pulled the pin, waited for the safety lever to pop, and dropped it squarely on the top of the bunker. He threw another. He called down to the men below for more grenades, and Sergeant Charles Hartman tossed him three. He dropped them, too.

He got a reaction. A door at the rear of the bunker opened, and a North Korean emerged and threw six grenades at Burkett. He slid down the hill to get away from them, but at the bottom, where Sergeant Hartman was waiting, one grenade came wobbling down and exploded just as Burkett arrived. Both men were wounded. Burkett told his men to pull back beyond grenade range and wait for Captain Kryzyzowski to send help.

The afternoon had worn along, and Colonel Bishop decided it was time to stop and regroup. He ordered the battalion to establish a defense perimeter for the night. Captain Kryzyzowski sent up men with stretchers, and they moved the wounded back. The platoon moved to the company area.

That night was quiet. When dawn came on September 1, it was clear and fogless. Colonel Bishop put Company A in the attack position this day. He could now use artillery, and he called for a barrage along the ridge line between Hill 773 and Hill 940. He also asked for mortar fire from the supporting companies. Company C set up two heavy machine guns to fire on Hill 773.

Under this fire support, the men of Company A advanced to the second knoll, where Lieutenant Burkett had been wounded. Once again, the advance was halted by machine gun and small arms fire from that same bunker. Several members of the forward platoon were wounded. Lieutenant Elden K. Foulk, commander of Company A, started forward but was hit in the leg. He dragged himself back to Company C and told Lieutenant Mallard that he needed help up front. Then he collapsed from shock.

Mallard called Colonel Bishop, who told him to commit Company B again. Captain Kryzyzowski led the company up this time. The machine guns and the BARs from Company C fired on the bunker, and Company B moved up in a grenade assault that took the position. The first man to be wounded was an officer who had joined the company fifteen minutes before it began the attack.

The bunker was taken at ten o'clock that morning. Most of the ridge line to Hill 773 was now under control. What remained was to take Hill 773 itself, which was about two hundred yards away. From here on, the ridge line turned around like a question mark with Hill 773 at the hook on the end.

The cost of taking the second bunker had been high. Company B was now down to fifty men, but it resumed the advance. Halfway along the question mark, the men came upon three more bunkers. North Koreans emerged from each, throwing grenades, and five Americans were wounded. Captain Kryzyzowski stopped. A machine gun began firing down on them from Hill 940. He moved back beyond range and called on Company A for a bazooka. He told Company C to adjust the mortars so the shells fell on the crest of Hill 773. Under the covering fire, the bazooka team came up and silenced the first bunker.

Private First Class Edward K. Jenkins crawled up to the second bunker and dropped three grenades into it. He ran out of grenades, and from below someone threw up three more. He moved to the third bunker and threw two grenades inside. That ended the opposition from that set of bunkers.

But the enemy had more bunkers. Fire began coming from another, twenty-five yards up the ridge line. One American fired several rifle grenades at the bunker but the fire continued. It kept the men of Company B from moving north. They moved south to flank the bunker, but then they came under fire from the machine gun on Hill 773 and from another on Hill 940.

Once again, Colonel Bishop pulled back the battalion for the night. Captain Kryzyzowski moved the company back to the last knoll they had captured. Company A and Company B then mustered: there were twenty-two men left in Company A and twenty in Company B.

Colonel Bishop called for reinforcements, and early on the morning of September 2, replacements, including six officers, joined the battalion. Companies A and B each received two officers and sixty-five men, and Company

C received two officers and twenty men. Six men were sent to the rear for a quick course in the use of flamethrowers.

Getting ready for a new assault, Colonel Bishop moved a tank and a quadruple .50 caliber flakwagon onto the Worun-ni road so they could bear on Hill 940.

In addition to his temporary company command, Lieutenant Mallard reverted to his job as battalion intelligence officer. He set up an observation post on the last knoll captured and from there prepared to direct by radio the fire of the tank, the antiaircraft half-track and the heavy mortars. An artillery observer directed the fire of the artillery on Hill 940. Battalion called down air strikes on the west end of the ridge.

All day long on September 2 the artillery and the airmen hit the ridge line. The infantry remained virtually static. Twice patrols from Company C probed the approaches to Hill 773, but each time the enemy bunkers erupted with machine gun and grenade fire and drove the patrols back.

On the night of September 2 the situation was the same, except that the replacements had one day of experience in the line. On the morning of September 3 Lieutenant Mallard informed Lieutenant Arnold C. Jones that he would lead the next assault with his platoon. Jones was one of the replacements. Before the platoon could move out Colonel Bishop had some second thoughts and told them to await a new series of air strikes to soften up the position. During the morning, planes of the Fifth Air Force made almost perfect runs over the enemy-held ridge line. Four fighters came in with eight napalm containers. One napalm bomb hit the top of the hill. The seven others fell on the reverse slope, but they had to be effective because the Americans on the near side could feel the heat from the burning napalm across the hill.

A second flight of fighters came in, carrying antipersonnel bombs fixed with proximity fuzes. They dropped, then returned and strafed. They had hardly left the ridge line when Lieutenant Mallard was calling in fire again, and the artillery was shooting once more.

At two o'clock Company C resumed the attack. The eighty-five men were divided into three platoons, two of them experienced and one made up of tyros. Lieutenant Jones led an experienced platoon around the neck of the question mark. His men reduced two bunkers, but at such cost in casualties that they were stopped at the third. Lieutenant Jones was wounded, and his platoon was no longer effective. Lieutenant Mallard committed the second platoon then. Jones told him that most of the fire had been grenades lobbed over the sharp ridge by enemy troops on the far side. The second platoon bogged down in the face of this problem. Mallard got ready to send in the third platoon, but he also called up Colonel Bishop and asked for the three teams of newly trained flamethrower men. They came up and began to crawl up the ridge line.

One flamethrower was disabled when an enemy bullet hit the pressure tank. The other two teams managed to reach the crest of the ridge, pointed the nozzles up and sprayed the far side as far as they could reach. The operation was effective—no more grenades came over the ridge line.

Company C then continued around the bend of the question mark and destroyed two more bunkers. Late in the afternoon the company took the top of Hill 773. Lieutenant Mallard then sent a platoon from Company A up to the top to help hold the position, in case of counterattack from Hill 940, a thousand yards to the west.

Getting ready for the night, Mallard asked battalion to let him consolidate Company C and Company A since Company C was now back down to thirty effective riflemen. That permission was granted, and he moved up to tell the men. Just then a "friendly" round of artillery fire fell short and wounded him. He turned over command to Lieutenant Robert D. Lacaze, another battalion officer who had been put in charge of Company A after the original command became a casualty.

Mallard headed back for the aid station. On the way he encountered Captain Kryzyzowski, the last remaining officer of the original contingent of the battalion in the line, and they spoke a few words. Almost immediately after that, Kryzyzowski was hit by the machine gunner on Hill 940 and killed. That left Lieutenant Lacaze and one other officer in charge of all the men of the three rifle companies, and not a single company officer from the battalion as it had existed at the end of August.

The enemy had suffered even more, and two days later, the battalion occupied Hill 940 and Hill 983, without opposition. The cost had been enormous. Small wonder that bit of Korean real estate has come down in military history as Bloody Ridge.

20

Heartbreak Ridge

As the battle of Bloody Ridge indicated, the Chinese and the North Koreans had been using the Kaesong truce talks as a camouflage for the rebuilding of the armies that had been so badly battered by the attrition tactics of the UN forces from January through June. Apparently, someone high in the Chinese establishment still believed they could drive the UN forces out of Korea.

With the attack on Bloody Ridge, General Van Fleet had authorization from higher headquarters to renew his offensive activity, at least to the extent of taking some positions deemed necessary to the health of the UN forces on the line. In particular, the offensive was intended to drive the Chinese and North Koreans back from the Hwachon Reservoir area since it was the source of water and electricity for the capital at Seoul.

A heavily augmented 1st Marine division was to go into action once more; it now numbered nearly 1,400 officers and 24,000 enlisted men, plus 4,000 Korean porters. On the military side it also included Korean marines.

On August 27 the 5th Marines, the 7th Marines, and the Korean Marines moved up from Tundong-ni to the combat areas south and west of the Punchbowl. (See Map 40.) The area in which they would operate was dominated by Yoke Ridge, with high points at Hill 930, Hill 1000, Hill 1026,

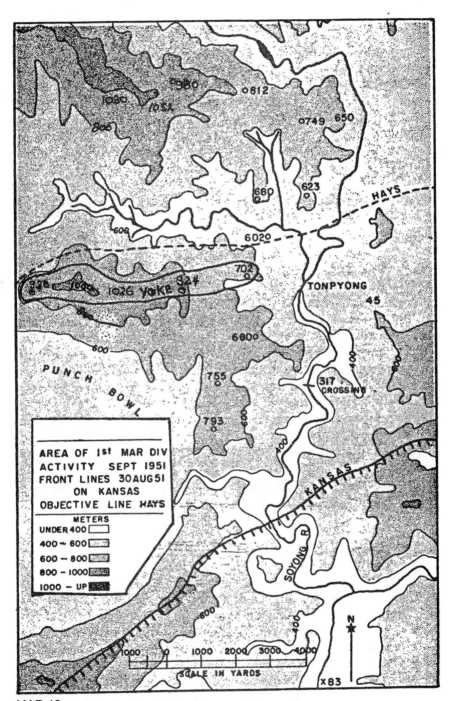

MAP 40

and Hill 924. Two smaller hills lay east of the Soyang River. On both sides of the area were other sharp ridges, each presenting a potential problem.

The enemy troops in the area were mainly from the 6th Regiment of the North Korean People's Army. They had a number of heavy mortars, machine guns, and some small artillery.

It was raining hard as the 7th Marines and the KMC Regiment moved up to relieve the units on the Kansas line, and the trucks did not arrive until nine o'clock at night. The rain grew worse and the men did not make their position for a full twenty-four hours and then discovered that the bivouac area was full of water. They stayed in the trucks and caught what sleep they could.

The 3rd Battalion of the 7th Marines was to cross the Soyang to reach its assembly area. The river was badly swollen, and after Company H had struggled across, nearly losing equipment and men, amphibious tractors were brought up to let the others cross. The two forward battalions of the 7th Marines did not get into place until the afternoon of August 29. The Korean marines were in place on the 30th.

There were indications that the Chinese might be ready to launch their "Sixth Phase Offensive" at any moment. Several enemy regiments were reported moving south into the Punchbowl area. It was important to work fast. On August 31 the South Korean marines attacked toward Hill 924 against light resistance. They had more trouble with enemy minefields than anything else. So did the 3rd Battalion of the 7th Marines, attacking against Hill 702. East of the river, the 1st Battalion of the 7th Marines moved up at the same time.

The attack resumed on September 1. For two days the 3rd Battalion of the 7th Marines fought a North Korean battalion that made four counterattacks and, for a brief time, penetrated the marine positions on the northeast fork of Yoke Ridge, but, as so often happened, the enemy attacks were broken up by a combination of air strike and artillery fire, two weapons in whose use the marines excelled. The North Koreans, as always, were proving to be formidable fighters, and in a surprise counterattack at midnight they drove the South Korean marines off Hill 924. But the Korean marines were also formidable fighters, and by noon they had recaptured the hilltop from the enemy. The 1st Battalion of the 11th Marine artillery fired 1,700 rounds of 105 mm ammunition in support of the Korean marines—that made the difference.

The U.S. marines and Korean marines continued to move along the ridge line, always against strong opposition. The 5th Marines came up the Soyang valley behind them, and they, too, ran into the same sort of fighting—attack, counterattack, and attack. Nonetheless, at six o'clock on the evening of September 3 the marines had taken the ridge line. On the west, elements of the

U.S. 2nd Division had also captured important positions along the rim of the Punchbowl. The next step was to be the capture of a series of ridge lines extending about four miles ahead of the Main Line of Resistance.

The marine attack was stalled because of the need to bring up supplies. It got going again on September 9, once more in heavy rain. The North Koreans had moved their 2nd Division out of the line and replaced it with the 1st Division, which was equipped with 76 mm artillery. The going was hard and when the 1st and 3rd battalions of the 7th Marines reached the ridge that led to Hill 749, they were stopped about halfway up. Napalm, rockets, and strafing made the difference. The 2nd Battalion moved up in a night flanking operation, and at daybreak on September 12 swept up Hill 673, completely surprising the North Korean defenders. All that saved the North Koreans from entrapment was a minefield between the 2nd and 1st Marine battalions.

On September 12 the 7th Marines were relieved in the line by the 1st Marines. By dawn two of the battalions had changed over, and the 3rd and 1st battalions of the 7th marines were on their way to the reserve station at Wontong-ni. The 2nd Battalion of the 7th Marines, however, was stuck in the middle of North Korean positions, and one of its companies was separated from the other two. The 1st Marines were to attack to get them out. At nine o'clock in the morning of September 13, a new sort of military operation was launched. It was the movement of troops in force by helicopter.

The world's first helicopter squadron, HMR-161, had been formed in January 1951. It consisted of 43 officers and 244 enlisted men, manning fifteen HRS-1 Sikorsky helicopters. The helicopters were about sixty feet long and each could carry six men with combat equipment.

At eight thirty in the morning of September 13, Lieutenant Colonel George W. Herring, commander of the squadron, was informed that the helicopters would leave their base at Airfield X-83, south of Sohwa-ri, to lift one day's supplies to the 2nd Battalion of the 1st Marines over a distance of seven miles.

Each helicopter loaded up about 800 pounds of supply. At three o'clock in the afternoon the loading began, and half an hour later seven 'copters were ready to fly. Four others went on ahead to take the landing point section of officers and men to the landing site.

The 11th Marines began firing smoke shells along the proposed route. The helicopters lifted off and flew down through the valleys as much as they could so as to avoid discovery and enemy fire.

After the four 'copters with the landing party reached the site, in twenty minutes they cleared an area twenty feet by forty feet and marked it with fluorescent panels. Just after four o'clock in the afternoon the first cargo ship arrived, carrying its cargo in nets suspended from a hook that was released manually. The cargo came down, the helicopter landed, and a few minutes later took off with two wounded men in litters and five walking wounded.

This *was* something new in warfare, and it was to have enormous significance in the handling of military casualties in the future. One marine, wounded in action on the line, arrived at a hospital clearing station seventeen miles behind the line thirty minutes later.

In two and a half hours that day the helicopters made twenty-eight flights to the position. They brought in 19,000 pounds of cargo and took out seventy-four casualties before the day's end.

Two days later the first helicopter lift of combat troops into battle was carried out. As the marine historian put it, "a new era of military transport had dawned."

The 2nd Battalion of the 1st Marines attacked toward Hill 749 on September 13, to pull out the 2nd Battalion of the 7th Marines. The 3rd Battalion of the 1st Marines was fighting on the left but was held up in its movement by the fighting on Hill 749. The 2nd Battalion drove forward to the summit at three o'clock in the afternoon and reached a point an hour later about three hundred yards from the two companies of the 7th Marines that were cut off. They had to fight all the way to get there, and it took until eight o'clock that night. The 7th Marines were taken out, and the 1st Marines settled in.

That night they were harried by mortar fire from the ridge lines around them. The 3rd Battalion was attacked that night by the North Koreans in one of their burp gun and grenade counterattacks, but it held them off.

At 8 A.M. the marine attack began again, against bunkers from which the North Koreans fought tenaciously with mortars, automatic weapons, and artillery.

The worst resistance in the area was on the north slope of Hill 749. Here the North Koreans had established several bunkers, all of them concealed from view. They had to be destroyed one by one, a process that kept the marines from advancing more than three hundred yards to the summit of Hill 751 by dusk. The tanks made the advance possible, firing four hundred rounds of ammunition directly into those bunkers.

Private First Class Edward Gomez of Company E and his squad were moving up the hill when an enemy soldier lobbed a grenade into their midst. Gomez dived atop the grenade and took the impact with his body, sacrificing his life to save four other men. For that, he was awarded the Medal of Honor.

September 15 was quiet. The marines spent the day consolidating positions, and the 2nd Battalion continued its advance north of Hill 749. The attack began just after five o'clock in the evening but was stopped forty minutes later by heavy mortaring from the North Korean forces on the hills.

The enemy had been given plenty of time to prepare. His machine gun cross fire was deadly in the ravines, and the marines had to withdraw short of their objective under artillery cover.

The North Koreans were using their bunkers most effectively. So stoutly constructed were they that the enemy did not hesitate to place artillery fire directly on his own positions. And the machine guns were so situated as to provide an almost classic maneuver, known to naval men—the crossing of the T. The guns were situated on the ridge lines in the fashion of the T crossbar. As the marines came up the hill they were subjected to simultaneous fire from several guns, "crossing the T."

The solution was artillery fire, and time after time, the 11th Marines were called on to knock out machine gun positions.

Just after midnight on September 16, the marines who had achieved control of Hill 749 were hit by a savage North Korean counterattack. The first indication was an artillery barrage—the toughest the marines had yet encountered in Korea. The enemy used 76 mm guns, 105 and 122 mm guns, and 82 mm guns, and many mortars. They had plenty of them, and the shells screamed in one atop the other. Then the barrage was followed by assault troops charging furiously. The enemy attacked for four hours.

The marine line bent several times, but it did not break. Corporal Joseph Vittori of Company F saw one platoon giving ground. He rushed up alone and started a counterattack. Others came along behind, and in a few moments the enemy was stopped.

Vittori kept up a ceaseless personal attack. He hurried from one foxhole to another, covering the wounded, taking over a machine gun when the gunner fell, and then bringing up ammunition for the besieged marines.

Vittori fought all night. Just as the enemy was preparing to withdraw he was hit, and when the aid men got to him, they saw it was a mortal wound. Vittori became the second marine to win the Medal of Honor within those forty-eight desperate hours on Hill 749.

The fighting continued for hours more. Not until four o'clock in the morning of September 16 did the enemy stop counterattacking. Four hours later the tired marines of the 2nd Battalion were replaced in the line by the 1st Battalion, under a new commander, Lieutenant Colonel John E. Gorman. The previous commander, Lieutenant Colonel Horace E. Knapp, Jr., had been seriously wounded shortly before. Such changes, which were all too common, were predictable. In fact, through rotation, wounds, fatalities, and other exigencies, the 1st Marine Division of the fall of 1951 was almost entirely a new unit; more than 90 percent of the "old" men had been replaced.

The next hill to fall to the marines was Hill 812. Again the fighting was furious, a fact that caused higher headquarters to note a basic change in enemy strategy. Chairman Mao's elastic warfare policy had been at least temporarily abandoned. Instead of giving ground in the face of attack, the enemy troops were contesting every foot. Holding a position to the last man seemed to be the rule. Of course, in this area the marines were facing North Korean troops, but apparently their orders were similar. Every marine attack was followed by an enemy counterattack, and these could be costly.

On the morning of September 18 the enemy still held Hill 980 and Hill 1052. The marines were determined to take these key points and straighten out their control of the ridge line. The key was a granite knob called "the Rock," which stood seven hundred yards west of Hill 812. The marines held the top and west side, and the enemy held the east side. On the north, were the dug-in forward elements of the 2nd Battalion. They needed supplies and fortification materials. In this new war, there was a way to supply them without excessive danger: by helicopter. And that is how it was done by sixteen flights in a single hour.

On September 19 in the hard fighting the 2nd Battalion took heavy casualties, and at the end of the day it was relieved by the 1st Battalion of the 5th Marines. They moved up to stretch the marine line two miles east along the ridges, nearly to the Soyang.

At 3:15 in the morning of September 20, the North Koreans made a new effort to recapture Hill 812. They pushed Company E back. That company and Company F counterattacked and regained all the lost ground. The front quieted down then, after a battle that had lasted ten days. The 1st Marine Division had taken many casualties in this battle, but the enemy had suffered far worse, a thousand dead and more than a hundred taken prisoner.

The bitter struggle for the key positions around the Punchbowl was going on up and down the line. The U.S. 2nd Infantry Division fought a similarly wearing battle for Heartbreak Ridge, the main north-south ridge line in the area that extended for seven miles. In the spring and summer months the enemy had built scores of bunkers and trenches in the area, and the army infantrymen had to fight for every foot they gained. By the second week of October, most of the ridge line had fallen into UN hands, but there was still one small eminence left, Hill 520, joined to the main ridge line by a series of little humps. On October 10 the 23rd Infantry Regiment had the responsibility for reducing this last strategic strong point, and the 2nd Battalion was ordered to make the attack. The battalion commander chose Company G for the job.

The fighting on Heartbreak Ridge had been so desperate that early in October that company numbered only twenty-three men. But by October 10

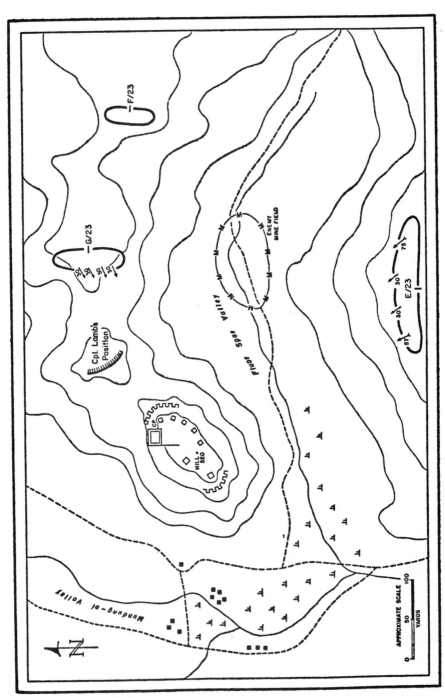

MAP 41

enough replacements had come up to bring the company up to about two-thirds normal strength.

Lieutenant Raymond W. Riddle, who was in command of the company, chose the 3rd Platoon to make the assault on the hill. The men would be supported by Company F and Company E on other ridges parallel to the one attacked. (See Map 41.)

Hill 520 was flat at the top, and the enemy were dug in all around the upper edge. The trouble was that no one knew how many men were up there. Lieutenant Riddle ordered his whole company to fire on the hill for thirty seconds, attempting to draw some counterfire that would tell him, but no fire came back. Riddle then called for maximum support fire from the artillery, machine guns, and the recoilless rifles held by Company E. On the ridge line halfway along from the Company G point of departure was another small knoll. Lieutenant Riddle decided to make a direct assault along the ridge because he knew the valley on both sides was alive with mines.

At 1 P.M., after a ten-minute barrage, the 3rd Platoon moved out, led by Corporal David W. Lamb. The men ran to the knoll in the middle and set up their machine gun. Under cover of that gun and the fire from the rear, Lamb deployed his men around the base of the objective. So far he had not suffered any casualties, although the infantrymen were drawing fire from the top of Hill 520 by this time.

Most of the riflemen were firing at bunkers on the east end of the hill. Corporal Lamb ordered one squad around to the left side, but they were driven back almost as soon as they set out. The fire was so heavy that several men were wounded. The barrage from the rear had not done much good. Lamb radioed Lieutenant Riddle for reinforcements.

Riddle sent up his 1st Platoon then. Theoretically, the platoon was under the command of Lieutenant Jay M. Gano, a brand-new replacement, but Lieutenant Riddle quietly told Private Cliff R. High, who had been leading the platoon for a week, that he was to continue in charge. That was just as well, for on the crawl up to the 3rd Platoon position Lieutenant Gano, who was in the lead, was killed. Two other men were wounded, and the platoon was pinned down by fierce fire from the hill.

Suddenly the 3rd Platoon's machine gun quit.

"I'm out of ammo," shouted the gunner. And with that a handful of enemy soldiers rose out of their bunkers and headed down the hill toward the 3rd Platoon riflemen. Fortunately the riflemen were able to put up a sufficient volume of fire with their M-1s and carbines to stop the enemy and turn them back.

Somehow, either from enemy fire or by accident, a brush fire had started between the objective and the battalion forces in the rear, and the smoke now made it impossible for the supporting troops to see what was going on. Nonetheless, Riddle ordered his machine guns to continue firing on Hill 520. Lamb reported back that the machine gun fire was just right.

On the ground, Private High moved his men slowly toward the 3rd Platoon position, passing wounded men of the 3rd Platoon who were making their way to the rear. Riddle sent up a squad from the 2nd Platoon, carrying eight boxes of ammunition for the machine gun, and they arrived along with High's platoon. The two platoon leaders planned an assault on the hill.

The enemy now opened up with mortars, and six more men were wounded. High's platoon was reduced to eleven men and Lamb's to twelve. They left six men behind to man the gun and fire rifles from the knoll and called on Lieutenant Riddle to stop the support fire. Then they assaulted the hill in a skirmish line, firing as they moved.

They had to cross sixty yards of open ground to the enemy positions on the slope of the hill. Halfway across the enemy started firing automatic weapons, but this fire was not effective. The men pushed on. When they reached the base of the hill, the enemy started throwing fragmentation and percussion grenades. Corporal Lamb was wounded. Seeing the skirmish line stop, back on the knoll Corporal Arne Severson picked up his machine gun and walked it forward, firing as he went. At the base of the hill an enemy grenade exploded at his feet and broke both his legs. He dropped to the ground but did not stop firing the machine gun. The attack was still stalled, however, and two men dragged Severson back to the covered position.

High radioed Lieutenant Riddle for more help. Meanwhile, he decided to make a second try and led a dozen men down the hill to the south, where they could move around without being seen by the enemy. Then they climbed Hill 520. When they appeared the enemy again began throwing grenades. One knocked High down, and the attack broke up. Believing High dead, the men abandoned the body. But High regained consciousness and, returning to the hill, reorganized his twenty men for another attack.

In the meantime, the battalion had received three flamethrowers from regiment; Lieutenant Riddle sent all three up with a man for each to help High. One man was wounded on the way up, but the other two made it. High sent one flamethrower up front, covered by two riflemen.

They crawled up to a point where they could fire the napalm into the eastern bunker (the front one). In a few moments this bunker was destroyed. High was right behind, and, leading the rest of his platoon around to the left, they formed a skirmish line. He signaled the flamethrower operator to fire on the next bunker, but the flamethrower would not work. High decided to assault the remaining bunkers, anyhow. He saw only two in operation. Each was firing a machine gun.

He sent a BAR team to one bunker, and he took two riflemen and the other flamethrower toward the other bunker. They walked, because High was afraid that if they crawled they would be pinned down. As they approached the bunker, the flamethrower operator pressed his trigger, but this flamethrower refused to work as well. The operator stood and tried to repair his weapon, until High ordered him back lest he be shot.

High and his riflemen kept the occupants of that bunker down with rifle fire. Then another bunker came alive on the left with automatic weapons fire. High sent Private Joe Golinda to that bunker and covered him. Golinda threw a grenade into the bunker and, after it exploded, the bunker was quiet.

High and his handful of men then assaulted one bunker after another, moving around the hillside, firing into the apertures. All the bunkers were empty. When they reached the top of the hill, they saw eight enemy soldiers running off to the northwest and fired after them. On the north side of the hill they came upon another bunker and just outside found eight men huddled, still holding their weapons but not pointing them. High fired, and they all surrendered. From another bunker emerged four other soldiers, who also surrendered. Meanwhile, a number of other soldiers were scurrying down the hill and off to the northwest. At four o'clock in the afternoon Hill 520 was secure, and Heartbreak Ridge was in UN hands. Like the assault of the marines on the ridge line, it had been a costly campaign. The 2nd Division had been hard hurt in the fighting of these past few months and bore a higher casualty rate than any other unit in the Eighth Army. The 23rd Infantry had been so badly hit that its commander had told division and Eighth Army that to continue these assault tactics would be suicidal for the units involved. That word got to General Ridgway and got home to America. The reaction in America was swift and negative. It seemed apparent both in the field and at home that the current strategy was not working and was costing far too much in terms of men and materiel. General Van Fleet continued the assault tactics a little longer, moving to what was called the Jamestown line, a bulge out of the Kansas line that removed a threat to the Chorwon–Seoul railroad. But in Tokyo General Ridgeway was rethinking the conduct of the war. Out of this planning came a new strategy of "active defense," which was really a warfare of position, maintaining the line. This new warfare brought change in many ways, not least of them the growing use of helicopters to supply forward positions, evacuate casualties, and get units out of traps. Once again, the fighting in Korea assumed the nature of a whole new war.

21

Negotiate and Fight

The bloody assaults of the UN forces of August, September, and October 1951 did have an effect not fully appreciated in a restless America: they forced the Communist side back to the peace table it had deserted in the hope of achieving a victory through strength. On October 8 the delegations of the UN and the Communist forces began meeting again, this time at the deserted mud hut village called Panmunjom, on the Munsan–Kaesong road. .

Once again, the Chinese and the North Koreans were playing games, using stalling tactics at the conference table, while they rebuilt the military machine so badly battered in recent weeks.

A new element of that machine had been brought into play this year. The Chinese were serious about trying to oppose the UN forces in the air, and they demanded further assistance from the Soviet Union in this regard. They had been getting it all through the summer of 1951.

During the late spring the UN air forces worked overtime, bombing the Yalu bridges, and by the end of May they had dropped parts of all of them, except one bridge at Sinuiju that had a charmed life. A few of the B-29s were shot down, but in the larger view the big bombers were enormously successful. They adopted some new techniques of bombing for this war. The B-29s came into the conflict using 1000-pound bombs. These were not powerful enough to do the job on the Yalu bridges, particularly with the difficult conditions of bombing in that area, and soon the B-29s switched over to 12,000-pound bombs. One of these could knock out two spans of a Yalu bridge.

The spring of 1951 also saw the emergence of the first jet "ace" of the Korean War on May 20. The Americans by this time had converted largely to the F86A Sabrejet fighter-interceptor. Captain James Jabara of the 334th Fighter Interceptor Squadron had already shot down four MIGs. He was flying a fighter sweep down the Yalu River that day when his bunch were called excitedly on the radio by other American pilots who reported they had just been jumped by an enormous "gaggle" of fifty MIGs. Jabara's team immediately jettisoned their auxiliary fuel tanks and climbed to 35,000 feet—except that one of Jabara's tanks hung up and would not part company with the aircraft. Standing orders told a pilot to head for the barn under such circumstances, but Jabara was nearing the end of his tour of duty, and he wanted that last MIG, so he ignored orders and headed into the fight, with his wingman.

They found half a dozen MIGs. One pair of Sabrejets dived on the formation and split it up, and Jabara and his wingman went after three of them. Just then, another three MIGs came down on the Americans, but they were too hasty and overshot. Two of them broke off, but Jabara got on the tail of the third. That third pilot was hot and tried everything in the book to shake off the American jet, but Jabara managed to get within 1,500 feet and put three bursts of armor-piercing fire into the enemy plane. The enemy pilot did two snap rolls, but the plane did not respond further and went into a spin, going down fast to 10,000 feet. The pilot bailed out just before the MIG exploded in midair.

Then Jabara and his wingman were in the middle of a melee, with fifty or more MIGs buzzing around some twenty-five Sabrejets. Jabara climbed back up to 20,000 feet and there saw six more MIGs below him. He and his wingman bounced them. Jabara closed fast, got in several bursts, and one of the MIGs flamed out. Black smoke came pouring out of its exhaust. Another burst in the middle of the fuselage set the MIG to burning, and it started down.

Jabara cut his power and followed the enemy plane down, to make sure it hit the ground so he could claim the victory. Suddenly he heard popping noises and turned. Two MIGs were on his tail.

Jabara broke to the left, goosed the throttle up to full power, and began running. The MIGs chased him, and they were very skillful about it. Jabara looked at his fuel indicator and saw that it was coming very close to the danger point. Then he heard someone on the interphone:

"There's an F-86 in trouble down there," said the voice.

"Roger," said Jabara. "I know it too damned well."

"Call us if you need help."

"I sure could use some."

He saw the F-86s wing over, and then they were coming down. One of the MIGs saw them and broke away from the chase to head for the Communist side of the Yalu. The second MIG was too intent on destroying Jabara and kept after him firing. The MIG nearly had him, close on his tail, closing the gap and firing all the while. They went around and around, and the other two F-86s came down. One of the pilots began firing on the MIG, and the other kept watch so that no other enemy planes jumped them. Jabara kept running. The pilot on the tail of the MIG—Captain Gene Holley—got in several effective bursts, and the MIG started to smoke. The pilot headed for the river, and there was no chance of giving chase because all three F-86s were virtually out of fuel. They made it home safely, and Jabara claimed his fifth and sixth kills of the war.

In June the Communist camp introduced a new wrinkle to the air war. They brought in "the big team"—Soviet instructors who flew combat with Chinese and North Korean pilots. The Americans could tell when the Soviets came in because of the dangerously improved caliber of the pilots they faced.

In July the MIGs began moving south in their effort to control the air. They came as far south as Pyongyang, and they brought new jet fighter tactics from Moscow. One was the "Yo-yo," a modification of the old Lufbery circle of World War I. The Lufbery was a vertical circle, in which a group of outnumbered pilots could protect each other's tails by flying around in giant loops. The Soviet wrinkle was to work the Lufbery circle at high altitude, above a group of American jets. The Soviet jets performed better at high altitude than did the American, so it was easy for a MIG to break out of the circle, make a pass at a UN jet below, and then zoom back up into the protective circle again.

Although the tactic worked very well at high altitude, the Americans learned to tempt the MIGs down to lower altitudes, where the F-86s could outperform the MIGs, and there the story changed.

Another Soviet addition to the air war was the "Zoom and Sun." The Soviet fighters would stay high—perhaps 48,000 feet—and when they saw F-86s coming they would zoom down, make a fast pass, and then climb back into the sun. With the MIGs superior climbing ability, this tactic was extremely effective.

Where the American planes showed superiority was at low altitude. The MIGs could not stay with any of them there, jet or propeller-driven craft. The F-51, the F-80, and the F4U could all outperform the MIGs. The smaller wings of the MIGs simply did not have the airfoil capability. The propeller-driven planes seemed to be at a great disadvantage as the jets closed in on them, but all the pilot had to do after the first pass was cut his throttle, and the MIG would scream by and be fifteen miles away before the pilot could turn. In fact, several UN pilots shot down MIGs from propeller-driven aircraft. Flight Lieutenant Peter Carmichael of the Royal Navy got his MIG while flying a Sea Fury from the deck of HMS *Ocean.* Captain Jesse Fulmar of VMF-312 also got one while flying an F4U from the carrier *Sicily.* His flight was jumped by four MIGs. They shot on past. The second section of MIGs was just turning left and climbing when Fulmar turned with them, climbed, and sent a five-second burst of 20 mm cannon fire into one MIG. The enemy plane belched, black smoke came out, and the plane burned. The pilot jumped, but his parachute was already on fire and did not open. Fulmar had made a lucky pass, but the proof that it could be done was a great comfort to the UN pilots of propeller-driven planes.

The change to a defensive posture by the UN forces not only gave the Communists an opportunity to rebuild their land armies, but it changed the air war again. The activities of the Far East Air Forces of the UN also changed the air war. In the spring of 1951 the Americans rebuilt Kimpo airfield and extended the runway at Suwon to handle jets and big cargo planes. A new airfield was built at Kunsan. The Taegu field got a concrete runway.

When the truce talks languished, the air war stepped up. In September Lieutenant Richard Becker got his fifth MIG to become an ace, and so did Captain Ralph Gibson. But many American and other UN planes were lost. Small wonder. The Chinese and Soviets and North Koreans were often putting as many as a hundred planes in the air over MIG Alley. The result was that Far East Air Forces decided to pull its fighter bombers out of that area. As soon as that happened, the enemy moved south and brought the MIGs down to Samcham, Techon, and Uiju airfields. These fields were changed over to accommodate the MIG-15. This tactic hurt the fighter bomber activity over the fighting line, but the answer was to send more Sabrejets into Yalu territory, and this was done. The jockeying continued. The B-29s moved back to the Yalu in daylight raids. The first of these caught the enemy by surprise, but when they hit Namsi on October 23, a hundred MIGs came up to go after the thirty four F-86s that were screening the B-29s. Actually, the escorting was being done by F-84s. But the MIGs did their job, keeping the F-86s so occupied they could not protect the big bombers. Then another fifty MIGs went after the B-29s and sliced right through the F-84s. Three B-29s and one F-84 were lost that day, and *every single B-29* that came home suffered major damage. This result was so staggering that the Far East Air Forces reversed itself and put an immediate end to daylight bombing raids by the B-29s.

The American reaction to this turn of events was to send in more F-86 jets. Seventy-five new jets were put aboard two carriers in the United States and brought to Japan.

More MIGs were also coming into Manchuria and Korea. The pilots, Chinese and Soviet, kept trying new tactics in the air war. What the Americans called "Bandit Trains" would form up in Manchuria and then cross the Yalu in groups of seventy five or so, flying forty to fifty miles apart at 40,000 feet. They would fly down to Pyongyang, intersect paths, and swing back north, jumping any and all UN aircraft they came across. With such a formidable armada of perhaps a hundred and fifty planes, they moved where they would. Meanwhile, as they started back toward the Yalu, another "train" of about seventy five MIGs would come out to cover them on the way home. If the F-86s chased the enemy planes north, they found that at the Yalu they would be getting near the critical point on fuel, while the new train of MIGs was coming down, tanks full and ready for action. This tactic was potentially disastrous for the UN forces. Fortunately for them, most of the Chinese pilots were not well enough trained to take advantage of the situation, and the Soviet pilots did not seem to be very aggressive.

That could not be said of the UN pilots. On November 27 Major Richard Creighton got his fifth MIG. Three days later a force of thirty Sabrejets caught two big flights of enemy planes as they were moving into the new Chinese base at Taehwa-do. The enemy planes—sixteen La-9 and twelve Tu-2 propeller bombers—were escorted by an overflight of MIGs. The F-86s split the air cover, and then half of them went after the propeller-driven aircraft below. In twenty minutes they knocked out eight Tu-2s, three La-9s, and one MIG. Major George Davis shot down three Tu-2s by himself. He also shot down the MIG, thus becoming the fifth MIG ace in Korea. Major Winton Marshall shot down a Tu-2 and an LA-9, to become the sixth air ace.

So while the Communists were constantly changing tactics, bringing in more Soviet instructors, and loading the air with Soviet-built planes, the UN forces continued on the aggressive in the air and did their job, keeping the enemy off balance and interdicting his supply lines, while the fighter bombers worked over the tactical situations, giving extremely effective air cover to the ground forces fighting below.

The ground forces situation was changing, too. In the winter of 1951 the army did what Major General William Kean, commander of the 25th Division, had advocated months earlier: integrated the military forces fighting in Korea. In the summer of 1950, when the U.S. 24th Infantry Regiment had come to fight in Korea it had come as an all-Negro outfit. The result had not been happy. The 24th's performance was the worst of all units on the American side, hardly better than the performance of the ill-trained ROK

Army. The reason was not that blacks could not be good soldiers, although many of the men in the 24th were not good soldiers. The reason was that the whole military system had for years militated against blacks being able to rise and to perform properly. During the hardest days of the war, incoming black troops were integrated in other units because there was no option—the units had to have replacements, and the blacks were there. These blacks performed far better than the ones lumped into the all-black units, and the army began to learn. By the midsummer of 1951 the all-black unit was a thing of the past in the forces that fought in Korea. The 24th Infantry was now a proper fighting unit that could be trusted in the line.

Another change was a new emphasis by General Ridgway on the retraining and proper use of the ROK forces. He saw to it that the South Korean forces got an artillery of their own and that they learned how to use the guns. The retraining of troops, particularly officers, changed the military situation so that the ROK Army could be trusted far more than it had been in the past. During the fighting for the Punchbowl, the ROK I Corps did a good job in its own sector. The ROK 1st Division had fought with gallantry since the first days and continued to do so.

As the negotiations dragged on in the fall of 1951 and the winter months of 1952, the fighting continued, although it was now what the marines called "warfare of position." The UN line was strung out from the mouth of the Imjin River on the west, to a point about twelve miles south of Pyonggang in the center, and over on the east to the coast well above Kansong. (See Map 42.)

On the west was the U.S. I Corps, with the ROK 1st Division holding the left anchor in the Munsan-ni area. Across the Imjin on the northeast were the British, now strengthened and reorganized as the 1st British Commonwealth Division. Farther to the northeast in the Yonchon area was the U.S. 1st Cavalry Division, with Greek and Thai battalions attached. Their lines abutted those of the U.S. 3rd Infantry Division, in the Chorwon area, with the Belgian battalion and the Philippines contingent attached.

Next to this group was the U.S. IX Corps, with the U.S. 25th Infantry Division on the left (including the 24th Infantry), and the Turkish brigade attached. The ROK 2nd Division held a sector east of Kumhwa, and next to it was the U.S. 7th Infantry Division, with the Ethiopian battalion attached. Next came the ROK 6th Division, extending to the Pukhan River, and the U.S. 24th Infantry Division, with the Colombian battalion attached.

On the right of the IX Corps was the U.S. X Corps, General Almond's organization. The ROK 8th Division was on the left flank of this corps, and next to it was the U.S. 2nd Infantry Division, with the French and Nether-

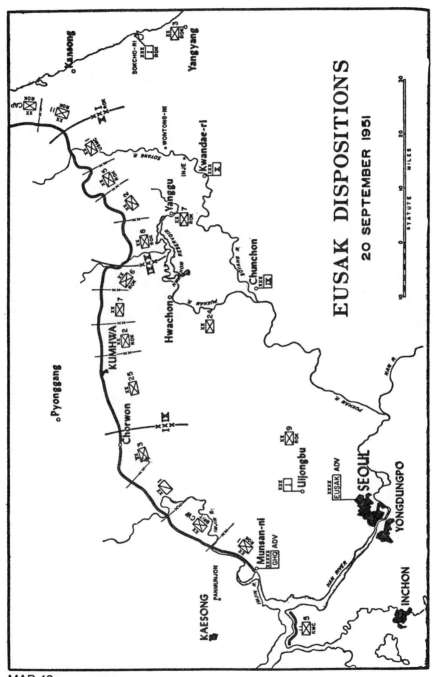

EUSAK DISPOSITIONS
20 SEPTEMBER 1951

MAP 42

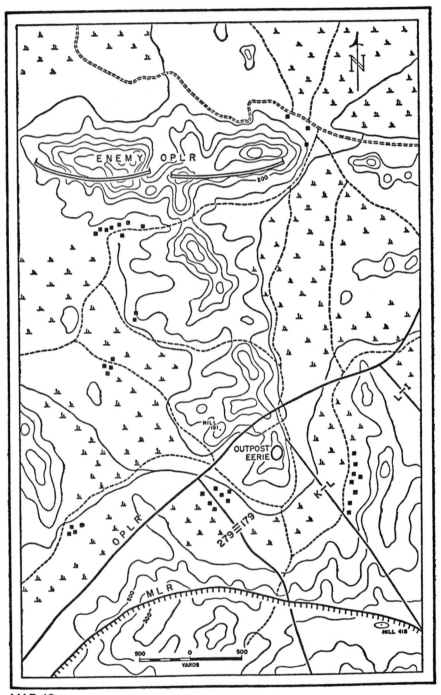

MAP 43

lands battalions attached. The ROK 5th Division came next, and the U.S. 1st Marine Division held the right side of the corps line.

Finally, on the far eastern side of the peninsula, the South Koreans had total responsibility. The ROK 11th Division was on the left, the Capitol Division in the center, and the ROK 3rd Division was in reserve.

Altogether, the UN forces numbered some 600,000. And so did the Communist forces facing them, including some 7,000 troublesome guerillas still behind the UN lines. This new positional war found the UN forces on high ground, so that they could, as General Van Fleet said, "look down the throat of the enemy."

Generally UN operations that winter were devoted to brief raids into enemy territory to capture prisoners for intelligence purposes. The enemy, however, had greater ambitions, as shown on March 21, 1952, in the 179th Infantry Regiment sector near the rubble that had been the town of Chorwon. Ten miles west of Chorwon and a mile south of the enemy's line of resistance, lay the UN outpost known as Eerie. It was the particular responsibility of Company K of the 179th Infantry. Two rifle squads, plus a machine gun and mortar section, maintained the post, which lay at the very southern tip of a T-shaped ridge. The enemy had placed his outposts on the T-bar and could look down with annoyance on the Americans whose presence made their outpost less useful than it might have been. (See Map 43.) Most annoying was the fact that using Outpost Eerie as a base, the 3rd Battalion made nightly patrols along each shank of the T.

The enemy did not like that a bit, and from time to time attempted to change the line. Such an incident occurred in the third week of March 1952.

On the afternoon of March 21 Lieutenant Omer Manley led most of the 3rd Platoon out from the Company K command post on the Main Line of Resistance to take over Outpost Eerie for the next five days. It was a nasty spring Korean day, with sleet and rain pelting down as the men started toward the rice paddies in the valley that lay between the MLR and the outpost. Through the valley and up the hillside in single file, they moved along, toward the southern tip of this two-mile-long ridge. Outpost Eerie was located at the peak of this ridge dip. A look at the map shows why the Communists would have wanted to take it back: the outpost controlled the high ground all the way back to the enemy line of resistance. As a strong point it was not much, just a rocky hill 120 feet high, with dugouts surrounding the point peak and a few scrub bushes and patches of grass growing on a surface that had been badly plowed by shellfire.

The best thing that could be said for Outpost Eerie was that the Americans had taken great care in constructing the defensive positions. (See Map 44.)

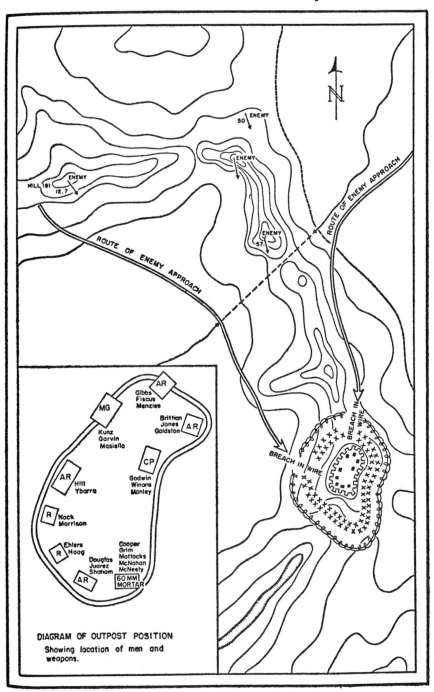

DIAGRAM OF OUTPOST POSITION
Showing location of men and weapons.

MAP 44

Fifty yards below the peak the high ground was encircled by three separate barbed wire entanglements, a coiled barrier, and then two double apron fences. The soldiers passed through by a gate entrance built across the trail to the hilltop. There were nine bunkers around the top, built to hold three men each, double layers of sandbags and logs on the sides, and three layers of logs and sandbags on the tops. These were built for shelter only. The firing positions were located in a trench that circled the hill adjacent to the bunkers or ran through them.

Most of Manley's men had spent time on Outpost Eerie before so they trudged into their assigned bunkers. The most important were three bunkers that guarded the north end of the hill. Manley assigned three men to each of these, armed with a light machine gun and two BARs. Immediately behind these bunkers was the command post. Three of the other bunkers were manned by two-man teams, one by another three-man team, and the five-man mortar squad was located in the southern bunker. All the bunkers were connected by a telephone system. Communication was made to company headquarters and battalion headquarters by line telephone and radio. Knowing the propensity of the Chinese for cutting wires, the communications men had laid four separate lines from the Main Line of Resistance to the outpost.

Manley knew that two patrols were scheduled by battalion for this night. One of these was Raider Patrol, coming out with the mission of catching an enemy soldier for interrogation. Raider Patrol came through Outpost Eerie at 7 P.M. on March 21 and set up an ambush on the east side of the ridge, six hundred yards north of Outpost Eerie. Its orders were to stay on post until 1:30 the next morning and then return to Outpost Eerie.

A second patrol, King Company Patrol, from Company K's 2nd Platoon, left Outpost Eerie at the same time to set up an ambush northwest of the post. It was to stay out until 2:15 and then go back directly to Company K.

After the men of the outpost had arrived, Korean Service Corpsmen brought up rations, water, and fuel for the bunkers' stoves. As dusk fell the men took position: one man in each bunker stood guard while the others slept or relaxed.

By eight o'clock that night the two patrols were out, the rain had stopped, and all was quiet. It was dark, misty, and cold. The infantrymen sat, waiting. Lieutenant Manley had told them to expect something to happen, because the enemy had probed around Outpost Eerie on the two previous nights.

Sure enough, King Company Patrol reported in by telephone that a large enemy force was approaching them. The enemy was setting up a machine gun. Just after that, the Raider Patrol reported that a platoon-sized enemy force was moving south in its area. Raider Patrol opened fire, but the Chinese did not stop. They moved on toward a deserted village that they checked frequently. Raider Patrol reported that it was moving out.

Lieutenant Manley relayed the message back to Company K. Raider Patrol had made contact with the enemy and was moving back to the Main Line of Resistance, he said. "We're cocked and primed and ready for anything."

At 11:30, two trip flares exploded down below the lower barbed wire entanglement. The men of Outpost Eerie were not quite sure of the circumstances. They heard movement outside the wire down there, but, since the commander of Raider Patrol had not said which route he was using to get back to the MLR, some of the men thought it might be Raider Patrol, or else the flares might have been tripped by the odd Chinese trying to escape them.

But seconds later two red flares went up, and Sergeant First Class Calvin P. J. Jones and the other men at the northern end of the outpost opened fire with their automatic weapons and rifles.

Lieutenant Manley rushed up.

"Don't fire," he shouted. "It's Raider Patrol returning."

"Like Hell," shouted Sergeant Jones. "They're talking Chinese. Come on."

Two machine guns then began to bark, sweeping the outpost region. The guns were about eighty yards apart on high ground northwest of Outpost Eerie and were able to place grazing fire across the Eerie position. On the north end of the outpost, Corporal Nick J. Masiello was manning the machine gun. He alternated his fire between the two machine gun positions and the Chinese who were trying to break through the wire down below him. The Chinese machine gunners then concentrated their fire on Masiello's position, and a third Chinese machine gun joined in. They also brought up several 50 mm grenade launchers to a hill on the north.

Back at the American Main Line of Resistance, Captain Max Clark, commander of Company K, watched the blue and white and red streams of fire from the machine gun duel. He could see the tracers ricocheting off the shields of the guns. He signaled for supporting machine gun and mortar fire. The guns and mortars had been zeroed in during daylight. One .50 caliber machine gun in front of Clark's observation post on Hill 418 fired directly over the heads of the men of Outpost Eerie and made it so hot for one of the Chinese machine guns that its crew moved it back.

From Outpost Eerie, Lieutenant Manley gave correcting information to bring the mortar fire into position. Then he moved out of his bunker to find Sergeant Jones. As he started out, machine gun bullets ripped through the shelter half that covered the entrance to his bunker. Manley dropped onto his knees and crawled out into the communications trench.

As he was moving, he heard the shout "Medic." Corporal Masiello had been hit at his machine gun, taking a whole burst from one of the enemy heavy machine guns. Corporal Herman Godwin came up. He was a medic, but also a rifleman; he preferred not to claim the immunity of the medic who did not bear arms. He rushed to Masiello's side and saw that it was no use.

Masiello's assistant, Private First Class William Kunz, was shaken so badly he had to go back to the bunker for a few minutes.

"He's not feeling anything," Godwin said to Masiello's ammunition carrier, Private First Class Theodore Garvin. Godwin stayed at the bunker, helping Garvin get the machine gun into action again. They straightened out a twisted belt, and Garvin began firing once more. Godwin became his temporary assistant.

They got down to one last belt of ammunition. Garvin went back for more, and Godwin manned the gun. He yelled at Kunz to come and help him.

The Chinese were busily trying to break through the wire at two spots, on the north and northeast. The defenders kept firing and held them off for another three-quarters of an hour. Lieutenant Manley asked for artillery fire: concentration No. 304, which meant the ridge finger called Hill 191. The fire came in.

The Chinese were using bangalore torpedoes to try to blow the wire concentrations below the outpost. As long as the mortars back at the company line were able to fire illuminating flares, this activity was a great help to the defenders. But at about 1 A.M. the illuminating fire ceased, and the Chinese were then able to spot the flash of the defenders' weapons. Private First Class Robert L. Fiscus, a BAR man in the bunker to the right of the machine gun, was wounded. Corporal Godwin left the machine gun and found Fiscus and carried him into the bunker to dress the wound. Sergeant Jones sent Private Elbert Goldston, Jr., to take over the BAR. Then Private Hugh Menzies was wounded, by grenade fragments. Godwin saw it happen, and he pulled Menzies into the bunker with Fiscus and dressed his wounds.

What Manley needed, he said, was more illumination. Captain Clark told battalion, and battalion told regiment, and regiment tried to get a "firefly" into the area, a plane equipped to drop flares. But none was available. The only air help was a B-26, which came in and dropped its bombs on the enemy positions at the north end of the ridge line. That was of no immediate help to the defenders of Outpost Eerie.

By 1 A.M. the industrious Chinese had broken the wire barrier line in two places. They started up the hill.

"Get up and fight or we'll be wiped out," Manley shouted.

Nine men had occupied the three bunkers directly facing the enemy attack. Two had been killed, and three had been wounded. Now Goldston was hit at his BAR by a burst of burp gun fire and a mortar round at the same time. Godwin dragged him down through the bunker where Fiscus and Menzies lay and into the trench on the other side. Sergeant Jones and Private Gibbs carried him into the bunker on the east, which was empty. Corporal Carl F. Brittian took over the BAR left by Goldston.

The Chinese were crawling up the hill. Goldston noticed that all the grenades in the center bunker were gone. Just then the Chinese appeared at the edge of the hill. Goldston grabbed his rifle and began firing at them. He fired all his ammunition and then threw his rifle down the slope and saw the butt of it hit a Chinese in the face and knock him head over heels back down the slope.

Corporal Brittian fired until all his BAR ammunition was gone. Corporal Godwin ducked down into the bunker to see how Fiscus and Menzies were doing, and, looking over his shoulder, saw Brittian throwing empty BAR magazines at the Chinese on the slope below. That was the last he saw of Brittian.

It was now about quarter past one. Kunz and Garvin were still manning their machine gun in the eastern bunker under heavy enemy fire. Godwin was alone with the wounded in the center bunker.

Suddenly, the Chinese gained the top. Jones, Gibbs, and Goldston heard the firing stop when Godwin ran out of ammunition. They saw enemy soldiers on top of Godwin's bunker and decided that all those on the north side must be dead. Jones and Gibbs helped the wounded Goldston, and they all climbed out of the trench and rolled down the hill halfway to the wire, where they lay quietly to avoid detection.

In the center bunker Corporal Godwin had the feeling that everyone must be dead but himself, Fiscus and Menzies. He stepped outside the bunker for a look. He saw a Chinese soldier coming along the trench toward him. He stepped back against the bunker and waited until the Chinese was at point-blank range and then shot him in the head with a .45 caliber pistol.

He knew this shot would be heard by the enemy. He jumped back against the side of the trench. An enemy soldier saw the movement and fired a burst from a burp gun at him. It missed, doing no more than denting his helmet. Godwin jumped back into the bunker. As he did so, a Chinese soldier on the other side threw a concussion grenade through the entrance to the bunker. Godwin fell unconscious.

In the left rear bunker, Sergeant Kenneth Ehlers warned Lieutenant Manley by telephone that the enemy was coming around the west side of the position. He requested mortar fire from the 60 mm mortars in the rear. But there was only one round left, and Manley said to hold up.

Ehlers moved up to the bunker behind that in which Kunz and Garvin were still operating their machine gun. Lieutenant Manley and Corporal Robert Hill and Corporal Joel Ybarra also came up and they fought the Chinese with their automatic rifles, M-1s, and grenades. Ehlers and Hill were killed. Manley ran out of carbine ammunition. He threw the carbine at the Chinese and then started throwing grenades. That was the last the others saw. In a few moments all action there stopped.

In the next bunker to the south, Private Elmer Nock and Private Edward Morrison fired until the enemy started through the trench into their position. They moved back to the next bunker south, while Corporal Albert W. Hoog, who was already there, covered them and shot two Chinese.

Private Winans, the platoon runner, was the only man left in the command post bunker. He called Captain Clark and said it looked as through they would have to surrender. Clark said no, and he told him to find Manley. Just then an enemy shell made a direct hit on the command post bunker, and all sound from there ceased. The telephone lines were cut, and Outpost Eerie was out of communication with Company K.

In the rear automatic rifle position, Corporal Robert Shoham and Private First Class David Juarez and Private First Class Francis Douglas did not see much action until the Chinese came up the communications trench. Then the Americans began firing. Shoham had the BAR, Juarez was loading for him, and Douglas had his M-1. An enemy mortar shell came in and hit Juarez directly on the leg. It was a dud, and he suffered only a bruise.

When the enemy got on top of the command post, the noise level suddenly went way down. Corporal Godwin noticed that as he regained consciousness in his bunker. Hazily he saw a Chinese reach in and grab a BAR. He also saw that Menzies was dead. Apparently some Chinese had come up to Godwin when he was unconscious and thought he was dead, for his hunting knife was missing from his hip. He stayed quiet in the bunker.

Back at the Main Line of Resistance, when communications with the outpost failed, Captain Clark ordered an artillery barrage placed right on top of the outpost. The bunkers could stand it, and the Chinese ought to have it. In a few minutes 105 mm shells with proximity fuzes began bursting over the position. After a minute or so of this, a Chinese bugle blew three times, and then enemy activity on the outpost stopped. Thus were Nock and Morrison and the 60 mm mortar position saved from attack. The Chinese withdrew through the breaks in the wire, leaving two of their dead.

At 1:30 Colonel Frederick Daugherty, the regimental commander, ordered Captain Clark to take the company up to relieve the outpost. Half an hour later the company moved out across the valley. They found Sergeant Jones and his two companions lying wounded near the creek at the base of the outpost, and they met the men of Raider Patrol, all of whom were safe. The patrol had been caught on open ground at the beginning of the raid and had been unable to help in the action.

Captain Clark left them and moved on. He reached Outpost Eerie at four o'clock in the morning. One platoon moved around the east side and climbed up. Another platoon used the direct route. They searched the area and accounted for all the men but Lieutenant Manley and Corporal Ybarra. The wounded were evacuated immediately. Captain Clark counted noses. Eight men were dead, four wounded, and two missing in action. Clark found only two dead Chinese inside the position but twenty-nine Chinese bodies on the north and northwest, the route of the Chinese advance and withdrawal. They also found one wounded Chinese. He reported that the attacking force had consisted of about sixty men. Their mission, they had been told, was to capture some U.S. soldiers. Apparently they had.

Captain Clark rounded up all the weapons and took the company back to the Main Line of Resistance. Regiment decided then that the outpost was not to be manned on a regular basis, and it was not for several months. Patrols were sent up often enough to keep the enemy from taking over, but Outpost Eerie was just another victim of the war of position, which demanded constant changes of attitude regarding what was important to hold and what was not.

22

The Bargaining

The Korean War changed again. In May 1952, General Mark Clark came to Tokyo to take command of the U.S. Far Eastern forces and the UN armies. General Ridgway was made NATO commander and took command of American forces in Europe, because General Dwight D. Eisenhower had returned to the United States to begin his campaign for the Republican nomination for president. Korea was obviously going to be a major issue in the campaign, a fact that was no help to the political leaders in deciding which way to go in the endless "bogdown" of negotiations with the Chinese and North Koreans, who seemed only interested in embarrassing the Truman administration. This was, indeed, a central factor in the war; the enemy miscalculation of the American will to fight was based on a misreading of the American media and the degree to which it represented the government and public opinion. They believed that by making sufficient propaganda they would be able to sap the American will, and there were signs in certain quarters that this was so. The *weltschmerz* that would drive the United States out of the Vietnam War was already setting in. It might be said that the propaganda of the Chinese in this war was successful enough to set up the destructive forces that eroded the will of a strong and confident United States by 1972. The pax Americana, established in 1945, had lasted less than five years.

To the soldiers in the line, as much as to the generals in the Pentagon, the year 1952 brought worries, doubts, and confusions. As military men, General Van Fleet and General Clark chafed constantly under the political restrictions imposed on them from Washington. They wanted to win the war. They wanted to build up the South Korean forces. Clark, at least, wanted to employ Chiang Kai-shek's Nationalist troops in Korea. None of these wishes were granted by Washington. Instead, the war continued, bloody, confused, and indefinite, and the political leaders on both sides planned, delayed, pushed, and pulled.

A few days after Clark's arrival in Tokyo the prisoner of war issue broke wide open when riots were staged by the ardent Communist POWs in the prisoner compounds, especially on Koje Island. This resulted in an intensified Communist propaganda drive, which so angered the American negotiators that they broke off talks on June 7, 1952, for several days.

As for the war, it went on in much the same way, except that in the summer and fall of 1952 the Chinese and North Koreans decided they would make another attempt to push the UN line farther south. That meant a new offensive. It began in August 1952, and soon Americans were hearing and reading about Big Nori, Kelly Hill, Old Baldy, Sniper Ridge, Finger Ridge, Heartbreak Ridge once more, and the Punchbowl again. Typical of these fierce and extended battles was the fight of the 1st Marine Division for Bunker Hill.

In the spring of 1952 the 1st Marine Division had been moved to the extreme west side of the UN line to shore up the defenses there. They operated along the Jamestown line, southeast of Panmunjom.

The rains came in July, and they effectively suspended major ground operations until the second week of August. Just before that, the 7th Marines had been assigned the task of developing a secondary defense line on the right side of the division, which meant crossing the swollen Imjin. But the river subsided, the flooded bridges reappeared, and ground operations stepped up. The Chinese and North Koreans had literally been creeping forward from their own main line of resistance toward the Jamestown line. Since April, division intelligence had noted a continuing extension of enemy trenches in the direction of the division's Main Line of Resistance. The Chinese technique was to occupy the high ground at night, work on the bunkers and trenches, and then evacuate the area just before dawn. When several nightly excursions had allowed them to complete a position, they moved in and occupied it. Thus, the Chinese were, in effect, trying to crawl their way to Seoul. Their goal in the 1st Marine Division area was Paekhak Hill, or Hill 229, the key marine point a mile east of the road from Panmunjom to Kaesong.

At the beginning of August the 1st Marines were manning the line around the central position. The dominating height here was Hill 201, 660 feet high, in the left sector. Southwest of this point was the marine stronghold—Hill 229. These hills were festooned with sandbag bunkers the marines had been ordered to build. The war had developed into a trench war of the 1914–1918 sort, which was not something the marines were quite used to. Both sides built defenses, stockpiled artillery ammunition, and sat, waiting for the command to do something.

To the northeast, separated by a wide saddle, was Hill 120, which was held by the enemy. A mile to the east was Hill 56-A, called Samoa. Another position was Hill 58-A, or Siberia, which overlooked Hill 1220 and Hill 120. These were held by marine squads. Another squad occupied Hill 52, on the other side of the Changdan road. The whole area was cut up by numerous gullies and draws.

Across what was now sometimes called "no-man's-land," again in the tradition of 1914, were two Chinese divisions, the 194th and 118th. The Chinese 352nd Regiment held most of the line around Bunker Hill. The key Chinese position was a 775-foot hill called Taedok-san, north of the marine center. Another important Chinese position was Hill 122, adjacent to the enemy outpost line. This hill was called Bunker Hill because of the large number of bunkers there.

The battle began just before 1 A.M. on August 9 on Siberia, or Hill 58-A. A force of about four enemy squads attacked the single marine squad from Company E that was guarding the hilltop. At almost the same time another force of Chinese attacked the Jamestown line held by Company E. The squad on Siberia withdrew and returned to the main marine line. The men of Company E broke up the direct enemy assault with a mortar barrage. Captain Jesse F. Thorpe then made plans to retake Siberia. At 3:55 the 11th Marine artillery began to fire a five-minute preparation barrage on the hill, and a reinforced platoon headed for Siberia once again. The marines moved quietly, so as to avoid detection. By 5:25 they had reached the base of the hill, but then they were discovered and the enemy artillery, which had been as careful to zero in the various positions as had the marines, opened up on the hill and the area around it and forced the marines to draw back to the Main Line of Resistance once more. Thus far the action had caused the death of one marine and the wounding of thirty-two. The Chinese casualties were not known.

At 2nd Battalion headquarters Lieutenant Colonel Roy J. Betterton could see that more softening up was going to be necessary if Siberia was to be recaptured. He asked for air help, and, at 6:50, four Marine F9F jets worked the hill over with napalm and 500-pound antipersonnel bombs. Just before 10

A.M. a flight of Fifth Air Force F-80 jets came in to drop eight 1,000-pound bombs on the hill. The marine artillery again opened fire. Five minutes later another marine platoon, this time from Company A, started its attack. The enemy waited until the marines reached the bottom of the hill and then plastered them with a furious barrage, but this time the marines were not driven back. They captured the hill, and the platoon immediately began organizing a defense.

Anticipating a prompt Chinese reaction, Colonel Betterton had already sent up a platoon from Company E to support the attack unit. It reached Siberia just seven minutes after the attackers took the hill. They were told to dig like hell, and they did. Yet the enemy barrage of the hill that came in a few minutes later was so powerful that all the marines had to seek shelter behind the southern side of the hilltop. From here they directed marine mortar and artillery fire on the top and on the opposite slope of Siberia and used their infantry weapons to attack the Chinese, who were trying to gain control from the other side of the hill. In spite of this support, the enemy had committed so much artillery and so many men that by midafternoon the marines had to withdraw again and return to the Main Line of Resistance. With the abandonment of Siberia, the squad manning the Samoa outpost also had to withdraw. They estimated that the Chinese had used 5,000 rounds of artillery so far.

Company E had borne the brunt of this day's activity, and it had been badly shot up. The company was withdrawn for reorganization, and Company C came up to take over. Captain Casimir C. Ksycewski led Company C up from the rear area to stage a night counterattack. Without artillery preparation, the company moved out at 10:45 and crossed into no-man's-land. At one o'clock in the morning of August 10 they made the assault on the hill. Some of the Chinese fought to the death, but most resisted only briefly and then crossed over to the north side and moved down the hill. The marines had taken Siberia once again. This time Captain Ksycewski sent a platoon down the north side to rout the enemy remaining there. As dawn came, so did the enemy infantry once more, preceded by an enormously powerful barrage, and, again, the marines retreated back down the hill and to the marine line. Siberia had changed hands three times in less than twenty-four hours.

This sort of fighting was hardly productive, and it was enormously expensive in terms of men and materiel. The marines had suffered casualties of 17 killed and 243 wounded, most of them by artillery fire. Colonel Walter Layer, commander of the 1st Marines, called a staff conference to determine what should be done. The key to the enemy success was the intensive shelling by their artillery, and this was possible because of observation from Bunker Hill and Hill 110. The colonel decided that the best course of action was to take Bunker Hill and thus cut out the enemy's "eyes." Bunker Hill also had the advantage of neutralizing enemy control of Siberia, and of making it possible to observe enemy rear outposts.

To assist in the attack, the colonel planned a diversionary strike against Siberia once again. The enemy, having seen how the marines had operated for twenty-four hours, would expect them to continue that assault, and, made by a reinforced rifle platoon and a unit of gun and flame tanks, it would look good. For the main attack against Bunker Hill, the colonel would employ a reinforced rifle company and whatever else was needed, armor, artillery, flamethrowers—the lot.

To insure surprise, it would be a night attack. To add to that surprise, there would be no preliminary artillery barrage.

During the afternoon of August 11 the artillery plastered Siberia and also hit other targets, including Bunker Hill. The 5th Marines on the right showered the Ungok area with artillery fire, and air strikes were called down along the line to keep the enemy off balance. The Chinese had no reason to believe anything special was planned for Bunker Hill.

At dusk on August 12, eight tanks from Company C moved out of their assembly area, half a mile behind the marine line, and up toward the takeoff point. They would lead the feint assault on Siberia. Four medium M-46 tanks, mounting 90 mm guns and four flame tanks moved up the Changdan road. The flame tanks each carried a flamethrower and a 105 mm howitzer. Each tank was equipped with an 18-inch searchlight with a shutter over the lens, to be used to illuminate the battlefield when desired.

They crossed the road, turned north and prepared to fire on Siberia and its environs. Just after nine o'clock, the tanks opened first with their 90 mm guns. Two flamethrowers moved up along a stream bed that lay between the marine line and Samoa, spurting brief bursts of flame to light their way. When they reached the slope they began firing longer bursts, searing the vegetation as they moved to the top of Siberia; they lumbered over the top and down the far side, burning the ground ahead of them. Then they turned around and came back.

The gun tanks fired on Siberia for a while and then shifted their fire to Hill 110. Meanwhile, the 3rd Platoon of Company D advanced on Siberia to complete the diversion. Guided by the tank fighting lights, the infantry swept up the crest of Samoa, and then down and up the top of Siberia. Once again the marines held the hill. Once again the enemy reacted with an assault on the hill. The marines then withdrew, having completed their part of the operation.

At the same time that all this excitement was occurring on Siberia, Captain

Sereno S. Scranton, Jr., led the main attack force of Company B to cross the line and head out toward Bunker Hill. By eleven thirty on the night of August 11, the lead elements of the company held the top of the hill, and another platoon was at the bottom, making its way up. As the marines came up, they came under fire from Chinese positions on the flanks of the hill. As the Chinese realized what was happening, they turned artillery and mortars on the hill as well. The defenders on top began sending out a hail of grenades. But on the eastern side the marines pushed the Chinese back up the hill and over, and then held the summit. By 3 A.M. on August 12 the hilltop was quiet and the marines were in control. They organized a defense there. The quiet continued for a while, but then a bypassed contingent of Chinese on the side of the hill came to life and started an assault. Two fire teams from the 1st Platoon were detailed to resist the Chinese and put them out of action, while the marines and Korean Service Command workers hauled fortification materials toward the hillside.

Obviously the area was alive with Chinese positions, for at 3:45 a new firefight broke out in a draw below the hill. The exchange of small arms fire continued for two hours. The Chinese made no major attempt to counterattack. As dawn came on August 12 the marines were in control of Bunker Hill. One marine had been killed and twenty-two injured in the assault. The diversionary attack on Siberia had cost one casualty. All the wounded were cared for speedily, most of them evacuated by helicopter from the area.

The marines expected a powerful effort by the Chinese to retake the position, so they spent the remainder of the morning of August 12 digging in. They continued digging until three o'clock that afternoon, when the expected attack materialized in the form of an intensive mortaring, followed by artillery barrage. The marines grabbed their rifles and got ready.

An hour passed, and nothing happened. The hour had been hurtful. Company B had suffered so many casualties from the shelling that it had to pull back from the ridge line and take positions on the reverse eastern slope of the hill. Captain Howard Connally came up at about this time, bringing a platoon from Company I. They had scarcely settled in when 350 Chinese came charging along the line west of Bunker Hill trying to find a weak spot in the marine line. They finally concentrated on the southwestern part of the hill. The attack continued until 5:15, when the fire from the combined weapons of Company B and the Company I reinforcements discouraged the Chinese. The enemy mortaring and artillery fire stopped, and the enemy infantry disappeared. They did not go far, just beyond the opposite hill. And they soon returned to occupy positions on the north side of Bunker Hill, while the marines held the reverse slope. The marines counted the casualties of the action so far. They had been heavy: thirty four men killed, mostly by the artillery barrages, and twenty-nine men wounded.

Meanwhile, the 1st Marines had taken other action to assist in the holding of Bunker Hill. Colonel Layer had moved more troops of the 3rd Battalion up to another hill adjacent to Bunker Hill. Units of the 7th Marines were brought to assist the 1st Marines in this effort. The 4.2-inch mortars of the 7th Marine were turned over to the 1st Marines for action. Two provisional platoons were moved out of the reserves of the 1st Battalion of the 1st Marines. All the 81 mm mortars in the area were sent to the support of Bunker Hill. All the 60 mm mortars that could bear on Hill 122 were also ready. Machine guns from the Main Line of Resistance were aimed at the crest of Bunker Hill. So were 4.5-inch rocket launchers. This relatively new weapon was usually set up in units of six. They could fire twenty four rounds in rapid succession, and each of these firings was called a ripple. A set of six launchers could fire fourteen rounds on target in less than a minute. Gun and flame tanks were assigned to protect the right flank, where the steep draw between Bunker Hill and the line offered the most ready access for the enemy. All this activity was hurried; the marines knew that at nightfall the Chinese would begin their move.

At eight o'clock that night, Lieutenant Colonel Gerald Armitage, commander of the 3rd Battalion, reported that the force on Bunker Hill occupied the entire reverse slope and were preparing for action. Enemy shells were falling on both Bunker Hill and the adjacent marine positions. Armitage estimated that about 400 Chinese occupied the reverse slope of the hill. But if they tried to come up, the marines had a fine field of fire along the gentle incline of the Bunker Hill crest. Further, the top of the hill was in clear view from the Main Line of Resistance, and the guns there could sweep it nicely.

The Chinese began the night's work with a diversionary attack. They engaged a marine outpost east of Bunker Hill. They also sent a platoon farther to the east, and it walked smack into an ambush set by the Korean marines. Before midnight both the Chinese units had withdrawn.

Then, early on the morning of August 13, Chinese infantry without any fire support attacked Hill 48-A, far to the east of Bunker Hill. The marines there held. Almost immediately came another attack way off to the right. Here Captain Clarence J. Moody's Company F fought back and pushed the Chinese away from the Main Line of Resistance.

On the Main Line, before Bunker Hill, the Chinese were increasing the tempo of their bombardment. They were not assaulting Bunker Hill, but the line all around it. In each case the marines held, and the Chinese gave up after a time and returned to their own area.

The most vigorous Chinese effort was against the hill called Stromboli, or

Hill 48-a. It was held only by a squad at night, and it was attacked by a Chinese platoon and surrounded. But at 3:25 in the morning, after the squad had been repeatedly attacked, Captain Moody sent out a rifle platoon to relieve the marines up there. The Chinese at that same time sent in more troops and a hand-to-hand fight developed on the slopes of the hill. The marines had the best of it. They penetrated the encircling line and went up the hill to join the beleaguered outpost. Seeing the outpost reinforced, the Chinese disengaged and moved off to the north.

All this had been the feint; in the middle of the fighting the Chinese attacked. First came the increase in mortaring and then the artillery fire. The Chinese infantry began to move on the slopes of the hill, and when that happened Captain Connally asked for box-in fire from the 11th Marines around the marine positions on Bunker Hill. It was delivered immediately.

At 1:30 the Chinese deployed into a skirmish line on the center and right side of Bunker Hill and began to move up, covered by machine gun and rifle fire. But they did not count on the heavy fire that could be laid onto the hill from the Main Line of Resistance, and this was delivered by various marine units. The Chinese threw men into the battle as quickly as they could. They assaulted from the front. They tried to move around the gullies to assault from the rear. But the marine artillery and machine guns, rockets, tank guns, flamethrowers, and mortars delivered destruction in large doses. The tanks used their fighting lights to illuminate the enemy on the battlefield. The rocket launchers fired nine ripples. It was the sort of firepower the Chinese had early learned to respect, and it did precisely what it was supposed to do: it kept the enemy waves from engulfing Bunker Hill.

The Chinese were determined. Seeing that they had not made much headway, they sent in a reinforced battalion to take Bunker Hill. The marines had sent up a reinforced Company G under Captain William M. Vanzuyen, and those troops arrived at the height of the battle just before sunup. The reinforcements and the increased marine fire stopped the Chinese, who withdrew, taking their dead and wounded. Their casualties had been heavy, and the marines knew that, but they did not know their full extent, for in typical fashion, the Chinese policed the field. The shelling began again, which meant the Chinese did not intend to attack at the moment. A marine platoon swept the northern slope of Bunker Hill a few hours later and did not find a single Chinese body. They did find seven enemy soldiers, apparently stragglers, remaining on the hill, and they killed them.

The fighting had been costly. Colonel Layer reported that the Bunker Hill action had resulted in 24 marines killed and 214 wounded, plus 7 killed at

Stromboli. The marines figured that in the last twenty-four hours the positions of the 1st Marines had taken 10,000 rounds of enemy artillery and mortar fire. Two hundred and ten Chinese bodies had been counted, but marine estimates added another 470 fatal casualties to the figure, plus 625 wounded. No one knew for sure.

For the moment Bunker Hill was secure. But the marines were under no illusions. They increased their defense preparations. A blocking company was moved up to protect Stromboli, where the threat had developed the night before. Reserves were brought up to the line opposite Bunker Hill to strengthen the position.

At dusk on August 13 the Chinese tried again. They began with a new diversionary attack, this time at the height overlooking the Panmunjom peace corridor. Shelling there lasted ninety minutes and caused a number of casualties. At the same time, the Chinese shelled parts of the Main Line of Resistance, as though they were going to launch a frontal assault on the line. The truth was that they wanted Bunker Hill back, for the same reason that the marines insisted on keeping it: it gave the marines a good view of activity inside the Chinese lines and prevented them from using the hill as an artillery spotting post for attack on the marine Main Line of Resistance.

All day long on August 13 the Chinese had shelled Bunker Hill. The shelling was sporadic, sometimes heavy, sometimes light, but the pressure was continuous. Mortars found the trail used for resupplying the hill and caused casualties among two resupply groups working their way up.

When night fell the shelling increased until about 9 P.M. when the enemy lifted the barrage to allow a reinforced company of Chinese infantry to make a new assault. Captain John G. Demas's Company H of the 7th Marines had replaced the marine company on the hill, and Demas called for box-in firing all around his perimeter, to seal off the positions. He also asked for illumination shells to locate the enemy. The Chinese came up against the center of the line and also against the right flank. Some Chinese broke through to the American positions, but they were eliminated by grenades and small arms fire.

The marine artillery and mortars and other weapons were again blasting the hillside and the top, and the Chinese could not stand the gaff. They withdrew just after ten o'clock that night, and the marines estimated that they took at least 175 dead with them. The marines found 20 bodies on the slope.

The Chinese shelling began once more.

Under the shelling, marine and Korean stretcher bearers brought casualties to the Company I command post, to the rear of the front line, and there the critically wounded were airlifted by helicopter to the hospitals in the rear. The less seriously wounded were taken by jeep ambulance to the battalion aid station two miles behind the line.

The marines on the line settled in to wait again.

Intelligence indicated that the night attack of August 13 had been made by an enemy battalion, and that same unit made another foray at 12:25 the following morning. Again it failed, this time after four minutes. No one could figure out why the Chinese had made such an assault, unless it was to retrieve dead from the lower slopes of the hill.

It was now certain that the battle for Bunker Hill was going to be a major action. The marines brought in more reinforcements to the hill and to the line around it. On the morning of August 14 Company E of the 1st Marines moved up to the Siberia sector, to reinforce the whole area. There the marines waited.

At midnight the whole area suddenly lapsed into an eerie quiet. There was no activity at all around Bunker Hill. Captain Demas sent a patrol down the hill toward the Chinese lines. The patrol returned to report no sign of Chinese activity. But at 1:18 A.M. on August 15 a firefight suddenly broke out on the left flank of Bunker Hill. At first the marines thought it was a patrol action, but it increased. The artillery was called, and the box-in fire begun. Once again, it was effective in stopping the attack.

Just then, a tank using its fighting light searched out a large unit of Chinese massed in the draw along the northeast side of Bunker Hill, just ready to make an assault. Seconds later the American fire began falling on the Chinese in sufficient strength to scatter the formation.

The surprise attack failing, the Chinese reverted to traditional tactics: the artillery barrage, the mortars, then the infantry. The barrage began at 2 A.M. and rose to a crescendo of a hundred shells a minute. The Chinese command reorganized the infantry, and they came up the hill toward Bunker Hill. The marines replied with rifle fire from the hill, automatic weapons fire, and all the support of the past few days, coming from all around the ridge. Once again the Chinese backed off. The marine front was entirely quiet.

The enemy losses this time were placed at 350. Captain Demas's company suffered 7 dead and 28 men wounded. They moved back, relieved by Company B, and on the way to the MLR they were hit by Chinese mortar fire, and four more men were hit, two of them killed.

The Chinese kept up a running mortar barrage on Bunker Hill and soon were inflicting casualties on Company B. During a thunderstorm in the afternoon, they tried an attack, but it failed, and just before six o'clock that evening they withdrew.

The marines waited.

Just after midnight on August 16 the Chinese again tried a major assault on Bunker Hill, using a battalion. A company assaulted the hill and broke through the defense line. Captain Scranton called for reinforcements, and a platoon from Company I was sent. By 3:15 the enemy began to withdraw, and more marine reinforcements went up the line. Three more marines fell in this fight, and twenty-seven more were wounded. Enemy casualties, estimated as usual, were about seventy.

Company B was hit three more times that day and night of August 16. On the morning of August 17 the company was relieved by Company C of the 1st Battalion of the 1st Marines. And that was the end of the battle for the time being. In the next few days, however, the enemy made seven more attempts to dislodge the Americans from Bunker Hill. All of them failed, but in every one of them the marines suffered casualties. It was the sort of war that sapped morale. There was no victory. There was only never-ending fighting. And no one could say when or how it was going to end. That is the sort of nightmare the Korean War had turned into by the autumn of 1952.

23

Not with a Bang . . .
. . . but a Whimper

In the summer election campaign for the presidency of the United States, the Korean War loomed large. It had become a major issue with the American people. Given the backing and filling of American Allies and the decision of the Truman administration that Korea was not to become the site of the "final" battle against communism, what else could be expected?

Those who believed the Communists had their right to a sphere of influence and that Korea lay inside that sphere opposed the war from the outset. Those who believed with General MacArthur that Korea offered the opportunity to do away with the Chinese Communist and, perhaps, the Soviet menace once and for all were completely disaffected by President Truman's refusal to broaden the war, use Chinese Nationalist troops, cross the Yalu River into Manchuria, and destroy the Peking regime.

Even those who backed the Truman war policies could not but be discouraged by the never-ending pressure, the ceaseless casualties, the frustrations and feeling of going nowhere that accompanied all that was happening in Korea.

On the military front, there was an endless repetition of Bunker Hill and Outpost Eerie under different names. A man died, and his buddy would be hard put to say what he had been fighting for. Certainly, he was fighting against the Chinese Communists and the North Koreans who were hurling grenades at him, but what was he fighting *for*? Not for victory certainly, that had already been decided. For peace? What sort of peace? That was the problem that worried the generals, the politicians, and the negotiators at the truce table. By the end of 1952 it had to be apparent to all that the sort of peace that could be obtained was not really going to be a peace at all but an armed truce. How long it would last, no one would know. The only thing to be gained in honor was the right of the thousands of North Korean prisoners of war who did not wish to return to the Communist sphere to begin new lives. That was an honorable motif, and it is to the credit of the UN negotiators that through thick and thin they stuck to it, despite the barrages of propaganda and the occasional outbursts of military fury that their insistence generated.

The issue brought about the total suspension of peace negotiations. After listening to Communist harangues for months and offering three separate plans to cover the problems of prisoner repatriation, only to see each proposal rejected and made the object of more Communist propaganda ploys, on October 8, 1952, Major General William K. Harrison broke off talks with the Chinese and North Koreans. Until they were willing to talk sense, he said in effect, there was no use in continuing the talks. The negotiations had become a charade.

During the 1952 election campaign the American people sensed that nothing would happen in Korea until the election was over. They also sensed that the UN policy, geared to a truce, was now bankrupt of ideas. Thus, when during the height of the campaign General Eisenhower announced, "I will go to Korea," the words reverberated from the American rooftops. As Governor Adlai Stevenson's backers said, if and when Eisenhower went to Korea, what could the trip possibly accomplish? They were right, of course, but the announcement galvanized the inchoate feelings of Americans. Somehow, the people believed, in growing numbers, that General Eisenhower would find a way to do what the politicians had failed to do: end the Korean War, stop the bloodshed, and call a halt to the endless parade of meaningless communiqués across the printed page.

In November 1952 the American voters went to the polls. Not quite 34 million voters chose General Eisenhower to lead the nation for the next four years. Just over 27 million chose Adlai Stevenson. One could not, then, say that the victory of General Eisenhower was "overwhelming," or that Korea was the central issue of the campaign. But the victory was certainly impressive, and the Korean War certainly played its role.

General Eisenhower did go to Korea, as promised, in December 1952. He surveyed the scene and came away convinced, as had been President Truman, that the course pursued by the Truman administration had been sound. He indicated that he would continue it. He did have the advantage of having come late to the scene, and his endorsement of the Truman position cut the legs from under those in the Communist camp who expected they might be able to force new concessions from a new President. President Truman had warned at the end of his term that America's patience was not inexhaustible, and that if the war could not be stopped, then perhaps it would, after all, have to be won. That would mean the use of atomic weapons if necessary. This was no idle threat: many in the military were pushing for such a policy, the shadow of General MacArthur stood behind it, and in 1953 the Soviets knew that in a final confrontation they would lose to the atomic bomb.

When President Eisenhower reiterated that position in his State of the Union address, any feelings of hope the Communist camp had about schism in America were dampened.

By the spring of 1953 it became apparent that China was as sick of the prolonged struggle as America, and in April Foreign Minister Chou En-lai visited Moscow to talk over the problem. Out of the Moscow visit came conciliatory statements from Peking and Moscow, and the Americans thought highly enough of them to reopen negotiations on April 16 to discuss repatriating prisoners. The real interest, of course, was in closing down the shooting war. The negotiations for armistice began again at Panmunjom on April 27.

The talks proceeded along a rocky road, for the war aims of the UN and the war aims of the South Korean Republic no longer coincided exactly. President Rhee was particularly concerned about establishing a climate in which the Republic of South Korea was sure of survival, and this did not always seem to be foremost in the minds of the UN negotiators. Nevertheless, the talks did proceed. The biggest threat to them came in July 1953, when the Chinese armies struck once more in a paroxysm of fury.

The 1st Marine Division had been in reserve for several weeks and was ordered back up to the line in the first week of July to replace the 25th Infantry Division. This was the same general sector in which the marines had been operating for many months, alternating with other divisions. (See Map 45.)

On July 6, the 7th Marines began moving up to positions on the right held by the U.S. 14th Infantry Regiment and the Turkish brigade. Even as they came in, the men of the 4.2-inch mortar company were pushed into action by a troublesome enemy machine gun across the line. Then enemy mortars opened up from behind a ridge and from the Reno and Elko fortified positions on the west.

The weather was, as usual in Korea in July, marked by blinding rainstorms.

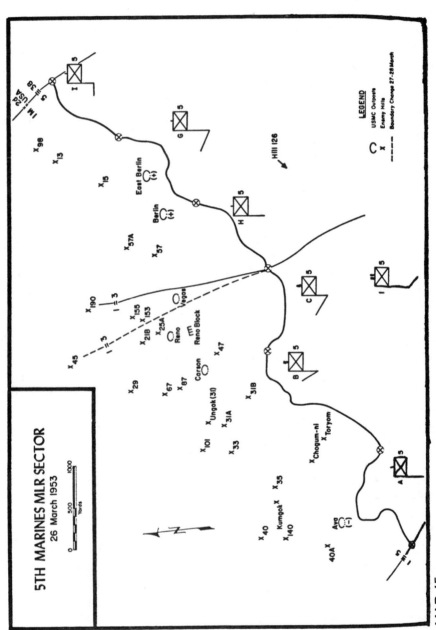

5TH MARINES MLR SECTOR
26 March 1953

0   500   1000
Yards

N

LEGEND

USMC Outposts   C

Enemy Hills   X

Boundary Change 27-28 March   -----

X 98
X 13
X 15
East Berlin C (+)
Berlin C (+)
X 57A
X 57
X 190
3
X 155
X 153
X 218
X 25A
X 45
3
Reno O
Reno Block
X 47
Vegas O
Carson O
X 29
X 67
X 87
X Ungok (31)
X 31A
X 31B
X 101
X 33
Chogum-ni X
X Toryom
Kumgok X   X 35
X 40
X 140
40A X
Ave C

HIII 126

I 5
G 5
H 5
C 5
D 5
B 5
A 5

MAP 45

Slogging through the rain on July 7, the 5th Marines came up to take over the center and left side of the line, and the 1st Marines moved up behind these two regiments, in reserve. The marines were just south of the Imjin River.

The line had changed since they were last holding it. The Chinese had captured outposts Carson, Elko, and Vegas in May, but the UN still held Outpost Ava and the Berlin–East Berlin complex. A major Chinese stronghold on Hill 190 lay northeast of the Carson–Elko–Vegas complex, and from there the Chinese tried to exploit the changing of the divisions as it was being carried out.

At nine o'clock on the night of July 7 the Chinese began a barrage of artillery and mortar fire. A reinforced enemy infantry battalion then stormed toward the positions of the 2nd Battalion of the 5th Marines, and soon the marines were engaged in hand-to-hand fighting on Berlin and East Berlin. Just before midnight the Chinese overran the East Berlin outpost.

A provisional platoon from the Headquarters and Service Company of the battalion was quickly brought up to reinforce the main line, because it was only three hundred yards behind the East Berlin outpost. The 3rd Battalion was ordered up to retake East Berlin.

Just before 4 A.M. Company F started for the outpost but was thrown back. Another unit coming up walked into twenty-five rounds of incoming artillery fire, and fifteen men were wounded. East Berlin still lay in enemy hands at dawn.

The Chinese obviously had much more on their minds, for early on July 8 great numbers of them were observed around the Reno and Vegas outposts. The marines blanketed the outposts with ripples from their 4.5-inch rocket launchers. The artillery also began firing at enemy positions in the whole area. At this time the artillery consisted of all four battalions of the 11th Marines, and seven U.S. Army and Turkish artillery battalions.

Early in the morning it was learned that while the East Berlin outpost had fallen to the enemy, the Berlin outpost had held and that eighteen marines were still up there. It was not feasible to reinforce them, said regiment, because the area could only accommodate a small garrison. The enemy simply had to be moved back along the line, and that meant retaking East Berlin.

The 7th Marines were chosen to make a massive counterassault on that outpost. At 10 A.M. a barrage of 1,600 mortar and artillery shells began falling on the enemy there. Two platoons then began the assault but were caught in enemy artillery fires, and in about fifteen minutes they were so reduced as to be ineffectual. Company G moved up to continue the assault. At 11:30 the marines were involved in hand-to-hand combat on the main trench line of East Berlin.

They were supported by tanks, artillery, and mortars, all firing just a few feet ahead of their own troops. Then up came the 3rd Battalion, and the fighting increased in ferocity. Marines were actually throwing Chinese soldiers down the reverse slope of the hill. By noon the marines had regained control of Outpost East Berlin, but only twenty marines in it were still on their feet. A reinforcing platoon from Company I was sent up the hill to help.

That afternoon artillery and mortars pounded the Chinese positions all along the line. F9F Panthers of VMF-11 dropped five tons of bombs and napalm on the enemy positions around these hills. By 3 P.M. on July 8, the transition of control of the UN line was completed in spite of the enemy effort to take advantage of the changeover. It had been quite a fight. The Chinese had thrown in 19,000 rounds of artillery and mortar fire, and the UN forces had delivered 20,000 rounds back.

Still, the Chinese seemed to have ambitions, and that was a little unusual in this period of the war. On the night of July 8 they probed the American positions along the line. They sent patrols up to the outpost again, but when they found them stoutly defended and the artillery and mortars zeroed in for box-in fire, they pulled back.

For the next ten days the marine sector was quiet. Patrols into no-man's-land reported that they found no evidence of Chinese anywhere outside their own line. There was very little reporting from the air, because heavy rain, fog, and haze played hob with the airmen during this period. The only sign of change was the sudden development of several new minefields in no-man's-land, which cost the marines some serious casualties among their patrols.

On the 5th Marine front, the enemy's activity was marked mostly by propaganda. For months the Chinese had attempted to wreck UN morale by using the "Tokyo Rose" technique of playing nostalgic music, and in between songs indicating to the married marines that they were being cuckolded at home by overpaid slackers, and to the unmarried marines that they were losing their girl friends to the same sort. The Dragon Lady was the local siren, who intoned these baleful and mournful sentiments night after night on the midnight broadcast.

From Tokyo and Panmunjom came reports that the war was really winding down and that an armistice could be expected at any moment. That sounded good, but it did not make much difference to marines under mortar fire. Firefights seemed to come almost daily, even when nothing really was happening. Meanwhile, from the central and eastern sectors of the line came the disturbing word that the Chinese had thrown five armies against three ROK divisions in a furious attack. This was seen at Eighth Army headquarters as an attempt by the Chinese and the North Koreans to punish the South

Koreans and convince them that continuation of the war (which President Rhee sometimes advocated) would be a bloody and losing business.

No such major activity was expected along the marine end of the line, just gruelling bloody encounters that never proved much, as on the night of July 16, when a fifteen-man reconnaissance patrol from the 2nd Battalion of the 5th Marines encountered a patrol of Chinese at least twice as numerous. The Chinese were obviously looking for prisoners, for they were deployed in the inverted V formation designed to entrap a smaller force. The marines set up a base of fire and beat off the enemy with rifles, BARs, mortars, and fists. A relief unit was sent up but was hit by heavy mortaring from the Chinese side. The whole detail was wounded. A second squad came up and also was brought under mortar fire. The fight lasted two hours. At the end of it at least ten Chinese were known to be dead, an estimated nine more were presumed dead, and three were wounded. The marines found seven men missing. The next day they discovered six bodies. So, if the Chinese were after prisoners, perhaps they got one. At this stage of the war, when the lines were so static that major movements were predictable, when the talks were nearing their final stage, what was to be gained by all this?

The Chinese had been told that they were to conduct a major offensive all along the line, and on the night of July 19 they hit the Berlin and East Berlin outposts again in great strength and captured them once more. This time the reply of the marines was to unleash an artillery, mortar, and air attack on these pieces of real estate more powerful than any that had yet been seen. Tanks, rocket launchers, and every other sort of weapon were involved. All the bunkers were demolished, and all but fifteen yards of trench line on East Berlin were thrown into rubble. Fighter bombers delivered tons of napalm and bombs. At the end of July 20 the two outposts were no longer worth anything to anyone. The enemy had lost at least seventy-five men killed and three hundred wounded, and the battalion involved was so beaten down by casualties in other sectors that it had to be replaced in the line.

Considering the problem, the divisional commander suggested that the enemy might be trying to seize Hill 119, south of Berlin and East Berlin, in order to strengthen a position for the final truce line, to deny to the UN part of the Imjin River. Reinforcements were brought up to the marine line to guard against such a contingency.

No attack materialized in the next few days, but on July 24 division's hunch seemed to be borne out when at dusk a heavy concentration of artillery and mortar fire began falling on Hill 119. Enemy troops were reported to be massing for an assault, and two battalions struck Hill 119, at about eight o'clock. The reinforcements that had been carried out meant more artillery, more mortars, and more rockets were available to the marines, and they held their positions, until 9:20, when the enemy faltered and began to withdraw in one sector, around Hill 111. The attack on Hill 119, however, continued; indeed, it increased in power, and by midnight the marines were beginning to fall back around the slopes of the hill on both sides. Company G of the 1st Marines was in the line, and it was down to 25 percent effectives. The men were holding on with the help of sheer guts and a little ammunition. Company I was sent up but fell under enemy mortar fire and was badly cut up. The Chinese were also suffering severely from the marine artillery that fired continually from 9 P.M. until midnight. The rocket launchers put out four ripples.

The Chinese tried to break through in the 5th Marines sector, with another heavy attack against Outpost Esther. The marines used tanks, flame tanks, and every other weapon and finally drove the Chinese off with heavy casualties. The enemy lost about five hundred men in the assault, while the marines suffered a hundred casualties, including a dozen dead.

On the morning of July 25 it became apparent that the enemy had thrown at least three thousand troops into this battle for position, and they had lost. Hill 119 remained in marine hands. July 26 was quiet, until night, when the Chinese made another desperate effort to seize Hill 119, failed once again, and retreated.

Before dawn the Chinese assault all along the Eighth Army line had come to an end. To attempt to change the configuration of the line, the enemy had sent in at least six armies, along the Iron Triangle, the Punchbowl, and the Kumsong Bulge (see Map 46), and they had failed. They had been willing to sacrifice 75,000 men to this end.

On July 27, 1953, it was all over. The UN delegates and the Communists met at Panmunjom, and, without speaking a word to one another, signed eighteen copies of the armistice agreement. The fighting was officially ended.

At 10 A.M. a flash message was sent to the troops all along the Eighth Army line. There would be no celebrations, no firing, no fraternization with the enemy. The troops were to be ready for a Communist trick at any moment, but they were not to fire their weapons unless attacked.

On the line the marines watched as the Chinese came up to police their area, removing their dead, and clearing the minefields away. One group approached a marine post and wanted to talk. Others hung up gift bags at the base of Outpost Ava and shouted, "How are you? Come on over and let's have a party." The marines just sat and looked at them.

The general feeling in the UN military camp was that the war was over, and "so what?" It had been a "so what" war since the Chinese attack in

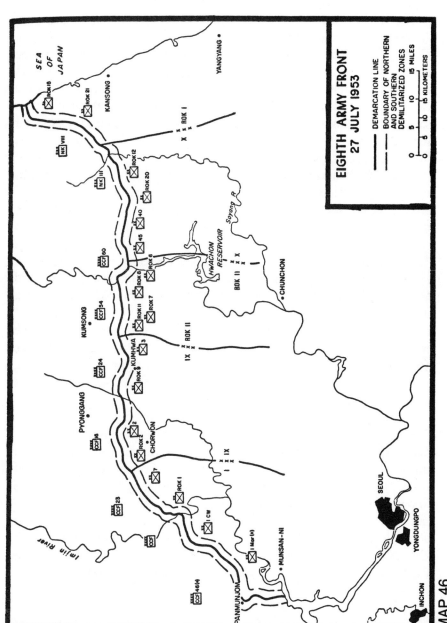

EIGHTH ARMY FRONT
27 JULY 1953

DEMARCATION LINE
BOUNDARY OF NORTHERN
AND SOUTHERN
DEMILITARIZED ZONES

0   5   10   15 MILES
0   5   10   15 KILOMETERS

SEA OF JAPAN

YANGYANG

KANSONG

ROK 15

ROK 21

NK VIII

ROK 1

NK III

ROK 12

ROK 20

40

45

Soyang R

CCF 60

ROK 6

ROK 8

HWACHON RESERVOIR

ROK II

CHUNCHON

ROK 11

ROK 7

CCF 54

KUMSONG

ROK II

ROK 9

KUMHWA

3

CCF 24

IX

PYONGGANG

CCF 46

2

ROK 2

CHORWON

7

IX

CCF 23

ROK 1

I

1 CW

I Mar (-)

MUNSAN-NI

SEOUL

YONGDUNGPO

CCF

PANMUNJOM

CCF 46(-)

Imjin River

INCHON

MAP 46

November, and the politicians had decided that the war would not be won by the arms of the Americans and their Allies, but would be fought to a stalemate. Military men cannot get excited about a war like that.

The Korean War was written into the history books as a failure of American arms, and it became a matter Americans did not like to discuss. More than a hundred Medals of Honor bespoke the valor that had been expended on Korea's soil, fifty thousand casualties told more. But for what had it all been done? The negative attitude of most Americans persisted; the Korean War was succeeded by the Vietnam War, and in the public consciousness they were too often equated. The decision was made not to fight Korea to a finish and not to fight to the end in Vietnam. Thus, both have been lumped together as failures.

In the 1980s, however, it was becoming clear that the Korean War was not a failure, but a success, in the end. It started as a brave action. One man, General MacArthur, changed the nature of the war, when he insisted on driving to the Yalu River. Had he stopped at the 38th parallel and been content to repel aggression, the war would have been "won" in the fall of 1950. Instead, it took the UN nearly three more years to achieve the same end.

Yet, for the first and only time in history, men of many nations banded together in the common cause of preventing an aggressive force from having its way in world politics. The Communists did not have their way because of the bravery of South Koreans, Americans, British, Turks, French, and the men of many other nations. There are monuments around Korea to the heroic Gloucestershires, virtually wiped out on the line; to the Turkish brigade, which stopped a Chinese drive; to the French, who held their little hill and saved a segment of the Eighth Army.

Korea created its thousands of heroes, none more brave than those of the 3rd Battalion of the 8th Cavalry, caught in that first explosive drive of the Chinese against the Eighth Army line in northwest Korea. And the story of the marines at the Changjin Reservoir is another tale of valor that has gone down in military history, and properly so. There are many, many others, little known to Americans because they do not like to read about wars that have not been won. But they will be reading about Korea in years to come and about the Korean War and how, for once at least, when trouble came the United Nations was able to pull itself together and maintain a generally united front to stop a catastrophe. That is the real meaning of the Korean War.

Chapter Notes

1.
The Chinese Change the War

Even today, thirty-five years after the Chinese entered the Korean War, there is a paucity of information available to the Western world about the history of the Chinese intervention. Most of what I have is a matter of historical record, as carried in the press of the time. I wrote to friends in Peking, seeking material, and got nothing. I checked with the various agencies and bookstores in the United States that sell China's books and found an absolute blank on the subject. Finally, I did get some information from Japanese sources, but not much. Therefore, most of my sources are American and subject to all the error that implies.

The material about the background of the Korean War is from the first volume in this series, *The Pusan Perimeter,* also published by Stein and Day.

The discussion of motivations and the opinions expressed are my own, based on experiences in Korea and elsewhere as a journalist. As a correspondent in Korea and China in 1946 and 1947 it was evident to me that the United States was following an Asian policy that was myopic and would lead to disaster. I have not wavered from that view.

The story of the 3rd Battalion of the 8th Cavalry at Unsan on the Nammyon River is a tragedy to rival Custer's Last Stand and one that deserves more attention than it has hitherto enjoyed. The abandonment of the battalion seems to me unnecessary and occasioned by a general panic on the part of the senior officers of General Milburn's corps. That panic persisted for weeks and became the gravest problem General Ridgway assumed when he took command of the Eighth Army following General Walker's death.

2.
The Battle of Sudong

From the beginning of the operations in northeastern Korea the marines were uneasy, for they saw how General MacArthur had opened up his lines for a drive down the center and encirclement of the right. MacArthur's intelligence was dreadfully faulty; indeed, the whole intelligence operation of the United States forces in the Korean War was a military disgrace. The British in the field and at home knew far more of the enemy's intentions and capabilities than did the Americans, but nobody listened to them. Again, this difficulty seems to me to be a hangover from the China policy of the 1940s that got the United States moving entirely the wrong way. The fact that the marines were able to withstand the initial Chinese assault so well was an indication of the reasonableness of their suspicion of General Almond's orders and their concomitant troop disposition.

3.
The War Changes

The fact that General MacArthur's intelligence officers were so easily confused by the Chinese method of misidentifying their military units is an indication of how little the Americans knew and how willing they were to ignore those who did know. Lieutenant Colonel Evans Carlson of the marines spent many months in northeast China with the Chinese Communist armies, which operated in this fashion. But Carlson's utilization of Chinese methods and his obvious admiration for the Chinese were suspect even in World War II, and the military establishment ignored his findings and those of others who lived with the Chinese Communists in the days before they took power.

4.
The Wrong Moves

General MacArthur's backing and filling as to the Chinese intentions in

Korea as of November is a matter not sufficiently explored as yet by MacArthur's biographers. The most sensible officer on MacArthur's staff seems to have been General Beiderlinden, the personnel officer, who did not share the Tokyo illusions about the Chinese. Apparently he operated in a vacuum.

It is interesting to see how a legend can outlive its time. MacArthur was certainly a legendary figure in 1950, but the legend seems to have lost its military acumen. MacArthur's performance during World War II was sometimes brilliant, as exemplified by his insistence on the "island hopping" campaign in the South Pacific that resulted in the isolation of more than 100,000 troops in the Rabaul area without a battle, and in the saving of thousands of lives.

But in Korea in the fall of 1950 MacArthur has to be accused of resorting to low cunning in his relationships with the Joint Chiefs of Staff. The incident of the Yalu bridges resulted in General Stratemeyer's correct guess that MacArthur was trying to bulldoze the Joint Chiefs into a major shift of policy.

The story of Captain Tanner's exploits is from *MIG Alley*. Once again the American high command seemed to have underestimated the enemy—this time, his capability of putting modern military equipment into the air.

The difficulties of the airmen in Korea, occasioned by the political policies followed, should be studied as a case history by every Air Academy cadet. It must be evident that military campaigns cannot be won if the campaigners are restricted in their scope of activity. This lesson was first taught in the Korean air war, but it was not learned. MacArthur insisted on going ahead with his drive to clear Korea, despite restrictions that made success most unlikely.

The Big Push

A rereading of the Chinese appraisal of the American fighting man ought to be salutary for the militarists among us. The basic American problem that developed in Korea and was never resolved there or in Vietnam was the indoctrination of troops to give them a feeling that they were fighting for a cause. This failure, as much as shortcomings in training, resulted in a fighting man in the field who did not know why he was there. This situation ultimately led to new difficulties when Americans were captured. Since the troops had no basic political indoctrination, it was relatively easy for the Chinese to "turn" many of them into propaganda agents against their own kind. That is always a danger in a struggle against absolutist governments. In World War II the problem did not exist because Americans believed they were fighting for right against evil. There was no big problem in Korea during the first five months; the savagery of the North Koreans gave the Americans a temporary reason for fighting. The Chinese, with their well developed propaganda, were another matter.

In the matter of the guerilas, MacArthur's strategic failure to recognize the consequence of his rush to the Yalu came home to roost. It took General Ridgway months to undo the damage.

For the story of General MacArthur's paranoid behavior as army chief of staff I am indebted to Joseph Goulden's *Korea: The Untold Story.*

6.
MacArthur's Blunder

If General Smith was aware of the difficulties of military operations in a Korean winter, then why was not General MacArthur? The answer appears to be that MacArthur seems to flatly have refused to consider anything but immediate victory. He had already whined that the Chinese had unfairly upset his applecart and prevented the quick investment of the whole Korean peninsula. The Chinese did so because they read MacArthur's statements and were afraid that he would be allowed to do what he most wanted to do—carry the war to Peking and restore Chiang Kai-shek to power in China. There was no way the Chinese were going to allow that.

The valor of the Turkish brigade and other small units of various United Nations members is largely forgotten in the 1980s, but it was enormously impressive and has been detailed in the Republican of Korea's six-volume official history of the Korean War. That is my source for the story of the Turkish brigade on the Sunchon Road.

7.
General Smith Escapes a Trap

The story of the marines in the Chosin Reservoir area is from the official marine history of the Korean War. It is an impressive tale of bravery and spirit; the marines along that narrow road subsisted on guts and very little else in their efforts to get out of the trap, with Chinese on both sides of the only escape route. Whatever the Chinese propagandists had to say about the "American soldier" did not apply to the marines. The marines cost the Chinese thousands of their best troops in this "advance to the rear." Marine air cover here was vital to the success and salvation of the 1st Marine Division. It ought to have been a lesson to the army and air force in Korea, but, unfortunately, it does not seem to have taken. The coordination of air force and army units in the field never achieved anything like the effectiveness of the marine air and ground units. Later in the campaign, when air support was vital, the army units showed a marked preference for marine air.

8.
The Army Trapped

The sad story of the 32nd Infantry at the Chosin Reservoir is in sharp contrast to the story of the marines. Once again, the unrealistic attitude of General Almond, a hand-me-down from his mentor, General MacArthur, was a major factor in the entrapment of the troops. The story is from the marine history, Appleman, Gugeler, and the official Republic of Korea history.

9.
Breakout

MacArthur's enormous blunder created chaos in the UN high command. But, at least in Washington, the political leaders knew what they should have known earlier, that the Korean problem was not to be settled by military means. They had resisted the North Korean effort to do this but failed to comprehend the precisely similar reasoning of their own side. It was very late in the day, but Harry Truman could still learn.

The continuing story of the marine slogging march down the road to Hamhung is from the marine history and the Republic of Korea history.

10.
The Evacuation of X Corps

The story of the march is again from the marine history, for the most part. The ROK official history was another source.

11.
The Brink of Disaster

The discussion of the political and military arguments in Washington and Korea come from Goulden, Donovan, Appleman, MacArthur, Manchester, and Ridgway. The reaction of the marines is from the official marine history of the Korean War. The story of the evacuation is from the marine history and the navy history. Ridgway noted in his own book on the Korean War that the first problem he faced was American morale. The second was the even worse morale of the ROK forces and the incompetence of their high command. The story of the French stand south of Wonju is one of the great tales from the Korean struggle.

12.
Counteroffensive

It is too bad that the Korean War could not have been ended at the close of 1950, for everything that happened after that time was wasteful. The Chinese apparently truly believed the UN morale was so bad that they could push them out of the peninsula altogether, and that was the reason for the continuation of the war; the Chinese had to learn their own limitations, just as the Americans had learned theirs. Barring an all-out struggle that would have had to involve the USSR, there was no way either side was going to "win."

Ridgway's plan was to punish the Chinese, while keeping his own casualties low, and for the most part he managed this. The Twin Tunnels patrol, as delineated by Gugeler, shows the price that sometimes had to be paid by good men for a piece of territory that in itself was meaningless.

13.
The Battle for Chipyong-ni

The source for the material on the marine effort to clear out the guerillas south of the 38th parallel is the official marine history. That and the Gugeler book served as the basis for the story of Chipyong-ni, as well as Ridgway and the official Republic of Korea war history.

14.
Northward

Gugeler and the official Republic of Korea war history are principal sources for the story of the Crombez task force. As noted, General Ridgway came up to see what had happened and was mightily impressed.

The stories of the UN offensives of February and March are indicative of the changed nature of the war. So, too, was the negative reaction of the Pentagon and congress to the warlike code names Ridgway used for his war operations. There, indeed, was a sign of the confusion that had overwhelmed the American movers and shakers.

General MacArthur came over for the kickoff of the first Ridgway offensive—it was his last moment of glory in the field. Correspondents tried to portray General Ridgway as another grandstanding MacArthur, but it never would wash. Ridgway was concerned with the good opinion of his troops and never played to the great American audience as MacArthur had always done.

15.
The Recapture of Seoul

The second recapture of Seoul by the UN forces was essential for Korean political purposes, but in terms of material strength, Seoul was nothing but a liability at this point, a hundred and eighty thousand miserable people whose needs were added to the UN burden.

The stories of the fighting are from the Republic of Korea official history, Gugeler, Ridgway, and the official marine history.

The materials about changing political maneuvers is from Donovan's book on Truman, the Marshall biography, MacArthur, Acheson, and Goulden.

16.
The Chinese Spring Offensive, 1951

MIG Alley is a primary source for the story of the air war, along with the history of the air forces in Korea. The story of the marines in battle is from the official marine history.

17.
The Second Chinese Spring Offensive

The story of Hill 800 is from Gugeler. It is interesting because it shows once again the changing nature of the war. The Chinese were experts at building entrenchments and surpassed the UN forces all through the war at this. But the U.S. Army could do it, too, as the story of Hill 800 shows. In the end, of course, Hill 800 became as meaningless as had all these other prepared positions, for by the spring of 1951 the UN and Communist forces were fighting along the general line that would be the final line of settlement. Everything that happened from this point on was meaningful only in that the Communist world had to learn the hard way that they could not achieve by propaganda and attrition what they had tried and failed earlier to achieve by force and surprise. The lesson was learned at the cost of many thousands of UN and Chinese and North Korean lives.

18.
Punchbowl

There is no more famous name to come out of the Korean War than the Punchbowl. What a bloody battleground it was, that plateau surrounded by high mountains that the Communist forces wanted since it enabled them to assemble their troops for drives into the Iron Triangle and south toward Seoul. It was won, lost, and won again by the UN forces. It continued to be a major trouble spot all during the rest of the static war.

The story of General Almond's driving of the task force up to the banks of the Soyang River is presented by Gugeler as an example of creative leadership at the top level of field command. But my question was why? Even at the time the move seemed to have very little significance. History has pushed it into a much smaller mold, where it looks more like an exercise in command arrogance than a meaningful military operation. And coming from the man who went charging into the Chosin Reservoir area to decorate the doomed and assure them that they had nothing to fear from a handful of "Chink laundrymen," it seems to me doubly suspect.

19.
The Static War

The story of Million Dollar Hill is from the Republic of Korea official history, for the most part. Gugeler and Ridgway were also used here.

The story of Bloody Ridge is one of the most poignant to come out of the Korean War. Gugeler was vital to my account, the Republic of Korea war history was important. Certainly that struggle is a reminder of the high cost of leadership; virtually every officer of three infantry companies that began that struggle was killed, and one must assume that the same happened on the Chinese side.

20.
Heartbreak Ridge

Most important about Heartbreak Ridge was the inauguration of the helicopter into combat. Here was a change that would affect infantry warfare for all time. Except for that, the story of the fighting is just more of the bloody repetition that the Korean War had become by the fall of 1951. It had settled down into bunker and trench warfare.

21.
Negotiate and Fight

The stories of Captain Jabara and the other pilots are from *MIG Alley*. The stories about command problems are from Ridgway. The story of Outpost Eerie is from Gugeler.

22.
The Bargaining

The material about Mark Clark is from his own book. The stories about the marines are from the marine official history. The story of Bunker Hill is another tale of fighting for a piece of ground that had little value.

23.
Not with a Bang . . . but a Whimper

There was nothing satisfactory about the Korean War, except that it finally ended. The Chinese soldiers were closer to an understanding of it all than were the marines and American soldiers when it finally came to an end. As the marine history says, the Chinese came out of their positions, hung gift packages on trees, and called across the line to the Americans to come over and "have a party." The marines sat in their foxholes and looked at the

Chinese dumbly. Both actions were totally understandable: the Chinese *lao pai hsing* were as sick of the war as were the Americans. The marines, who had been told not to fraternize with the enemy, were by this time so numbed by the war that they did not know what to believe. As it turned out, the Chinese were right, although it took the U.S. government almost another twenty years to discover it. For the fact is that the United States and China are geographically and culturally natural allies. The worst tragedy of the Korean War was that Americans and Chinese were pitted against one another. The North Koreans deserved all that happened to them, but the entry of China into the war was caused almost entirely by the ego of one man, who was proved in the final analysis to be dead wrong.

Bibliography

Acheson, Dean. *Present at the Creation.* New York: W. W. Norton and Co., 1969.

Appleman, Roy E. *U.S. Army in the Korean War: South to the Naktong, North to the Yalu.* Washington, D.C.: Office of the Chief of Military History, Department of the Army, 1960.

Army Times, Editors, *American Heroes of Asian Wars.* New York: Dodd Mead and Co., 1969.

Berger, Carl. *The Korea Knot: A Military-Political History,* rev. ed. Philadelphia: University of Pennsylvania Press, 1964.

Clark, Mark W. *From the Danube to the Yalu.* New York: Harper and Bros., 1954.

Kojima, Noboru. *Chosen Senso.* Vol. 3, *Bei kai hei bu no chokyogun jui no toppa suru.* Tokyo: Bungei Shunju, 1977.

————. *Chosen Senso.* Vol. 6, *Chokyogun no kasei, roku senshi kenkyu fukyu kaitten.* Tokyo: Bungei Shunju, 1971.

Davis, Larry. *MIG Alley.* Warren, Mich.: Squadron/Signal Publications, 1978.

Donovan, Robert J. *Years of Decision.* New York: W. W. Norton and Co., 1977.

Fehrenbach, T. R. *The Fight for Korea: From the War of 1950 to the Pueblo Incident.* New York: Grosset and Dunlap, 1969.

Field, James A., Jr., *History of United States Naval Operations, Korea.* Washington, D.C.: U.S. Navy, 1962

Futrell, Robert Frank, Lawson S. Moseley, and Albert F. Simpson. *The United States Air Force in Korea 1950-1953.* New York: Duell Sloan and Pearce, 1961.

George, Alexander L. *The Chinese Communist Army in Action: The Korean War and Its Aftermath.* New York: Columbia University Press, 1967.

Goulden, Joseph C. *Korea: The Untold Story of the War.* New York: Times Books, 1982.

Gugeler, Ralph. *Combat Actions in Korea.* Washington, D.C.: Combat Forces Press, 1954.

Jacobs, Bruce. *Korea's Heroes: The Medal of Honor Story.* New York: Berkley Books, 1953.

Kim Il Sung. *Yesterday Today: U.S. Imperialism—Mastermind of Aggression on Korea.* Pyongyang: Korean People's Army Publishing House, 1977.

Korean Overseas Information Service. *A Handbook of Korea.* Seoul: Ministry of Culture and Information, 1979.

Leckie, Robert. *Conflict: The History of the Korean War.* New York: G. P. Putnam's Sons, 1962.

MacArthur, Douglas. *Reminiscences.* New York: McGraw Hill, 1964.

Manchester, William. *MacArthur.* Boston: Little, Brown and Co., 1981.

Meid, Pat, and James M. Yingling. *U.S. Marine Operations in Korea.* Vol. 5, *Operations in West Korea.* Washington, D.C.: Historical Division, U.S. Marine Corps, 1972.

Montross, Lynn, and Nicholas A. Canzona. *U.S. Marine Operations in Korea, 1950-1953.* Vol. 3, *The Chosin Reservoir Campaign.* Washington, D.C.: Historical Division, U.S. Marine Corps, 1967.

Montross, Lynn, Hubard D. Kuokka, and Norman Hicks. *U.S. Marine Operations in Korea.* Vol. 4, *The East Central Front.* Washington, D.C.: Historical Division, U.S. Marine Corps, 1962.

Ridgway, Matthew B. *The Korean War.* New York: Doubleday, 1967.

Russ, Martin. *The Last Parallel.* New York: Rinehart and Co., 1957.

Simmons, Robert R. *The Strained Alliance: Peking, Pyongyang, Moscow, and the Politics of the Korean Civil War.* New York: The Free Press (Macmillan), 1975.

Schnable, James F. *U.S. Army in the Korean War, Policy and Direction: The First Year.* Washington, D.C.: Office of the Chief of Military History, United States Army, 1972.

Stone, I. F. *The Hidden Story of the Korean War.* New York: Monthly Review Press, 1952.

War History Compilation Committee, Ministry of National Defense, Republic of Korea. *The History of the United Nations Forces in the Korean War.* Seoul: Ministry of National Defense, 1972.

Whiting, Allen S. *China Crosses the Yalu. The Decision to Enter the Korean War.* Stanford, Calif.: Stanford University Press, 1960.

Index